I and I

I and I

Epitaphs for the Self in the Work of
V.S. Naipaul, Kamau Brathwaite
and Derek Walcott

RHONDA COBHAM-SANDER

THE UNIVERSITY OF THE WEST INDIES PRESS
Jamaica • Barbados • Trinidad and Tobago

The University of the West Indies Press
7A Gibraltar Hall Road, Mona
Kingston 7, Jamaica
www.uwipress.com

© 2016 by Rhonda Cobham-Sander
All rights reserved. Published 2016

A catalogue record of this book is available from the National Library of Jamaica.

ISBN: 978-976-640-576-2 (print)
978-976-640-577-9 (Kindle)
978-976-640-578-6 (ePub)

Cover and book design by Robert Harris
Set in Scala 10.25/15 x 27
Printed in the United States of America

CONTENTS

Acknowledgements / **vii**

Introduction / **1**

PART 1. **V.S. NAIPAUL**

1   For Walter Raleigh / **21**

2   For C.L.R. James / **30**

3   For Blair / **50**

4   Last W/Rites / **60**

PART 2. **EKB**

5   For Kamau / **69**

6   For Son/Sun / **87**

7   For Edward / **99**

PART 3. **DEREK WALCOTT**

8   For Naipaul / **133**

9   For Brathwaite / **167**

10   For Walcott / **202**

Accidents: An Afterword / **240**

Notes / **245**

Selected Bibliography / **285**

Index / **293**

ACKNOWLEDGEMENTS

A book that has been as long in the making as this one accrues many debts. I wrote the first version of what became the Naipaul section while on a Humboldt Fellowship at the University of Bayreuth, Germany. Although this was not the project I was there to do, I am grateful to my sponsors for allowing me the freedom to take my research in an unexpected direction. Subsequent chapters were written during sabbatical leaves paid for by Amherst College, which also very generously financed my travel to archives in the Caribbean. The librarians in the West Indian collection at the University of the West Indies, St Augustine, allowed me unfettered access to the manuscript of Walcott's *Omeros*. Elizabeth Walcott-Hackshaw and the late Margaret Walcott provided me with details about Derek Walcott's career and obtained permission for me to cite from his manuscripts. Several Amherst colleagues read portions of the manuscript at various stages and offered wise counsel, including Andrew Parker, Karen Sanchez-Eppler and Jack Cameron. I am grateful to Jean Antoine, Timothy Reiss, Barbara Lalla and Jennifer Rahim for agreeing to publish early versions of three chapters in festschrifts they edited, even though they knew I intended to include the essays in this volume. Their editorial feedback has made those chapters much stronger. Edward Baugh, Paul Breslin, Biodun Jeyifo, Gordon Rohlehr and Reinhard Sander read sizeable portions of the manuscript with meticulous attention to detail and offered many useful suggestions for changes. Reinhard in particular kept me from giving up when administrative responsibilities threatened to derail my scholarship. Thank you for your support at a very crucial time.

    A project like this stands or falls on the reliability and professionalism of the assistants who help prepare the manuscript for publication. Neltja Brewster, Kimberly Bain, Sylvia Li and Sylvia Heredia ferreted out information for footnotes and made sure my page numbers lined up. Julie Howland was punctilious about formatting the quotes from Brathwaite's *Barabajan Poems*, and she worked hard to keep me from reintroducing typos into the final manuscript. Diana Babineau performed heroic feats of copy editing, challenging hazy footnotes, insisting that I revise impossible run-on sentences (like this one) and scolding me on a regular basis when I allowed myself to become distracted from the work.

I owe special thanks to the family members and close friends who have supported me through this process. Each time we spoke, my father-in-law, Robert Sander, never failed to ask how the book was coming along, although he does not speak English and could therefore never read it. Margit Wermter and the late Eckhard Breitinger made sure that my time in Germany went well. Patricia Haward spent many an evening feeding me delicious meals in her London flat and telling me stories about Naipaul and Brathwaite from earlier eras. My cousins Hazel Heath and Michael Charge and my sister Denise Cobham-Albo took care of me during my research trips to Trinidad – thanks so much for the rotis, Michael! Other sisters and cousins, scattered across the Caribbean, North America and England, continue to tolerate my obsession with literature, even when it leaves me less than capable of dealing with real life. To my daughter, Petra, who allowed me to alternately abandon her and drag her around the world while I was working on this project, I owe a special debt of gratitude. Thank you for believing in me and for holding me accountable. To Sebastian, Ian, Julian and Juliana, Pamela and Amanda, thank you for making our family dinners worth stopping work to enjoy. And to John, whose loving presence has given me the peace of mind to complete this project, thank you for sharing my passion for poetry. This book is dedicated to my new granddaughter, Leona. I hope that it will help connect you some day to one of the many worlds that have shaped you.

INTRODUCTION

> ... So much left unspoken
> by my chirping nib! And my earth-door lies ajar.¹

Only duppies dance at their own funerals. So it is hard to repress a shudder, an uncanny intimation that I am watching a ghost chisel its own epitaph into the page, when Derek Walcott invites me to his funeral near the end of *Omeros*, on the pretext of eulogizing his island/warrior Achille, "whose fist of iron", he claims, "would do me a greater honour if it held on / to my casket's oarlocks than mine lifting his own".² But Walcott is not the only Caribbean writer of his generation for whom, by the end of the twentieth century, writing had become a wager with death. Here is V.S. Naipaul in *The Enigma of Arrival*, lying in the bathtub, playing with himself:

> I used to have two baths a day. The first bath was after breakfast, to wash away the effects of the sleeping pill that had kept my mind quiet during the night, had stopped me dealing in words, solving the problems of the various parts of my book, had stopped me seeing all these problems come together into one unsolvable and alarming threat (in daylight I knew that writing problems were solved one by one).... One morning the idea came to me that I was like a corpse at the bottom of a river or stream, tossing in the current. I gave up the morning soak. But the idea of the corpse was hard to get rid of. It came back to me every time I had a bath.³

Kamau Brathwaite takes the deadly game one round further in *The Zea Mexican Diary* as he writes about his wife's cremated body: "Some is to go to Guyana, some to Barbados, a little I've decided to keep The rest I think I'll pour into her garden spot [in the end we poured that 'little' third into the planting of her tulip tree] & when I was going downstairs to get the second vessel, I put some of the ashes on my tongue & swallowed her."[4]

The desire to consume mortality is as old as the text. Unlike orators, authors of written works anticipate that their words will live on beyond their bodies. Indeed, for many readers a text only truly can be considered a classic if the author is dead. But in the Caribbean literary tradition there is no precedent for life after death: until the twentieth century no cohort of writers had managed to produce a body of work capable of surviving the amnesiac violence of a world without history. Naipaul has written eloquently in the essay "Jasmine" about how "landscapes do not start to be real until they have been interpreted by an artist, so, until they have been written about, societies appear to be without shape and *embarrassing*".[5] The threat of ephemerality, endemic to new societies, is also a threat of extinction, the crumbling of the edifice of selfhood that writers construct to announce their being in the world. Lacking a literary landscape, the true subject of the first generation of postcolonial Caribbean authors became the creation of selves they hoped would someday inhabit that imagined space.

In the late twentieth century, as the cohort of Caribbean writers who first took the literary world by storm faded into obscurity, the consequences of fame and death acquired new significance for Walcott, Brathwaite and Naipaul. At the time, all three writers were at the peak of their literary productivity. To different degrees they already had experienced the pressures of mortality and the privileges of literary canonization. In 1992 Derek Walcott became the first anglophone Caribbean writer to win the Nobel Prize for literature. Death had always overshadowed his experience of life. His father died when Derek and his twin brother, Roderick, were almost two years old. The poet's first mentor, Harold Simmons, committed suicide in 1966, just as Walcott was beginning to garner international acclaim for his writing.[6] By the time he received the Nobel Prize, Walcott had buried his mother, as well as an increasing number of "friends . . . who have been dying / as if from some medieval plague".[7]

Though he would not be awarded his own Nobel Prize until the turn of the century, Naipaul already had garnered almost every other accolade bestowed on literary prose. Not the least of these was the predictability with which his work was cited in the mainstream press to "explain" developments in the Third World. By the 1980s Naipaul also had dealt with his share of bereavement. To the untimely death of his father while Naipaul was an undergraduate at Oxford were added the equally premature deaths of two of his siblings: a sister, Sati, in 1986 and his brother and fellow writer, Shiva, in 1985.[8] Among anglophone writers in Africa and the Caribbean, Kamau Brathwaite was arguably the most influential of the three writers during the 1970s, defining the orientation and stylistic effects to which a new generation of politically committed writers aspired.[9] Brathwaite's enhanced visibility in the United States was a consequence in part of his relocation to New York University in the 1990s. But that relocation was itself the product of a series of devastating personal losses, including the loss of his first wife, Doris, to cancer in 1986 and the loss of his home in Jamaica to Hurricane Gilbert in 1988.[10]

Brathwaite, Naipaul and Walcott share more than the coincidences of fame and death, however. Taken together, they constitute the crest of the wave of West Indian literary achievement that began to build in the 1950s and 1960s. When they published their first literary efforts, there was no such thing as a Caribbean literary tradition beyond the small circles of struggling writers in each of the separate British West Indian territories. By the beginning of the twenty-first century, their feel for words and their experiments with form had come to define the standard by which creative writing was assessed across the English-speaking world. In different ways and to differing degrees they had achieved the dubious distinction of becoming institutions within their lifetimes.

To write an epitaph for oneself in the late twentieth century involved fantasizing about what comes after the self at a time when the very concept of self had become imperilled. As Jean-Luc Nancy contends in his introduction to *Who Comes after the Subject?*, "the inaugurating decisions of contemporary thought – whether they took place under the sign of a break with metaphysics and its poorly pitched questions, under the sign of a 'deconstruction' of this metaphysics, under that of a transference of the thinking of Being to the thinking of life, or of the Other, or of language, etc. – have all involved putting subjectivity on trial". Nancy maintains, however, that all these linguistic, psychoanalytical and metaphysical moves "point to the necessity . . . of a move forward toward someone – *some one* – else in its place". He asks: "Who would it be? How would s/he present him/herself? Can we name her/him? Is the question 'who' suitable?"[11]

Within the postcolonial context, questions like these are complicated by the writer's need to resist what Frantz Fanon in *Black Skin, White Masks* calls "the colonization of subjectivity" (as Diana Fuss explains in *Identification Papers*).[12] In Fanon's paradigm, "'White' operates as its own Other, freed from any dependency upon the sign 'Black' for its symbolic constitution." Or, as Fanon visualizes it,[13]

White
———————————
Ego different from "the Other".

This freedom to imagine itself without explicitly invoking a racialized Other enables the stability and authority that the white subject takes for granted, even as it disables blackness as both subject and object. Consequently, as Fuss points out, "'Black' functions, within a racist discourse, always diacritically, as the negative term in a Hegelian dialectic continuously incorporated and negated";[14] in Fanon's term, "the Negro is comparison".[15] Fuss uses Fanon to buttress her argument that, "read psychoanalytically, *every* identification involves a degree of symbolic violence, a measure of temporary mastery and possession", and that "a certain element of colonization is structurally indispensable to every act of interiorization".[16] However, she merely speculates in passing about how such symbolic violence affects the imaginary identifications of the colonized Other. The postcolonial writers I consider cannot sidestep such questions. They understand that "acts of interiorization" involving symbolic violence allow them, like other speaking subjects, to establish "temporary mastery and possession" over the landscapes in which they come into being. They also understand that each time they speak, they leave themselves vulnerable to colonization and erasure in other speakers' paradigms, since nothing besides whiteness exists above Fanon's line, and the non-white speaking subject's inevitable relegation to the space below the line remains unmarked. As these writers endeavour to represent and theorize their problematic relationship to subjectivity, the question for them is never merely "Who am I?" or even "What is an 'I'?" but, more crucially, "What can 'I' represent – and to whom?"

The manifold difficulties surrounding subjectivity that press in upon the Caribbean writer inform both parts of the title of this book. The phrase "I and I" articulates the trajectory of these writers' achievements: their movement during the late twentieth century from the periphery to the centre of Western literary discourse, which allowed each of them to fantasize that he stood above Fanon's line and that the self he was now in a position to define discursively could take its own world as its referent. This was the signal linguistic achievement of the phrase "I and I" when it entered Jamaican language via Rastafarian Dread Talk in the 1960s. With it, Rastafarians announced their subjectivity in language that circumvented the limited linguistic choices available to them at the time. These were either to assimilate their subject position to that of the colonial oppressor by using the Standard English form of the first-person singular pronoun *I* or to persist in using the Creole version of the first-person singular, *mi/me*. *Mi* had the advantage of sounding authentically folksy. However, when inserted into the heteroglossic space of the Creole language continuum, it relegated the speaking subject to the position of eternal object in relation to the parallel and interpenetrative grammar of the Standard English *I*. The relationship of the Creole form *me* – used for both subject and object – to the Standard English *I* thus reiterates the condition whereby the colonized "Other" can function only diacritically, in Fuss's terms, "as the negative term in a Hegelian dialectic continuously incorporated and negated".[17]

In the essay "Colin Ferguson, Me and I: An Anatomy of Creole Psychosis", I have written about how some forms of creole psychosis may have their origin in the speaking subject's inability to negotiate the linguistic and psychological distance between the pronouns *I* and *me*.[18] The problems of mimicry and alienation related to these imaginary identifications can have pathological consequences when colonized creole subjects confound their use of Standard English with literal access to social power and psychological agency.[19] In such a context, Rastafarians' recourse to the grammatical form "I and I" to represent their subjectivity has obvious appeal, because it allows the speaking subject to identify with a projection of the self rather than defining that self by reference to the subjectivity of an unattainable Other. To maintain such autonomy, however, the utterance "I and I" circumvents all other personal pronouns. This compensatory doubling of the subject in Rastafarian Dread

Talk may lead to the creation of a discursive world so circumscribed in its imagined range of interlocutors as to be incapable of communicating meaning. Dread Talk descends into solipsism when the line between subject and object becomes so blurred that *I* can only define itself in relation to itself.

The dilemma of Dread Talk's tautological subject is a useful image for thinking about Caribbean writers' relationship to language, as it brings us back to the paradox in Fanon's paradigm: namely, that the relegation of an unspecified Other to the space beneath Fanon's line in his model stands in for the work that the white Ego – any ego – cannot do for itself. Like the Rastafarian's "I and I", the white Ego too can represent itself only in relation to itself. Thus the sense of incompletion that assails colonized speaking subjects each time they cross the line separating self from "Ego different from 'the Other'" in Fanon's paradigm may be both a consequence of their inevitable relegation to the space below the horizon of self-consciousness by the politics of racism and the irruption of an older problem: the (im)possibility of the subject's autonomy.

This is the point at which the second part of this book's title, "Epitaphs for the Self", comes into play. The idea of writing for yourself the lines you would write if you could no longer write is one way in which all three authors I discuss here have attempted to erase Fanon's line. It is their way of avoiding – or repeating – the kind of distinction that Heidegger makes between *Dasein* and *Vor-* or *Zuhandensein* (between present and past or future being), and which his interpreters have critiqued for reintroducing on the sly a distinction between subject and object, even as it challenges the possibility of such a distinction. In "Eating Well", for instance, Derrida cites Heidegger's sleight of hand in order to talk about how most philosophical thinking about grammar depends on past, present and future states of subjectivity, to mask the reappearance of an object that can be re-ingested without fanfare to support the construction of a stable subject. He tries to find another way of thinking about *Dasein* through the idea of *Geworfenheit*, a German word that implies for him a primordial notion of "being-thrown" that precedes "the determination of a *subject* that would come to be *thrown*", and he speculates from there:

> Starting at "birth", and possibly even prior to it, being-thrown reappropriates itself or rather ex-appropriates itself in forms that are not yet those of the *subject* or the *project*. The question "who" [comes after the subject,] then becomes:

"Who (is) thrown?" "Who becomes – 'who' from out of the destinerrance of the being-thrown?" . . . The subject assumes presence, that is to say sub-stance, stasis, stance. Not to be able to stabilize itself *absolutely* would mean to be able *only* to be stabilizing itself. Ex-appropriation no longer closes itself; it never totalizes itself. One should not take these figures for metaphors (metaphoricity implies ex-appropriation), nor determine them according to the grammatical opposition of active/passive. Between the thrown and the falling (*Verfallen*) there is also a possible point of passage.[20]

Derrida's point is easier to grasp when applied to the actual dilemma discussed in this book. The claim that, in the process of identification, the subject needs an object whose origin lies beyond the self makes it clear that "I and I" can only ever be an exercise in iterability, a closing off of the self or a totalizing of the self. Yet that claim gives the object an aura of coherence and distinction that obscures the extent to which the object itself may be no more than a subject in disguise. By introducing the notion of a state beyond the determination of the subject, the state of "being-thrownness", Derrida demonstrates how our assumption that the positions of subject and object are impermeable is related to the function of space in the grammatical utterance, rather than time. Once we think about these writers as writing to and from themselves across the divide between "real" time and fictional time, or between something we think of as time and something else we call eternity, or canonicity (in both senses of the word), then their self-referentiality, their repetitions and the tautologies in their work can be read as stages of differentiation or acts of becoming.

The readings that follow reflect upon what it means for these writers to contemplate such questions: the licence their success has allowed them to experiment with forms, which in the work of writers of lesser repute might have been considered too eccentric for serious consideration, and the protected space it makes available for them to face up to issues that they were too insecure or too inexperienced to confront in their earlier work. They are about the temptations of narcissism and isolation this licence conceals; the seductive drift towards self-plagiarism and aesthetic stagnation it allows; the endlessly tautological conversation of I with I. Ultimately these readings constitute a reflection on the intimations of mortality that one senses in the mature work of all three writers, each entering his seventh decade at the close of the century, and each, at the apogee of his creative life, beginning to dread, as Walcott puts it, the possibility of his gift "fading out of this page".[21] At the height of their powers, these writers could dare to dream that their work would outlive them, and in the literary projects to which they turned in the late 1980s and early 1990s, all three were fighting for the right to influence how that legacy would be read. The readings I offer here, from Naipaul's *A Way in the World* (1994), Brathwaite's *Barabajan Poems* (1994) and Walcott's poetic works *Omeros* (1992) and *The Bounty* (1997), demonstrate how the project of writing one's critical epitaph – not only because one dreads death or fears obscurity but also as a way of circumventing the metaphysical impasse produced by the death of the subject – can be understood as an overriding thematic concern, as well as an important source of stylistic innovation in contemporary Caribbean writing.

Naipaul, Brathwaite and Walcott were the kid brothers within the fraternity of postwar West Indian writers. Separated in age by less than a decade from such writers as George Lamming, Samuel Selvon, Wilson Harris and Edgar Mittelholzer, and in terms of publication by an even smaller margin, the three nevertheless constituted a distinct subgroup within their cohort. For a start, all three were top students at the exclusive colonial schools they attended and, unlike most of their older compatriots, they all went on to earn university degrees. Naipaul went from Queen's Royal College to Oxford on a Trinidad Island Scholarship in 1950, and Brathwaite from Harrison College to Cambridge on a Barbados Scholarship in the same year. Walcott left St Mary's College, St Lucia, also in 1950 for the University of the West Indies, on a scholarship funded by the British Colonial Development and Welfare Organization, thus becoming one of that fabled first cohort of multifaceted postcolonial artists, professionals and intellectuals to graduate from the new regional university, who went on to dominate West Indian cultural and professional life.

All three men emerged early as critics of other Caribbean writers, and each has named the influence of those writers on his development. Naipaul claims in *A Way in the World* to have grasped the possibilities of his comic gift after observing the response of BBC *Caribbean Voices* producer Henry Swanzy to a comic passage in George Lamming's *In the Castle of My Skin*.[22] Brathwaite, in *Barabajan Poems*, reveals that he was discouraged from publishing his first semi-autobiographical novel because the Guyanese novelist Edgar Mittelholzer dismissed its style as too "Lammingesque". He goes on to add that Mittelholzer later encouraged his poetry when it began to appear from Ghana.[23] Walcott's reorientation from painting to poetry followed his recognition of the possibility of a Caribbean literary voice in the poetry of the Jamaican writer George Campbell. Walcott memorializes that shift in the opening chapter of his autobiographical poem, *Another Life*, when he describes how, while still struggling to establish himself a painter, he picked up a copy of Campbell's *First Poems*

> . . . and began to read:
>
> "Holy be
> the white head of a Negro,
> sacred be
> the black flax of a black child . . ."
>
> And from a new book,
> bound in sea-green linen, whose lines
> matched the exhilaration which their reader,
> rowing the air around him now, conveyed,
> another life it seemed would start again[24]

Like kid brothers everywhere, Vidia, Kamau and Derek were quick to spot the missteps of their older siblings and to learn from them. As editor of the *Caribbean Voices* programme for a short period in the mid-1950s after Henry Swanzy moved on, Naipaul regularly read and reviewed on the air the writings of fellow Caribbean hopefuls and established writers. The scripts of these broadcasts offer a fascinating insight into Naipaul's own struggles with language and form during the time he was completing *A House for Mr Biswas*.[25] Elsewhere, in a review of Lamming's *Of Age and Innocence* that appeared in the *New Statesman* in 1958, Naipaul faults Lamming for his move away from realism and for his choice of a hypothetical Caribbean island for his novel's setting:

> Mr Lamming . . . is not a realistic writer. He deals in symbols and allegory. Experience has not been the basis of this novel. Every character, every incident is no more than a constituent idea in Mr Lamming's thesis; the reader's

sympathies are never touched. San Cristobal, the imaginary island which is the setting of Mr Lamming's novel, could never exist. I can understand Mr Lamming's need for fantasy. His conception of the search for identity is highly personal; it has arisen from a deep emotion which he has chosen to suppress, turning it instead into an intellectual thing which is fine in its way, but would be made absurd by the comic realities of West Indian political life.[26]

Notwithstanding these reservations, Naipaul went on to produce *The Mimic Men*, which borrowed Lamming's technique of using children of three different races to represent the racial tensions in Caribbean politics, and which introduced Isabella, a hypothetical island as abstract and allegorical as Lamming's San Cristobal. Although he never lost his comic gift, over the years Naipaul, like Lamming, came to feel constrained by the demands of realism.

Both Brathwaite and Walcott authored important landmark essays on Caribbean writing early in their careers. As in-house critic for the *Trinidad and Tobago Guardian* between 1960 and 1967, Walcott reviewed practically everything that came his way from the regional literary and theatre scenes. As with Naipaul's *Caribbean Voices* reviews, these journalistic pieces are as valuable for what they tell us about the writers whom Walcott assesses as for what they say about his own creative development. Indeed, as Gordon Rohlehr shrewdly points out in his essay "The Problem of the Problem of Form", one of the surest ways to anticipate the shifts in Walcott's stylistic development is to take note of the features in the works of other writers that he criticizes most harshly in these reviews. On Walcott's dismissive comments about calypso as poetry and Carnival as theatre in the *Guardian* reviews, Rohlehr quips: "with Walcott nothing is that simple. Whatever he warns against, he's on the verge of attempting."[27] And indeed Walcott went on to use calypso rhythms in one of his most acclaimed poems in the 1979 *Star Apple Kingdom* collection, "The Schooner *Flight*".

A historian by training, Brathwaite's critical strength has been the literary retrospective. Essays such as "The Love Axe", which appeared in consecutive issues of *Bim* in 1977–78, and his tripartite series "Jazz and the West Indian Novel", published in *Bim* a decade earlier, offer authoritative assessments of the meaning and direction of Caribbean cultural production during the 1960s and 1970s.[28] Brathwaite used these critical retrospectives to gauge the extent to which other writers anticipated the concern with the region's African heritage and folk cultures so central to the themes and techniques of his own literary endeavour. Yet here again, as we shall see in the discussion of *Barabajan Poems*, it is possible to intuit in Brathwaite's reflections on other writers the germs of ideas that blossom in his later literary productions.

Critic, novelist and journalist; journalist, dramatist and poet; poet, historian and critic – these are only a cross-section of the literary roles that Naipaul, Walcott and Brathwaite's multiple presences within and beyond the literary and academic mainstream have allowed them to inhabit. These are writers determined to occupy all the available space within the literary world as they see it; artists who write with an eye to posterity and who would rather not publish than be considered second-rate; critics who aim to rewrite the meaning of the cultures that have produced them. Inevitably, the ambitious scope of their critical pronouncements and the innovative reach of their creative writing have contributed to the construction of all kinds of exaggerated, often acrimonious oppositions between their respective oeuvres among the critics who have appointed themselves champions of their causes – oppositions the writers themselves have not always been averse to exacerbating.[29] Yet the contrasts between their points of view are never as marked as the self-contradictions within their own respective oeuvres. As each writer struggled to come to terms with fame and death at the close of the twentieth century, what strikes me most is the extent to which their perspectives on what mattered in these struggles coincided. Their "kid brother" legacies as both observers of and participants in the growth of a Caribbean literary tradition left all three peculiarly vulnerable to the burden of witness – especially when that witness involved an estimate of their own achievements. The epitaphs for themselves and others written into the works I consider are meant to pre-empt their judgement by others, to tutor us in the proper ways of reading their achievements, and to insert into the literary tradition, against the metaphysical odds, a record of their subjectivity. They bring each writer face to face with his own most dreaded nemesis, even as they attempt to manipulate the ways in which we interpret that confrontation.

The epitaphs to the essays in the first section of this work delineate Naipaul in relation to three of the figures he eulogizes: the historical figure Walter

Raleigh, one of the first authors to write about the Trinidad landscape; a person Naipaul calls Lebrun, whom he models after the Trinidadian intellectual C.L.R. James; and a fictitious character, Blair, whom Naipaul assembles out of characteristics drawn from various black West Indian readers of his novels whom he has encountered over the years. Naipaul's decision to model his fictional character Lebrun on his fellow countryman C.L.R. James allows him to examine the problems of co-optation and appropriation that come with fame – problems with which both Naipaul and James struggled throughout their careers. Naipaul challenges readers who have seen him and James as representing diametrically opposed positions in Caribbean intellectual thought to acknowledge the angst and insecurity, the refusals and accommodations that must of necessity have lain behind James's poised public persona. Without an understanding of this angst, Naipaul contends, we cannot fully appreciate either the greatness of a figure like James or the limits of his vision. At the same time, his reading of the fictional Lebrun offers us strategies for understanding the fictional persona Naipaul has created for himself. My reading of Naipaul's take on Lebrun's inner life is framed by discussions of Naipaul's reflections on Raleigh and Blair. Naipaul asks that we read Raleigh's *Discoverie of Guiana* not as a historical document but as the explorer's attempt to write himself into history through the creation of an imaginary landscape. Conversely, Naipaul's deployment of the black Trinidadian Blair allows him to fantasize about who the local readers of such a text might be. As he examines the extent to which the Trinidadian landscape that writers such as himself and Raleigh and James created may never have corresponded with the imagined landscapes of their variously raced readers at different historical moments, Naipaul invites us to consider how reading any writer's legacy depends on distortions of time and space.

The essays in part 2 examine the names that Brathwaite gives his poetic persona in *Barabajan Poems*. "Kamau" and "Son/Sun" have histories that originate in Brathwaite's earlier poems and essays. Embedded here in the fantasy of an all-encompassing autobiography, the names the poet gives himself accrete new meanings as they are celebrated or rejected by the poet's interlocutors – the poet's first muse, Esse; the critic Carolivia Herron; and Barbadian society in general. My reading of the politics of heteroglossia enacted in Brathwaite's multilayered hypertext provides the point of departure for considering the writer's assumptions about his audience and what those assumptions reveal about the limitations and possibilities of his literary project. I compare Brathwaite's image of his Caribbean island as a submerged landscape to Naipaul's vision of a landscape terminally obscured by the infinite ramifications of its histories, and reflect on how these competing visions structure each writer's understanding of his subjectivity. This section's most sustained discussion examines Brathwaite's relationship to an identity he refuses. The search for the missing epitaph for "Edward" opens up to scrutiny Brathwaite's ambivalent relationship with his patrimony and the implications of this ambivalence for his literary legacy. By comparing the different approaches that Walcott and Brathwaite take in their work when representing black and white mentors and father figures, I offer a reading of Brathwaite's anti-colonial rhetoric that takes seriously the implications of Fanon's advocacy of the death of the racialized subject, whether that subject be the "native" or the "colonizer".

The final section, on Derek Walcott's *Omeros* and the poems in *The Bounty* collection, reprises the discussions that precede it while offering a reading of Walcott's approach to the subjectivity of his poetic persona. In chapters that open with the dedications "For V.S. Naipaul", "For Kamau Brathwaite" and "For Derek Walcott", respectively, I argue that Walcott always has been the most explicitly "literary" of the three writers, using references to a range of canonical writers, from Homer to Joseph Brodsky, to situate his poetic sensibility and to represent the literal and literary landscapes he inhabits. As the focus of his work shifts in mid-career from an almost narcissistic self-reflexivity to engagement with epic themes, those whom he seems most often to cite (albeit implicitly) are his fellow Caribbean writers – men like Brathwaite and Naipaul who have attempted to deal with the same themes of history, landscape and subjectivity that Walcott has made his own.

In the chapter that opens with the epitaph "For Naipaul", I examine how Walcott's apprehension of the St Lucian landscape in *Omeros*, through the figure of Major Plunkett, reverses and builds upon Naipaul's attempts to domesticate the English countryside in *The Enigma of Arrival*. The chapter "For Brathwaite" acknowledges that the journey back to Africa made by *Omeros*'s other protagonist, Achille, recalls the obsessive odysseys that have carried many of Brathwaite's poetic personae back to an imagined

Motherland. However, it argues that Walcott's less easily acknowledged debt to Brathwaite in *Omeros* lies in the way he builds on Brathwaite's experiments with Caribbean speech. Paradoxically, Walcott achieves this newly confident indigenous voice by submitting himself to the disciplines of "ancestral rhyme", so much of the discussion here is taken up with tracing the development of a new commitment to formal metrical structures at the same time that Walcott's language is moving closer to the St Lucian vernacular. The chapter on Walcott's relationship to Naipaul is most concerned with the autobiographical *I* in both writers' work, while the chapter discussing Walcott and Brathwaite focuses on how both writers represent *them* – the folk.

The final chapter, which opens with the epitaph "For Derek Walcott", argues that in *Omeros* Walcott eventually comes to a point where he can trust his own voice – mining his own archive of poems, plays and essays for the images and languages he needs – without becoming defensive about the perceived inadequacies of the Caribbean literary landscape, on the one hand, or the postcolonial subject, on the other. Counterintuitively, the pronoun that matters most in these closing readings is the dialogic *you*. In my closing meditations on *The Bounty*, a collection that reads for long stretches like an unbroken lament for lost parents, lovers, children, landscapes and words, I return to the problem of the subject. As Walcott asks himself and his readers, "can you genuinely claim these, and do they reclaim you"?[30] we again confront the dilemma of self-authorization. This final chapter addresses the artist's insatiable desire to fix – for *you*, his readers and himself – the version of that self through which he wishes to be known for posterity, even as he, like Brathwaite and Naipaul, confronts his fear that time, distance and the limitations of language already may have rendered him incapable of summoning those images through which he first immortalized his landscape and which in their turn earned him the accolades of canonicity.

Wrapping up *Another Life* with the death of his mentor, Harry Simmons, Walcott writes:

> Forgive me, if this sketch should ever thrive,
> or profit from your gentle, generous spirit.
> When I began this work, you were alive,
> and with one stroke, you have completed it![31]

And there is indeed something mildly opportunistic about the way in which Simmons's untimely suicide facilitates closure in Walcott's autobiographical poem, making possible the ghoulish perfection of a line like "Then, with slow strokes, the master changed the sketch".[32] Walcott, who was already writing eulogies when he first published *Twenty-Five Poems* as a nineteen-year-old, confesses in an unpublished interview with Kenneth Ramchand to often having felt guilty at funerals when, his consciousness still raw with grief, he would catch himself greedily cataloguing images to put into the poem he knew he would end up writing about his latest dead friend.[33]

I know what he means. When I first began to think about this project in the mid-1990s, the questions it raised were purely aesthetic. Naipaul, Brathwaite and Walcott were at the height of their powers, and though they had begun to worry about their literary legacies, they seemed nowhere close to the ends of their lives. Two decades later, as my project draws to a close, all three are old men battling the encroaching indignities of mortality: decreased mobility and mental agility; endless doctors' visits; growing reliance on wives, partners, children and batteries of caregivers to fend off the inevitable decline. At moments I have found myself guiltily assessing which will be the first to achieve completion – their lives or my project. Meanwhile, the hum of accolades for each man, at celebrations and in festschrifts like the ones in which excerpts from this study have appeared, approaches a crescendo.[34] Increasingly in that buzz of adulation, one divines an indecorous eagerness as admirers circle closer, hoping to land the final *coup de grâce* – the last interview, the last reading, the last signed copy, the last public sighting. Naipaul's description in *A Way of the World* of how he thought C.L.R. James was hounded in his final years by researchers, political disciples and sycophants seems uneasily apt. Brathwaite may have longed to raise "stammaments in stone" to his dead forebears, but during their lifetimes, fame may ultimately have entombed all three writers in the critically deadening edifices of official adulation.

This study inevitably contributes to the eulogizing project, but it aims to do more than that. For if it is true that these three writers represent the crest of the wave of West Indian writing that first began to build on the literary horizon in the 1950s, then those of us born in that decade constitute the first generation of West Indian readers to frolic in its cascading surf. That is, we were the first cohort of readers in the region to grow up taking the existence of an anglophone Caribbean literary tradition for granted. By the early 1960s, when our cohort entered high school, independence from Britain had come to many West Indian colonies, and novels, plays and poems by the region's writers had begun to find their way into our classrooms and onto bookshelves in our homes. But the writers themselves were still making their way in the world. Their success was not a foregone conclusion. They inhabited the same spaces that we did, and occasionally we witnessed their creative and personal vicissitudes, if not at first hand, then at only a slight remove.

Walcott's Theatre Workshop rehearsed in the auditorium of my school in the late 1960s, and its inaugural production of *Ti-Jean and His Brothers* in 1970 was the first grown-up theatre production I ever attended. Naipaul's first wife and his sister both taught at that same school while I was a student there. And though I already had fallen in love with *Miguel Street*, a book set in a part of Port of Spain not far from where I lived, there was no precedent at the time for considering people with names like Naipaul and Capildeo as international celebrities. At the University of the West Indies in Jamaica, Brathwaite – he was still Eddie then – had an office in the history department, just downstairs from the English department, where I was a major. As students we produced his plays and invited him to judge our Carnival competitions. But the jury of the day was still out as to whether the success of his first trilogy was more than a passing fad. We read these writers' works as they appeared, dismissing them, adopting them, celebrating them as we felt inclined, but we did not think of them as "famous" beyond our corner of the known world. We knew no more than they did what turns their literary careers would take over the next forty years. The questions they began to raise in the 1990s about their literary legacies prompted us to consider that their works might endure and that their audiences had expanded well beyond our parochial cohort of regional readers. Yet their bonds with us, their most intimate readers, also endure. In works that take the world as their stage, they continue to clamour for the attention and recognition of a local audience that has not always treated them kindly. My study attempts to unpack those local quarrels as a way to understanding more fully the global dimensions of their achievements.

Other things have changed. The worlds that Naipaul, Brathwaite and Walcott describe – the worlds in which they came of age – no longer exist.

Some aspects of these communities were already fading when their early works first appeared. However, the pace of that change quickened by the turn of the century. Brathwaite's fascination with computers and with the possibilities of his "video style layout", as he calls it in *Barabajan Poems*, seems quaint even by the technological standards of its date of publication. Many of the beaches that Walcott describes and the fields Naipaul remembers had made way for full-service hotels and expensive suburbs in Barbados, Jamaica, Trinidad and St Lucia by the time *Omeros* and *A Way in the World* were published. The gender roles and assumptions about sexuality that inform all three men's work also have come under greater scrutiny: new cohorts of Caribbean readers and writers have moved away from the normative heterosexual masculinities that circumscribed literary production in the mid-twentieth century. Globalization has replaced colonialism as the defining framework for representing inequality. Those changes have allowed me to uncover new possibilities and vulnerabilities in the work of all three writers, and part of my project here is to read their works through the enabling lenses of such change.

There are not many moments when readers or writers can lay claim to having participated in making literary history. Within the English literary tradition, one thinks perhaps of Chaucer's age or Shakespeare's or the Romantic era as having produced sea changes in language and culture that both shaped their respective writers' work and were enabled by them. In Britain's former colonies we can locate a similar cohort of writers, born in the 1930s, whose work redefined the language and transformed the literary imagination of the entire English-speaking world during the twentieth century; Naipaul, Brathwaite, Walcott, Achebe, Soyinka, Coetzee and Gordimer are among those whose work I know most intimately. These writers divined that the worlds into which they had been born were on the threshold of great change. Their literary productions have shaped the meanings we assign to those changes and to the era in which they lived and wrote. My study ends with a personal tribute to the ways in which Naipaul, Brathwaite and Walcott have shaped me as a reader. In offering that testimonial, I hope I can give back to them symbolically some of that sense of having been heard and seen that their literary legacies have bequeathed to me.

PART 1

V.S. NAIPAUL

1

FOR WALTER RALEIGH

> And year by year our memory fades
> From all the circle of the hills.
>
> Till from the garden and the wild
> A fresh association blow,
> And year by year the landscape grow
> Familiar to the stranger's child.[1]

Early in his chapter on Raleigh, about halfway through *A Way in the World*, V.S. Naipaul addresses the question of how a writer's work is read at different moments during and after his life. Although these insights come to us indirectly – by way of Raleigh's inquisitorial ship's surgeon as the explorer plays out his last wager with fame and death – Naipaul's tone here is unmistakably tutelary. The surgeon is complaining about how he must comb through Raleigh's account of his 1595 voyage to Trinidad and the Guianas for the facts upon which to hang an opinion – a judgement, really – about the explorer's achievement. What begins as an admission of frustration and disorientation in the surgeon's complaint, however, shifts unexpectedly into a treatise on the art of close reading:

> You slip about, you lose your footing. It's nice and easy and clear and brilliant for a number of pages, and then suddenly you feel you've not been paying attention. You feel you've missed something. So you go back. You've missed nothing. It's just that something's gone wrong with the writing. This happens many times. So even if you're a careful reader you lose the drift of the narrative. It's not easy, noticing first of all that the writing has changed and then finding exactly where. But those are precisely the places you have to identify.

Because those are the places where the writer decides to add things or to hide things.[2]

The shift in the surgeon's tone from complaint to instruction allows Naipaul to make the passage's stylistic progression enact the process that the surgeon describes: to display and conceal the meaning of his text. The overall structure of *A Way in the World* constantly reiterates this sly, frustrating process of slippage and excess. Like Raleigh's travelogue, Naipaul's eccentric mixture of loosely connected chapters – some autobiographical, some documentary, some the unfinished drafts of "unrealizable" screenplays and stories – is itself "a deliberate mixture of old-fashioned fantasy and modern truth".[3] As we make our way through what the American edition persists with perverse accuracy in describing as a novel – that is, a new mixture of genres and language registers – we constantly have to readjust our perspective. Naipaul makes us look at his world, "now sharp and small and not quite real, now standard size and real but blurred", in the way he tells us he played with his first pair of glasses, "moving between dazzle and coolness".[4] The reader drifts between rapid, practically effortless consumption of his language's spare cadences and a hesitant double-checking of the name of the chapter, the identity of the narrator and the dates of the historical period in which a particular piece is set. We flip back and forth between references we imagine have cropped up before, in other chapters or in other works by Naipaul.

If we follow Naipaul's surgeon's advice and read those moments of slippage as key structuring elements of the novel, several patterns come into focus. For a start, the novel is an unabashed exercise in self-plagiarism. Naipaul borrows almost all his characters and scenes from his previous works: the early colonial history of Trinidad presented in *The Loss of El Dorado*, on which he draws for the unrealizable screenplay about Raleigh, as well as the unfinished drama about the Venezuelan revolutionary Miranda, and the impressions of Obote's Uganda and Bokassa's Central African empire familiar from *In a Free State*, *A Bend in the River* and "The Crocodiles of Yamoussoukro", which provide background to the chapters on the black West Indian characters the narrator encounters in Africa. Naipaul also rifles his past works for familiar narrative perspectives and turns of phrase. The narrators of the opening two chapters, set in Trinidad, share much of their *naïveté* with the child narrator of *Miguel Street* and the memoirist in "Prologue to an Autobiography". There are echoes of *Guerrillas* in the descriptions of several of the lost revolutionaries who wander through *A Way in the World*.

The studied artlessness with which Naipaul juxtaposes new characters and old scenes, culled as it were from browsing his own archive, organizes the novel's overriding concern with the act of reading. Each of his loosely related chapters offers a rereading of the life that a specific character has constructed for himself. In the case of Raleigh and the Caribbean intellectual Lebrun, the readings are generated by the characters' published writings. For others, like Miranda and the remade Indo-Trinidadian (now Venezuelan) Sorzano, the documents the men carry with them to support fictive identities produce these readings. Other protagonists are trapped within narratives about their identities to which they have merely acquiesced. The son of a Caribbean Garveyite who actually goes back to Africa is one such man, as is the protagonist of "New Clothes, an Unwritten Story", who finds himself marooned in the Guianese interior, caught between the utopian fantasies of the revolutionaries who have hired him to organize their journey and the apocalyptic visions of the Amerindians who are their guides. Naipaul embeds in these accounts his reflections on the semi-autobiographical narrative persona he has constructed for himself over the years. Sometimes the shifts between character and author are as direct and unvarnished as the shift between the descriptive and the instructional in the surgeon's complaint. But at other moments Naipaul seems to struggle to contain the multiple readings of himself that his text sets free.

In the paragraph that follows the instruction in close reading quoted earlier, the surgeon launches into a detailed consideration of the "Advertisement" with which Raleigh prefaces his account of his earlier voyage of discovery: "One of the more extraordinary things in your book occurs in the 'Advertisement,' a kind of preface which you print between the letter of dedication and the book itself. It's very bold, very effective, to place something so important in that half-way-house place, where people don't read all that carefully."[5] The surgeon accuses Raleigh of embedding a disclaimer here, denying that his expedition found anything and admitting "that the so-called 'ore' . . . was really sand and that the piece of Guiana gold . . . was something . . . bought beforehand in North Africa".[6] It implies that Raleigh brought back the sand only because the forty men he had sent up the Orinoco in search of gold kept returning with different-coloured sands that they insisted were gold.[7] According to Naipaul's fictional surgeon, Raleigh's City of Gold is merely a mirage that his readers collude with his crew in imposing on the sand, by reading past and through the "facts" his text presents. In the process, they construct a glittering illusion. But of course that text is not quite nothing. Raleigh's fantasies and ambition endow it with a fungibility as palpable as the passion of his sand-bearing soldiers. His readers accept his fiction because, in spite of his disclaimer, he wants them to do so as desperately as those forty men needed him to believe that the glittering sand they had found was in fact gold.

Naipaul's surgeon's instruction in close reading, followed by his detailed account of how Raleigh positions his advertisement, sent me on my own search through the preamble to Naipaul's improbable novel. Like Raleigh in his account of the discovery of Guiana, Naipaul secretes in his novel's front matter lines that mask and reveal his authorial predicament. Between his novel's copyright page and its table of contents, he wedges in the lines of verse I have used as the first of my "epitaphs", in the epigraph to this chapter. Naipaul takes these lines from Tennyson's *In Memoriam*, without acknowledgement. Like the stranger's child they invoke, he appropriates the unnamed poet's landscape with scant regard for its original associations. For a start, he divides the citation across two pages, positioning the first two lines – "And year by year our memory fades / From all the circle of the hills" – on the front of one page while placing the remaining four lines on the back of the page, where a reader anxious to get on with the "real" story may easily overlook them. This fracturing isolates the sentiments expressed in the first two lines – about the fading of the writer's self – from the promise of recuperation contained in the next four lines, which describe the fresh associations that future generations may yet bring to the writer's work or his landscape. Seen as two separate statements, both portions of this epigraph become statements of loss. On the front of the page, the memory of the speaker's friend fades "[f]rom all the circle of the hills". Turn over the page, and the meanings the poet thought he had inscribed indelibly on the landscape disappear, replaced by the "fresh associations" of a stranger's child.

But even a careful reader may miss the epigraph's final travesty. In

Tennyson's original poem, memorializing his dead friend Arthur Hallam, the two lines from the end of canto CI that Naipaul cites first – "And year by year our memory fades / From all the circle of the hills" – actually come after the next four lines that he cites. Reversing their order allows Naipaul to excise the first two lines from canto CI's closing quatrain that read, "As year by year the labourer tills / His wonted glebe, or lops the glades".[8] Archaic words like *glebe* and *wonted* would have been considered quaint even when Tennyson used them. They signal the poet's nostalgia for a rustic innocence associated with an imaginary preindustrial England. Naipaul thus excises all references to the landscape that depend on a cultural knowledge he does not share. At the same time, by placing the lines about the stranger's child at the end of his citation instead of at the beginning, he gives the interloper the last word, denying the speaker in Tennyson's poem even that echo of a fading memory that would have lingered had the citation ended where Tennyson's canto ends, with the lines "And year by year our memory fades, / From all the circle of the hills".

The multiple dispossessions of the strategically fragmented epigraph anticipate the moments in the chapter "A New Man" in *A Way in the World*, when the narrator recalls the personal associations he brought as a child to the abandoned cocoa estate where his family once lived. The adult narrator remembers how he had struggled at the time to visualize the process by which a landscape he knew so intimately might one day be wiped clean of all traces of his sojourn in it, as well as that of other inhabitants from previous epochs:

> The idea of a recent wiped-out past was too big for a child in an elementary school to grasp. Later it became difficult in another way. As soon as you tried to enter that idea, it ramified. And it ramified more and more as your understanding grew: different people living for centuries where we now trod, with our own overwhelming concerns: different people, with their own calendar and reverences and ideas of human association, different houses or huts, different roads or paths, different crops and fields and vegetation (and seasons), different views, speeds, reasons for journeys, different ideas of the ages of man, different ideas of the enemy and fellowship and sanctity and what men owed themselves.[9]

The way in which the colon, the parentheses and the commas in this passage defer closure within its long central sentence mimics the process of ramification Naipaul describes. And the process does not stop there. Every category of difference that the narrator enunciates finds its echo in the endless shifts in characters and chronology his narrative performs. The stories present us with the half-Indian Don Jose's mystification at the rituals Raleigh's commander observes for the men he has killed; the changing settlements, accents and populations of the Trinidad to which the narrator returns in alternating autobiographical chapters and shifting historical periods; the way that being Trinidadian comes to mean different things in Trinidad, in London, in Africa, in Manhattan or on a plane to Venezuela. In the end we understand, from this perspective of endless ramification, how the world of Naipaul's narrator, like the experience of Naipaul's reader, "appeared to lose some of its substance; reality became fluid. It was more natural to let go, to let the mind spring back to an everyday, ground-level vision that took in only what could be seen."[10]

Naipaul presents this "everyday, ground-level vision" as the only reality anyone can grasp with certainty, even as he tries to understand and represent the wiped-out past. I think this is why he insists on describing Raleigh's and Miranda's historical dramas, as well as his story set in the Amerindian heartland of Guiana, as "unwritten" or "unrealized". Even as he attends to lived nuance and observed detail, Naipaul distrusts the authenticity of voices that he creates but cannot hear, whose socio-historical ramifications he can barely intuit. And so his native Amerindians, his Manhattan Jewish literati, his foreign mercenaries in the Guianese interior, even such meticulously researched figures as Raleigh and Miranda, all remain sandy mirages within his text, incompletely realized characters who have none of the immediacy, the recognizable idioms and physical gestures of the black West Indian educator the narrator meets in Africa, or of Sorzano, the remade Indo-Trinidadian he encounters on a flight to Venezuela, with his piratical braid, his Spanish doubloons and his Hindu devotional records. These characters have been produced by a Caribbean world that Naipaul knows intimately. Although his narrator meets them only briefly and knows of them only what they are willing to reveal in snatched conversations, Naipaul has no difficulty suggesting their complexity or helping us to divine their desires.

By contrast, the reconstructed historical characters who live out their lives in earlier Caribbean landscapes remain cardboard characters, incompletely animated figures in half-finished screenplays or dramas who speak most convincingly when they mouth the author's personal preoccupations. Miranda, for instance, whose complex revolutionary motivations leave me untouched as a reader of fiction (as opposed to history), suddenly springs to life when Naipaul allows him to commit to his journal his bitterness about the cavalier manner in which his fellow countrymen dismiss his hard-won achievements:

> Whatever I had done in the world I had done, according to this way of thinking, only because I was like them, my critics. Whether in Russia or England or France or the United States, there was nothing personal about my achievement. If they had been where I had been they would have done what I had done. I had gambled nothing of myself, taken no risks, exercised no personal will. . . . They had done it for me. I had done nothing. I was nothing.[11]

We know very little about the hazily sketched detractors whom Miranda refers to as "they". However, we know enough about Naipaul's *they*, from his previous essays and novels, to credit this outburst as something he himself might conceivably have said about his Caribbean critics. In fact, the passage reads suspiciously like a direct riposte to Walcott's critique of Naipaul's *Enigma of Arrival*. Walcott's 1986 review lectured Naipaul for making a myth of his exceptionalism, as if he were the only Caribbean writer to have overcome his parochial limitations and achieved literary renown. Here Naipaul seems to use Miranda to respond sarcastically to Walcott's sneering reproof, "how weak Naipaul's struggle would seem if it were communal".[12]

In attending only to surfaces, asking us to credit only what the lines on the page reveal or conceal, without claiming to have exhausted the ramifications of landscape and consciousness that have produced his characters, Naipaul plays with the possibility of his own extinction. Like every writer, he aspires to live on in his text. But once he claims the right to appropriate Tennyson's poem or to remake Raleigh and Miranda in his own image, according to his own experience of their landscapes, Naipaul has to acknowledge that his own writing and the meaning of his literary achievement are also infinitely appropriable by others. If he can deconstruct, recontextualize and even novelize whole epochs of history, like those he appropriates from Raleigh's text, then it stands to reason that someday, somewhere, if his work survives and achieves canonical status, some "stranger's child" will do the same thing to his writings and to him.

Naipaul confronts the fear of personal diminishment, to which Miranda gives voice and his novel's appropriations give substance, as he considers how his literary legacy will be read. And the method of his text suggests that the options are limited. He can risk the indignity of neglect, of becoming a faded memory, or he can succumb to the more sinister loss of appropriation: to be read only through the preoccupations of the children of strangers. Ultimately, their unknowingness about the landscape that produced him will constitute an erasure more complete than the parochialisms and distorting pettiness of his contemporaneous Caribbean audiences. The author's demise thus becomes an inevitable consequence of his work's endurance.

In his later works Naipaul attempts to forestall erasure by making his autobiography – his personal landscape – an integral part of the stories he invents. He smuggles into the fantasy world of his fiction an "advertisement" that both affirms and conceals what he wishes to be seen as the truth about his self. As in his other fictionalized memoirs, *A Way in the World* constructs a narrating persona to stand in for Naipaul the writer when he can no longer guide the reader towards this self. Here too his method mirrors what the surgeon says about Raleigh's account of his voyage. The surgeon tells Raleigh, "Everything you write about the Trinidad side of the Gulf is true. It's remarkable. Every tribe, every village, every river is as you say."[13] But once he turns to Raleigh's description of what it is like on the El Dorado side of the Gulf, the surgeon sees only fantasy and self-deception:

> The Gulf had always been a place of blood and revenge, of Indian dispossessions and resettlement. Even before the Spanish time. The man-eating Caribs were moving down. There were dreadful wars. You added to that. But you went away and wrote a book about an untouched paradise on the rivers, a place to which you alone had access, where the Indians lived in beautiful meadows and didn't know the value of the gold and diamonds by which they were surrounded, and where you alone had the secret to Indian hearts.[14]

Raleigh needs this blend of minutely observed fact and recklessly invented fantasy if he is to convince himself and his readers of a reality that his advertisement acknowledges is fictive. Similarly, Naipaul's hallmark attention to finely observed details and historical chronology creates the illusion of facticity that he needs to support our reading his novel as autobiography, even as he insists that it is a work of fiction.

In *A Way in the World*, all the descriptive passages set in Naipaul's Trinidad utilize this documentary style: Woodford Square; Parry's Funeral Home; St Vincent Street; the Registrar General's Department at the Red House, where Naipaul, like his narrator, worked as a teenager; the narrator's aunt fanning her coalpot on the back steps of the overcrowded house in Port of Spain; the food stain on the chief minister's tablecloth; the feel of the unread book by Lebrun that the young narrator discovers in his high school library; the smells of fish glue and rotting cocoa pods. The narrator delivers these descriptions almost clinically, as if from direct observation, so the reader experiences them as carefully observed fact. The relationships Naipaul invents between his semi-autobiographical narrator and two of his compatriots – the intellectual Lebrun and the fictionalized black Trinidadian character Blair – fall into this category. In the ensuing chapters I argue that, through the epitaphs he writes for them, these men come to embody achievements that Naipaul wants to claim for himself. His representation of them instructs us in the responses that Naipaul hopes his works may one day elicit from his readers.

2

FOR C.L.R. JAMES

> ... a man who had been born early in the century into a very hard world, whose intellectual growth had at every stage been accompanied by a growing rawness of sensibility, and whose political resolutions, expressing the wish not to go mad, had been in the nature of spiritual struggles, occurring in the depth of his being.... But perhaps, too, in extreme old age, he had become a child again, looking only for peace.[1]

When *A Way in the World* first appeared in 1994, reviewers noted as a matter of course that Naipaul had modelled the figure of Lebrun after the historical figure C.L.R. James, another Trinidadian who had achieved international celebrity during his lifetime. Naipaul's novel includes several such characters based on thinly disguised public figures. He models Foster Morris, the debonair English author of a book on Trinidadian politics called *Shadowed Livery*, on the English novelist Arthur Calder-Marshall, whose documentary *Glory Dead* (1939) provides a detailed account of the 1930s oilfield riots in Trinidad. De Groot, the white intellectual born and raised in Africa, in whose home the narrator meets Blair near the end of the novel, is based on James de Vere Allen, a white Australian expatriate who taught at Makerere University while Naipaul was in Uganda in the 1960s. Like his fictional double, Allen was gay, cultivated a beautiful garden and studied Swahili culture.[2] Naipaul's method of simulated facticity depends on readers who are "in the know" being able to pick up on these factual details, enhancing our sense that we are reading a historically accurate document. However, Naipaul does not change the names of all his historical characters; Raleigh and Miranda remain Raleigh and

Miranda. Henry Swanzy, an associate of Calder-Marshall and producer of the BBC's *Caribbean Voices* programme in the 1950s, remains Henry Swanzy. On the whole, it seems that only the characters whose life stories he manipulates to produce specific effects are given new names.

It is difficult, though, to decide what to make of Lebrun. The fictional relationship between him and the narrator corresponds closely with details of the actual relationship between James and Naipaul.[3] Moreover, the moments where they deviate can easily be identified in the numerous accounts of James's career that appeared near the end of his life.[4] James is such a well-known public figure in leftist and Caribbean circles that altering his name seems to be as futile a gesture as it would have been for Naipaul to alter Raleigh's name in his chapter on the explorer. Naipaul's insistence on distinguishing between Lebrun and James, therefore, signals his interest in imagining the private life of a public figure, in recreating through fiction the most intimate motivations of someone *like* James (or like himself), rather than presenting us with an accurate estimate of C.L.R. James the historical figure. This method allows Naipaul to use Lebrun as a foil and a mirror for himself in ways that he could not have done had he remained faithful to the historical record, even as he draws on that record to create the illusion of facticity.

James is one of the few Caribbean intellectuals – certainly the only other Trinidadian – to have attained through his writing an international reputation equal to Naipaul's. In spite of significant political differences between the two, Naipaul's semi-autobiographical account reveals that as a schoolboy at Queen's Royal College he was inspired by the accomplishments of this distinguished graduate of his alma mater. Like the fictional Lebrun, James anticipated many of Naipaul's themes, since, as Naipaul allows his quasi-autobiographical narrator to explain, they shared an interest in the history of the Caribbean and Latin America and in Trinidad's role within that history.[5] Indeed, Naipaul's awareness of James's literary reputation probably goes further back than the relationship he describes between his narrator and Lebrun. James had co-founded the early literary magazine the *Beacon* in the interwar years, and Naipaul's father interacted with members of that literary circle who were still active in Trinidad in the 1940s and 1950s.[6] Naipaul also drew inspiration from *Beacon* stories for his early novels. He refers in the essay "Jasmine" (reprinted in *The Overcrowded Barracoon*) to a handful of local short stories he encountered as a child, through which he "began to appreciate the distorting, distilling power of the writer's art. Where I had seen a drab haphazardness they found order; where I would have attempted to romanticize, to render my subject equal with what I had read, they accepted. They provided a starting-point for further observation; they did not trigger off fantasy."[7]

Seen through these connections to Naipaul's father, Naipaul's school, Naipaul's intellectual interests and the international literary scene, the historical James clearly was an early role model for Naipaul, as the younger writer acknowledges in his review of the 1963 reissue of James's *Beyond a Boundary*:

> To me, who thirty years later followed in his path almost step by step – but I only watched cricket, and I won the scholarship – Mr James's career is of particular interest. Our backgrounds were dissimilar. His was Negro, Puritan, fearful of lower-class contamination; mine was Hindu, restricted, enclosed. But we have ended speaking the same language; and though England is not perhaps the country we thought it was, we have both charmed ourselves away from Trinidad. "For the inner self," as Mr James writes, "the die was cast."[8]

In a moment of characteristic self-plagiarism, Naipaul recycles these lines in *A Way in the World*, not to describe Lebrun but to eulogize his fictional character Blair, in the longer passage from which I take the framing "epitaph" for my next chapter. The shift emphasizes the extent to which James remains a seminal figure for Naipaul, despite his critique of James's politics. James had had to struggle with the limitations of a colonial society not very different from Naipaul's; if anything it was, as Naipaul notes, a world much harsher than his own in its racial divisions. Yet James had made a way for himself in that world. He had established himself as a writer of international renown in all the ways that Naipaul, as a literary novice in the 1950s, also aspired to do.

Naipaul's respect for James as a fellow craftsman of words colours the estimation his narrator offers of the fictional Lebrun, who publishes a review article about the narrator's novel in "one of the Russian 'thick magazines'".[9] "The article seemed to me a miraculous piece of writing. It stuck closely to what I had actually written, but was about so much more. Reading the article, I thought I understood why as a child I felt that history had been burnt away in the place where I was born. I found myself constantly thinking, 'Yes,

yes. That's true. It was like that.' "¹⁰ The words *seemed* in the first sentence quoted and *I thought I understood* later on prepare the reader for the painstaking deconstruction of Lebrun's reading that follows this passage. Yet the tone of the narrator's response communicates an intuitive recognition of intellectual merit. As with the instruction in close reading we receive from Raleigh's surgeon, the narrator's initial response to Lebrun's reading of his novel is obliquely tutelary: Lebrun's essay grounds its explication of the text by attending to surfaces in the way that Naipaul tells us all good close reading should. Its thoroughness gives the novelist a satisfying assurance of having been seen and heard.

Naipaul even displaces insights onto Lebrun that originate in his own writing. His notorious pronouncement in *The Middle Passage* that "[h]istory is built around achievement and creation; and nothing was created in the West Indies" has become something of a byword.[11] In this rendering of his ideal reader, however, it is Lebrun who provides the narrator with the language through which to articulate his half-understood childhood intuition that "history had been burnt away in the place where I was born". Naipaul displaces his harshest judgements of Trinidad onto his reader via Lebrun, but in a form benign enough to suggest insight and acceptance rather than the embittered defensiveness in his original formulation. Through this displacement, he anticipates the absolution he hopes history will give to his political pronouncements. *Look*, he seems to say, *Lebrun can see what I mean. He has a wonderfully expansive intellect that is not afraid of the truth. He is willing to bear witness to what many others can see but are afraid to acknowledge in their readings of my work. He has anticipated what the world may come to understand about my aesthetic vision only many decades after I am gone.*

When the narrator finally meets Lebrun, he characterizes his conversation as being "like Ruskin's on the printed page, in its fluency and elaborateness, the words wonderfully chosen, often unexpected, bubbling up from some ever-running spring of sensibility. The thought-connections – as with Ruskin – were not always clear; but you assumed they were there. As with the poetry of Blake (or, within a smaller compass, Auden), you held on, believing there was a worked-out argument."[12] Never mind the tongue in cheek, the Naipaulesque insinuation – too mischievous to let pass – that there indeed may have been no worked-out argument beneath the elegantly formulated rhetoric. Naipaul is comparing Lebrun here to the literary models who dominated his colonial education and subsequent literary initiation at Oxford University. Lebrun's association with the mercurial genius of Blake, the perfect poise of Ruskin and the contemporaneous glamour of Auden (whose plays and poetry were much in vogue at Oxford in the 1950s) marks the narrator's enthusiasm as an initiate's naïve response to a specific notion of literary greatness he has been taught to admire. At the same time, however, it affirms that – in terms of what it was possible for a colonial to imagine attaining through language – Lebrun had achieved it all.

The relationship in *A Way in the World* between the semi-autobiographical narrator and the public oracle Lebrun allows Naipaul to foreground several similarities between himself and a historical figure whom many consider his black nemesis. For contemporary Caribbean aficionados, James epitomizes a black intellectual activist tradition associated with such figures as George Padmore and Frantz Fanon, a tradition from which Naipaul has often been accused of distancing himself. That perspective on their opposition plays well on both sides of the ideological divide, where Naipaul is ostracized by one camp as a betrayer of the Third World and lionized by the other as the consummate Hindu aesthete.[13] For both kinds of readers, the essential Naipaul is a man divorced from his Caribbean roots; he becomes the Hindu purist nauseated by filth and flesh or the racist anti-black who has forgotten his own family's sojourn in the cane fields of the New World.

Naipaul signifies on both the purist and racist readings of his work in his description of two meals, one of coo-coo with Lebrun and other West Indian writers in London, and the other of gefilte fish with Lebrun's influential friends, who belong to the prestigious circle of Jewish publishers and literati in 1980s Manhattan. The first meal is served in a Maida Vale flat filled with overstuffed furniture. Naipaul allows his narrator to describe those present with the meticulous attention to nuances of colour and ethnicity that West Indians invoke as a matter of course when describing themselves – as well as the vague generalizations with which they describe everyone else. Thus the host is identified as a Lebanese Trinidadian, and his wife as a creole who could pass for white but is from one of the smaller islands. Lebrun himself, though fairly dark in complexion, has a dash of Amerindian that gives his skin a reddish tinge. Lebrun's white woman friend, however, is described merely as Polish or Czech.[14] Their meal, which the narrator inaccurately identifies as coo-coo, is rendered in even greater detail:

> A heavy, glistening mound was placed on my own plate. I probed it: boiled yams and green bananas and possibly other tubers mashed together with peppers, the whole mixture slimy from the yams and – the Lebanese touch – olive oil. Below the pepper it had almost no taste, except one of a tart rawness (from the green bananas), and I thought it awful, the texture, the slipperiness. I didn't think I would be able to keep it down. I let it be on my plate. No one noticed.
>
> While Lebrun ate, and his dutiful woman friend ate, and the smell of meat and oil became high in the squashed sitting room with the old upholstered chairs, and people asked the Lebanese where they had got the yams and green bananas from, I (feeling that I was betraying them all, and separating myself from the good mood of the evening) remembered my aunt twenty years before, fanning her coalpot on the concrete back steps of our house in Port of Spain, and talking about Grenadians boiling their "pitch-oil tin" of ground provisions once a week.[15]

Naipaul sets up the moment of excruciating embarrassment and gross satire very carefully. He arranges the dinner guests' sophisticated cosmopolitanism against the backdrop of the crude peasant meal they make a point of eating with great gusto, and their stuffed mouths and the high smell of the food in the cramped room against the elevated intellectual disquisition Lebrun proceeds to initiate. This passage is one of Naipaul's most exasperating fabrications, since the meal he describes sounds more like a small-island dish called "oil-down" made from "ground provisions" – yam, dasheen, eddoes and the like – rather than the okra and cornmeal paste of coo-coo. However, the substitution allows Naipaul's narrator to draw on his aunt's memorable phrase – clearly a reference to oil-down – to produce that wonderfully gross description of the meal's contents without sacrificing the many Caribbean folk and literary associations that coo-coo evokes. In this way, Naipaul, like the stranger's child of the first epitaph, appropriates yet another landscape – this time a culinary one – without regard for the ramifications that others have brought to its naming.

Through the narrator's reference to his aunt, Naipaul draws into this moment all the ramifications the meal would have had for him in its original Caribbean setting. He associates its ingredients with the small-island labourers who periodically flocked to Trinidad in search of work. In the course of an earlier description, the narrator had introduced a satirical portrait of his aunt, now "an alert, generous, elegant woman" residing in Canada, but then a squalid, shrieking harridan fanning a coalpot on the back steps of the Port of Spain house, which is bursting at its seams with recently relocated country relatives.[16] The aunt's derogatory comments about small-island labourers' culinary practices indicate how the postwar influx of immigrants from Barbados, Grenada and St Vincent affected the status of Indo-Trinidadians. Darker in complexion than indentured labourers of Chinese and Portuguese origin, less urbane than black and mixed-race Port of Spain creoles, the Indo-Trinidadian peasant population occupied the lowest rung on the complex ladder of Trinidad class and colour hierarchies.[17] Consequently, Indo-Trinidadians who were making the transition from country to town in the interwar years may well have seen an opportunity to revise their humble public image when the number of black peasant immigrants to Trinidad from the smaller islands rose during and after the Second World War. The narrator's aunt does not need to acknowledge the squalid nature of her backyard coalpot if she can deride the small-islanders' living and cooking arrangements as even more primitive. At the same time she can transform her provincial unease with Port of Spain's cosmopolitan foods and customs into disgust, by redirecting her squeamishness towards the foods and customs of the new immigrants, with whom she dreads being lumped at the bottom of the socio-economic ladder.

In *The Middle Passage*, Naipaul had used small-island immigrants as proxies for Indo-Trinidadians' marginal ethnic status when he devoted an extended passage to describing the callousness with which children from the smaller islands were treated by Trinidadians. In *A Way in the World*, he uses small-island immigrants as both mirror and foil: the images through which he makes the coo-coo appear revolting extend the connections between small-island squalor and Indo-Trinidadian social angst. The way the meal's ingredients are mashed together recalls the overcrowded Port of Spain house that both the narrator and his aunt have since fled. Naipaul's need to mark the racial separation between himself and his fellow diners also recalls the urgency with which urbanized Indo-Trinidadians struggled to put space between themselves and the unassimilated small-islanders. The emphasis on the meal's indiscriminate mixing of African, Indian and even Lebanese ingredients that the narrator's probing fork uncovers signifies the racial mixture and sexual promiscuity associated with Trinidad creole culture, which the narrator, like a viewer of pornography, approaches with a combination of curiosity and revulsion. His characterization of the taste and texture of the meal as that of "tart rawness" overlaying blandness and "slipperiness" reinforces familiar sexual innuendos associated with tubers and green bananas. These are codified further for the Caribbean reader in the way a popular Trinidad calypso links the smell of dried salted codfish – a side dish often served with coo-coo – to the smell of female genitalia.[18] Finally, the meal's sexual connotations are reinforced by the narrator's mildly envious allusions to Lebrun's reputation as a successful womanizer, repeated throughout the chapter and indicated in the passage quoted above by the narrator's uncomfortable awareness of the devotional attitude that Lebrun's "Polish or Czech" woman friend assumes as she dutifully consumes the slimy meal.

Naipaul's emphasis on the racial and sexual connotations associated with creole food highlights cultural distinctions that persist between what some Trinidadians perceive as the Indo-Trinidadian population's homogeneity and the much-vaunted cultural and racial hybridity of the wider society. One reason the narrator cannot quite bring himself to eat this mushy meal with the aplomb of the other middle-class West Indians at the dinner party – for many of them it would also be an exotic peasant dish – is that his relationship to cultural mixture (coded here as culinary slumming) is complicated by the conservative notions about racial separateness that others assume he represents or endorses. Thus, when the narrator notes parenthetically that he feels as if he is betraying his fellow guests, he indicates his refusal to play along with what he perceives as a staged indulgence in the cuisine of a class of people to which no one at the dinner (including Lebrun) belongs: poor, illiterate, black small-island labourers. But he also recognizes that his inclusion at the table is a test of his Trinidadian authenticity that he is bound to fail. He knows that his Indianness will never be considered fully assimilable in this Caribbean context, even – especially! – when it is overlooked.

Critics in the "Naipaul as purist" cultural camp will be quick to jump on the narrator's squeamishness as evidence of his Brahmin sensibility, which Naipaul codes here through his narrator's references to the nauseating smell of greasy meat. On the other hand, critics of the "Naipaul as cultural betrayer" camp will want to claim his over-refined expressions of disgust as one more piece of evidence of his distaste for all things associated with black Trinidadians. But Naipaul's position at this stage in his narrative is a lot more complex. Earlier in the chapter on Lebrun, Naipaul makes a point of noting how George Lamming influenced his literary development. He tells us through his narrator that Lamming's successful use of comedy in his novel *In the Castle of My Skin* affirmed something he had been unable to acknowledge in his own attempts to write: that "comedy, the preserver we in Trinidad had always known, was close to me, a double inheritance, from my story-telling Hindu family, and from the creole street life of Port of Spain".[19] Naipaul thus uses his connection to a black West Indian writer to underwrite his creolized literary sensibility.[20] Within creole culture, no racial or ethnic trait exists beyond co-optation. A Lebanese Trinidadian may appropriate coo-coo with the same matter-of-factness that an Indo-Trinidadian writer emulates the satirical conventions of the calypsos he hears on the streets of his neighbourhood, or the regional folk tales he absorbs via Caribbean writers of African descent. Similarly, Lebrun's creole urbanity is one of the features Naipaul allows his narrator to admire in his fictional rewriting of James, whose 1936 "barrack yard" novel, *Minty Alley*, is a clear precursor of Naipaul's urbane, ironic style.

The problem with creole appropriation, however, is that it inevitably entails a loss of racial specificity. Trinidadians constantly negotiate a tension between their specific racial origins and their participation in a multiracial creole society. In fact, the elegance with which they finesse these contradictions constitutes the hallmark of creole cultural hybridity. But once we perceive this hybridity in terms of loss rather than opportunity, it is easy to read it as a denial of difference or a form of cultural erasure. This defensive perception fuelled aspects of the Black Power reassertion of African roots in the Caribbean during the 1960s and 1970s. It also feeds the social angst that constrains Naipaul's narrator: the minority sensibility that rewrites the inclusive gestures of Lebrun's dinner party as denial of the specificity of his Indo-Trinidadian background, including his embarrassing private insecurities about consuming or being consumed by small-island food and culture.

Naipaul exposes the tensions within creole identity when he chooses to identify the meal that his narrator cannot consume as coo-coo. Although what he describes sounds more like something Jamaicans call "rundown" or a mixture that various small-islanders refer to as "oil-down" or "blue food", Naipaul's calling it "coo-coo" facilitates a second intertextual reference to Lamming's *In the Castle of My Skin*. That novel's closing chapter contains an often-cited passage describing how G.'s mother prepares for him a final meal of coo-coo before he leaves Barbados for cosmopolitan Trinidad. In his essay "Cuckoo and Culture: *In the Castle of My Skin*", Edward Baugh reads this passage as marking the moment at which G. affirms and accepts the African/peasant roots of his culture, so that every movement of his mother's hands, every ingredient that is added to the meal, becomes a kind of last sacrament and celebration of a culture that the boy G., until this moment, has experienced with deep ambivalence.[21] Paradoxically, the insight comes at the point in Lamming's novel when the narration shifts from the third person – in which the boy is signified by the anonymous "G." – to the first-person "I", through which the young man finally becomes an independent, speaking subject. Separated from his mother and his mother's culture, he can now reify them both as Madonna and sacrament.

The meal of coo-coo in Lamming's text is thus both a gesture of cultural embrace and a sign of the process of individuation that severs the connection between mother and son. The narrating I who now reifies the folk is less enmeshed in the folk culture than the nameless boy G., and therefore in the culturally powerful position of being able to appropriate this meal as symbolic. By highlighting the difficulties that his Indo-Caribbean narrator experiences when invited to participate in a similar rite of passage, Naipaul reframes Lamming's earlier description of the meal of coo-coo as an aggressive act of cultural appropriation, similar to the culinary slumming for which he indirectly indicts his fellow Caribbean intellectuals at Lebrun's dinner party. He may also be pointing out the limits of cultural and literary convergence between himself and Lamming – or between his narrator and Lebrun – imposed by the differences in their racial origins. The apparent ease with which Lamming's narrator reifies his mother's dish of coo-coo does not automatically liberate Naipaul's narrator from the complexly different racial and cultural anxieties he brings to a similar meal.

Read in relation to G.'s maternal individuation, however, Naipaul's narrator's refusal to eat may also signal a failure in the maturation process: an inability to free himself of primal anxieties about status and identity that are embedded in his unconscious. Thus the flashback to his garrulous aunt and his recourse to her peasant utterances about ground provisions and pitch-oil tins may indicate that he has failed to complete his own process of separation from an infantile perception of an imaginary Mother India. The impressionable child, who never quite frees himself from the half-articulated fears and dreams of his maternal community, resurfaces in the hysterical man, gagging inexplicably when faced with a meal that triggers feelings of suffocation, vulnerability and inarticulateness. While these same feelings assault G., Lamming resolves them by creating an independent, speaking subject.

In Lamming's resolution, to be creole is to be mature, that is, to be capable of choosing to adopt or reject aspects of one's own and others' cultures, to perform an identity that one writes for oneself rather than acquiescing in a reading of one's identity assigned by others. The West Indian group at the dinner party celebrates this reading of creolization when they deliberately claim a humble small-island meal as part of their shared culture. And Naipaul seems to support their perspective on personal choice – or at least to accept it as an inevitable condition of modernity – in his emphasis on his protagonists' personal rewritings of the self in all the stories in *A Way in the World*. Yet in this story about Lebrun, he reminds us that the borrowed cultural practices in which these "new men" (and women) clothe themselves coexist with deeply held primal patterns of belonging from which none of us is ever fully liberated. Moreover, new identities can threaten or erase the subjectivity of others. Illiterate black small-island labourers, for instance, are conspicuously absent at Lebrun's cosmopolitan dinner, represented only by their signature dish. Ultimately, the promise of incorporation into African-based creole culture that the Indo-Caribbean narrator rejects is as problematic as the token assimilation that the dinner guests confer on Lebrun's "Polish or Czech" woman friend as a reward for dutifully consuming the slimy meal.

Naipaul uses his narrator's anxieties about cultural assimilation to reflect on the threat of appropriation inherent in Lebrun's consummate ability to read his work. "The man want to take you over", the chief minister says of Lebrun in the course of another significant meeting and meal.[22] Trinidad historian and prime minister Eric Williams, the model for this character, was one of the most famous of James's protégés to later part company with his mentor.[23] Through him, the semi-autobiographical narrator comes to realize that what he at first considered an ideal reading of his novel in Lebrun's review article may have concealed a gesture of political co-optation. It relegates his aesthetic vision to a preordained niche reserved for "Indians" within Lebrun's elegantly formulated materialist reading of global culture. From that perspective, there is something sinister about the way Lebrun cheerfully exoticizes the narrator's cultural specificity while at the same time expecting him to demonstrate his successful assimilation by consuming creole food. When Lebrun, between mouthfuls of coo-coo, launches into a consideration of the debate between "Lenin and the Indian delegate, Roy, at the Second Congress of the Comintern in 1920" – presumably for the Indo-Trinidadian guest's benefit – the narrator feels even more like the token outsider among the guests at the meal.[24] In the end, he concludes that the price he must pay for full inclusion in Lebrun's vision of community is simply too high. It demands that he trivialize his aunt's deep-seated fear of poverty and squalor – expressed in her racist attacks on small-island culture – by acting as if he no longer feels threatened by his proximity to the culture of the underdog in the national imagination. It calls upon him to fit his complex Indo-Trinidadian identity into the generalizations about "Indians" that structure the debate between Lenin and Roy. From Naipaul's perspective, such generalizations reduce his narrator to one more instance of local colour divorced from its original setting, like the quivering mass of small-island food served up in a Maida Vale flat.

Ultimately, however, racial or cultural difference may not be Naipaul's only point. There is a real distinction – one might say a disciplinary distinction – between his narrator's position and Lebrun's, which has everything and nothing to do with race. From Naipaul's perspective, a writer like James who comes at the truth by formulating a theoretical claim, and then trying to read the world around him in terms of that claim, attempts something quite different from a writer who works, as Naipaul does, from a specific gesture, an observable trait or an emotional insight towards a reading of his world. This is not to say that both writers do not start off with certain (perhaps identical) framing assumptions about their worlds, or that their works do not depend on similar images for their credibility and rhetorical force. Indeed, the two approaches to reading can complement each other. This is why, at a certain level, Lebrun remains the narrator's ideal reader. He can use his theoretically honed vision to excavate layers of meaning below the surface of the text, which the creative writer must leave the reader to infer through anecdote and elision. His approach, unlike that of the creative writer, is not bound by the limits of the worlds he can bring to life in fictional representations. His theoretical paradigms can generate speculative universes that abstract meaning to the point where it no longer depends on lived experience. By manipulating logic and language, he can make diametrically opposed concepts in the "real" world function as substitutes for each other, thus achieving a theoretical or political resolution where a lived contradiction may remain.

For Naipaul's narrator, these disciplinary differences acquire additional nuances when race and culture become part of their concern. For the narrator, racial attitudes and cultural perceptions have their origins in a plethora of factors that affect his characters, which his sentences do not pretend to exhaust. For his stories to work, he cannot merely summarize his racial situation – as part of an Indo-Trinidadian minority in a culture shaped by early confrontations and accommodations between Africans and Europeans – in the categorical terms I am using in this sentence. His harridan aunt may be expressing a racist stereotype when she dismisses small-islanders and their pitch-oil tins of ground provisions. However, in the context of a fiction, she may merely be articulating her desire to escape the heat of her coalpot, or repeating a catchy phrase she picked up from a creole neighbour, or invoking a barely remembered culinary taboo from her own, half-forgotten cultural antecedents. Or maybe she is just a cantankerous curmudgeon. There is, after all, something quite splendid about her theatrical dismissiveness that compels our attention as readers of fiction, the more so as the narrator tempts us to fantasize about how those qualities are subsumed in the façade of her later incarnation as a sedate, conventionally generous, politically correct Canadian dowager. The successful fiction must find ways to leave these possibilities open. It must move beyond literary cliché and theoretical paradigms, even as it abstracts this one characteristic impression of the aunt to convey the associations Naipaul imposes on her words in the context of Lebrun's dinner party. And indeed, the writer of fiction is never in control of how his readers will respond to such simplifications – as I demonstrate when I read Naipaul's lines alongside Lamming's, as a hysterical failure of the narrator's voice. Naipaul acknowledges the disciplinary and stylistic boundaries that separate a writer like him from a writer like James, when his narrator says of Lebrun, "we both soon got to recognize – what I feel sure we always knew – that the relationship between us was forced. We shared a background and in all kinds of unspoken ways we could understand one another; but we were on different tracks."[25]

The problem of appropriation, of what from Naipaul's perspective it means to be read through someone else's intellectual assumptions – whether it be through the reified creole norms and cultural posturing of educated West Indians in a Maida Vale flat or the intellectual paradigms of Lebrun's essay – is crucial for our understanding of the stakes the narrator assigns to the meal of gefilte fish he later shares in Manhattan with Lebrun's powerful friends. Through this second meal, the narrator comes to realize that Lebrun too has been the victim of co-optation, that what Lebrun describes as the "political resolution" through which he comes to terms with the humiliations of his racial history may be a form of spiritual capitulation to the readings others have imposed upon his body and his writing.

During the Maida Vale meal, Lebrun recounts his humiliation at realizing that his great-uncle's stories of being treated like a guest by the servants in the kitchens of London great houses in the mid-nineteenth century were fantasies he nurtured to deny the realities of servitude and racism. The narrator uses this anecdote to anchor his imaginative insights into Lebrun's inner life. Lebrun claims that he is released from the shame he connects with his own participation in his great-uncle's self-delusion only when he shares this anecdote publicly. But he also maintains that "every black man has a memory like that. Every educated black man is eaten away quietly by a memory like that."[26] And, indeed, the narrator remains unconvinced that the shameful desires associated with the great-uncle's fantasies of proximity to whiteness are not still eating away at Lebrun. He sees Lebrun's compulsive need to repeat his great-uncle's story as marking the persistence of the trauma of racism inscribed in this early childhood memory, just as the narrator remains unable to move beyond the angst-filled range of his aunt's racist invective when confronted by small-island food.

Naipaul invites us to read the meal of gefilte fish from the perspective of the shame surrounding this painful legacy of obsequious gratitude to one's oppressors that Lebrun's great-uncle bequeathed to his nephew. The narrator is horrified when he realizes that these cosmopolitan Manhattan intellectuals, into whose company he has been admitted by virtue of Lebrun's introduction, can see him only through the paradigms offered by Lebrun's article in the Russian "thick magazine". They have no inkling of the complex nuances of cruelty, betrayal, indifference and joy that separate and connect different regimes and racial groups in the oppressed communities with which they claim solidarity. All their vaunted knowledge of the islands has been siphoned second-hand from their readings of Lebrun and other radical political theorists. The narrator interprets their offer of the worked-over, indeterminate mass of gefilte fish as a token of automatic solidarity between oppressed Jewish and Third World peoples that, like the contrived paradigms through which they read him, he would do well to accept. He resists that co-optation by making it clear that he finds the proffered meal revolting:

> The idea of something pounded to paste, then spiced or oiled, worked on by fingers, brought to mind thoughts of hand lotions and other things. I became fearful of smelling it. I couldn't eat it. With the coo-coo or the foo-foo in the Maida Vale flat I had been able to hide what I did to the things on my plate. That couldn't be done here: everyone knew that the gefilte fish had been specially prepared for Lebrun's friend from London.[27]

Whereas Lebrun offered the narrator coo-coo but was at least willing to overlook the fact that his guest could not eat it, his Manhattan friends treat the refusal of their meal of gefilte fish as a form of political betrayal.

Naipaul never labels Lebrun's friends directly as liberal Manhattan Jewish intellectuals, just as he never goes further than identifying Lebrun's woman friend as "Polish or Czech". From his narrator's perspective they are all just powerful white people who take it for granted that they can appropriate and categorize his experience, even as they prescribe how they expect him to read theirs. Their claims of solidarity with the oppressed seem to have no visible connection with the squalor and social limitations of his Caribbean childhood. Thus the ramifications of their specific ethnic history remain opaque, just as someone who did not know the narrator's aunt before she became a gracious Canadian lady would have difficulty associating her with the shrieking harridan fanning a coalpot on the back steps of an overcrowded Port of Spain house. Similarly, someone who has not read the novel's earlier descriptions of Leonard Side, the Trinidadian descendant of Lucknow's Shia

Muslim dancing transvestites, whose long, perfumed fingers iced cakes and laid out dead bodies at Parry's Corner, might miss the necrophilic associations Naipaul brings to the description of the way his narrator imagines gefilte fish is prepared.[28] The narrator concedes in his story of Leonard Side that "we go back all of us to the very beginning; in our blood and bone and brain we carry the memories of thousands of beings".[29] But he sees that legacy as expressing only "a fragment of the truth" we understand about our racial inheritances. He distrusts his hosts' insistence that he equate their history of oppression with what they imagine is his own, that coo-coo is somehow equal to gefilte fish and that both meals confer on their eaters badges of authenticity as representatives of the oppressed. The distinctions between him and the other guests that he can gauge in the context of this meal have less to do with the coincidences of oppression within their respective histories than with the imperial ease with which his powerful hosts assume they can read him.

As he struggles with the social ostracism to which he imagines his refusal of the gefilte fish exposes him, Naipaul's fictional double begins to reflect on the difficult line that someone like Lebrun must constantly walk among such powerful patrons. From this perspective, Lebrun's global paradigms can be read as an attempt to protect himself from his patrons' appropriative power, even as they seduce him into simplifying the stubborn contradictions in his specific history. Thus Lebrun's consummate rhetoric and his air of having transcended the legacies of slavery and racial injustice merely conceal a sense of incompleteness, a desire to be accepted – like that of his nineteenth-century great-uncle – which betrays him into the false securities of unequal alliances.

Naipaul's speculations about the private motivations behind Lebrun's "political resolutions" produce one of the most directly autobiographical statements through which he explicitly distances himself from James. The narrator successfully refuses the form of solidarity that he imagines he has been offered over the meal of gefilte fish, because he values his personal integrity as a writer above his hosts' approval. By contrast, he reads Lebrun's consent to the appropriation of his ideas, by people who neither understand nor respect the moral ambiguities and personal humiliations out of which his political resolutions arise, as evidence of Lebrun's feelings of incompleteness:

> Few of us are without the feeling that we are incomplete. But my feelings of incompleteness were not like Lebrun's. In the things I felt myself incomplete Lebrun was – as I thought – abundantly served: physical attractiveness, love, sexual fulfilment. But there were other yearnings that no shedding of skin could have assuaged: my own earned security, a wish for my writing gift to last and grow, a dream of working at yet unknown books, accumulations of fruitful days, achievement. These yearnings could be assuaged only in the self I knew.³⁰

There is a double subterfuge at work in this passage. In the first place, Naipaul structures his observation in such a way that Lebrun's gifts and insecurities are reduced to those that Naipaul's narrator can read through his own limitations. So, in a way, Naipaul is asking us to read Lebrun through his narrator's limited paradigms, in much the same way that his narrator accuses the Manhattan crowd of reading his work exclusively through Lebrun's paradigms.

Moreover, it is difficult to avoid the impression that Naipaul is protesting too loudly, that he, like Raleigh, is still burying disclaimers in his advertisement. By distancing his narrator from a particular reading of Lebrun's capitulation, he masks his own defence against similar charges of having sold out to influential champions of his work within the literary mainstream. Naipaul presents his narrator as someone whose stubborn misanthropy has protected him from the kinds of compromises Lebrun has made, in order to counteract the image of himself as a writer who has made a fortune by saying the derogatory things his powerful patrons want to believe about his community. Thus, just as his writing seems most clear, most forthright, most free of elision, Naipaul, like Raleigh, conceals between the lines a passionate defence of himself from criticism of his work that remains unformulated as such within his text.

Perhaps, in the end, this is the point of Naipaul's estimation of James and himself through the character of Lebrun. For Naipaul, Lebrun is always most interesting when his façade of consummate urbanity cracks: when Lebrun's naked sexual envy of the writer Foster Morris flashes out just as the narrator's literary vanity is piqued by this same man; when his bitterness about a personal dilemma betrays him in Africa – as it at times betrayed Naipaul in similar settings – into vicious or reckless political pronouncements; when the old hurts and humiliation associated with his great-uncle's obsequious gratitude over being allowed to take tea with the servants expose his pain at having to acquiesce when powerful patrons appropriate his ideas. Similarly, Naipaul's inability to repress his aunt's voice throws into relief anxiety about how his ideas have been appropriated by readers on either side of the ideological divide, readers who imagine they can claim him or pass judgement on his work after having read only a review of one of his books.

Through Lebrun, Naipaul describes men like himself and James as men "on the run". Both writers relinquished membership in the communities of their birth in order to pursue fame, thus gambling with the possibility of co-optation by more powerful players on a global stage. Both claimed for themselves – as Naipaul's narrator notes of Lebrun – the licence to critique anything and anybody in their writing, wherever they found themselves, although neither committed himself for long enough to any one community to be forced to live with the consequences of his pronouncements.[31] But Naipaul's narrator insists that he is aware of the dangers and limitations inherent in this way of reading the world, whereas he asserts that Lebrun is shielded from the limitations of his vision by those who lionize him. Thus, while Naipaul's narrator must constantly revise his reading of himself in the face of relentless criticism, Lebrun remains "oddly pure", because the ideals of revolution and African redemption that he espouses have become fashionable political clichés whose inherent contradictions no one in progressive circles cares to challenge.[32]

Responding to the passage in *A Way in the World* used for this chapter's "epitaph", Kent Worcester in *C.L.R. James: A Political Biography* takes exception to Naipaul's portrayal of James/Lebrun as a tormented intellectual:

> to the degree that Lebrun is intended to represent James, the idea that he actively repressed an underlying madness is completely at odds with all other portrayals of a proud and dignified rhetorician. A closer approximation of the truth would be to say that James – "in the depth of his being" – had a pacific temperament, coated by a pride in achievement and aptitude. *Pace* Naipaul, James was never a Stalinist hack, nor was he in "anguish". James did not "become a child again . . . looking only for peace" in his old age. Instead, he remained a sane old man, waiting to be liberated from a sick body, committed to basic socialist principles.[33]

Worcester wants to defend James the historical figure. But Naipaul's point here is that a writer of fiction must go beyond the facts. He needs to be able to imagine the inner life of such a man as James. Naipaul's method builds upon the anecdotal. It incorporates into the character of Lebrun recognizable traits of C.L.R. James, as well as Naipaul's observations over time of other writers and colonial impresarios. And Naipaul offers little concrete evidence that James ever evinced the anxieties the narrator imputes to Lebrun. Instead his method attempts to persuade us that, to the extent that someone *like* James shares the humiliations of Naipaul's colonial socialization, there must be a level at which he, like Naipaul, remains traumatized by that experience.

Caryl Phillips seems to come closer to the spirit of Naipaul's comments when, in his review of *A Way in the World*, he places the passage that offends Worcester in its context. Phillips focuses on the moment when Naipaul's narrator asks rhetorically, "How could one enter the emotions of a black man as old as the century?" as "the most revealing passage in the entire novel". He goes on to link it to the moment when the narrator, speaking of "the profile-writers and television interviewers" who pestered Lebrun in his later years, attempts to imagine what the ageing public oracle must have felt about those swarming journalists who had little real interest in or understanding of his work.[34] Naipaul's semi-autobiographical narrators have often exhibited similar symptoms of personal angst in such situations. They know what it means, as the narrator says of Lebrun in my opening epitaph, to have one's "intellectual growth ... at every stage ... accompanied by a growing rawness of sensibility", to face the realization that one's "political resolutions, expressing the wish not to go mad, [have] been in the nature of spiritual struggles, occurring in the depth of [one's] being".[35] Phillips concludes: "In the light of this passage it seems remarkable that anybody could have ever charged Naipaul with possessing a dyspeptic attitude toward 'primitives', let alone pointed the stern, accusatory finger of Negrophobia in his direction."[36]

In fairness to both views, it must be said that James in his later years, for all his charm and conviviality, remained a very private person in the presence of most interlocutors, seldom allowing others to see him out of control. So it is really anyone's guess – Worcester's as well as Phillips's – as to what lay behind that carefully cultivated demeanour. Nevertheless, just as Worcester champions James, Naipaul needs Caribbean readers like Phillips who are willing to view his angst through the lens of their own experiences with patronage and co-optation, rather than dismissing it as a sign of racial insecurity or personal hypersensitivity unique to this writer. In imputing to James, via his construction of the character of Lebrun, all the real and imagined fears of appropriation he has experienced, Naipaul tutors us in the way he would most wish his pronouncements to be read.

Through this complex gesture of generosity and appropriation, Naipaul challenges readers – those who insist on seeing him and James as representing diametrically opposed strands in Caribbean intellectual thought – to acknowledge the anguish and insecurity, even the petty viciousness, that must of necessity have subtended James's perfectly poised public persona. Unless we are willing to entertain that imaginative possibility, Naipaul contends, we cannot fully appreciate either the greatness of a man like James or the limits of his vision. At the same time Naipaul presents himself, through his narrator, as better equipped to refuse some of the accommodations that a colonial subject in James's position would have had to accept. He claims this greater resolve as a consequence, in part, of the accidents of history that brought him into the literary world at a less brutal moment than James. These include the changes in the politics of racial patronage that separate a Caribbean intellectual impresario of the 1930s from a Caribbean Oxford graduate of the 1950s, as well as the disciplinary distinctions that Naipaul sets up between a creative writer and a political theorist. Finally, Naipaul sees the double dispossessions of his Indo-Caribbean heritage as rendering him less susceptible to myths of racial affirmation that, in his opinion, create the dissonance between the expansive themes of global transcendence and the defensive subtext of cultural nationalism found in James's political pronouncement.

3

FOR BLAIR

> Remember him now, in the office at the Red House: at that mid-point in his career, when with his extraordinary gifts he could have gone one way or the other. Remember him (like me) trailing all the strands of his own complicated past, animated by that past, feeling the current running with him (as the lawyer Evander did), and feeling (again like me) as he studied after work that he was at the most hopeful time of his life.[1]

One of the clues the surgeon uses to debunk Raleigh's account of the 1595 voyage, during which he claimed to have discovered El Dorado, comes from a detail it incorporates about a Negro's death. The explorer had said that there were no Negroes in his crew, yet the surgeon finds one in Raleigh's account:

> I am thinking about the Negro who suddenly appears in your book when you are on the Guiana river, and see the meadows and fields and flowers near the falls. The river is full of crocodiles, thousands, you say. And the Negro – who would know about crocodiles – jumps in from the galley – for a swim, you say – and is immediately eaten alive. And that's that. There's nothing more about crocodiles or Negroes in your book. I have thought a lot about that vanishing Negro of yours, and I'm certain you borrowed him from John Hawkins's account of his voyage to Guinea in West Africa and the West Indies in 1564. In Guinea Hawkins saw a Negro who was snatched by a crocodile and pulled under as he was filling water at the river's edge. That's a better story.[2]

The surgeon does not distinguish between fact and fiction but between worse and better stories. Hawkins's story is better than Raleigh's not because it is more factually accurate but because it attends to the details that make a story credible. Both explorers sacrifice their Negroes to crocodiles as a way of marking their culture's ambivalence about the exotic natives and terrains they present to their readers. But Hawkins's story does not patronize its Negro by imputing to him an infantile ignorance about local dangers more appropriate to a European newcomer.

At every opportunity in *A Way in the World*, Naipaul returns to this preoccupation with what it means to read a culture or person faithfully, even when that reading is a fiction. At one point he critiques nineteenth-century British and twentieth-century American travel writers who reduce their West Indian subjects to black buffoons in squeaky shoes or exotic coolies, described as "a people apart" about whose language and religion very little is known.[3] He dismisses such writers as men "acting being writers, acting being travellers, and, especially, acting being travellers in the colonies".[4] At the same time, however, he sees their misreadings – even their clichés about local customs, inefficient public services and postcard-perfect sunsets – as instructive. In a perverse sense they offer the colonial subjects whose lives they distort fresh, imaginative angles on how to read their societies.[5] Thus the blasé world-weariness affected by one 1930s travel writer – when he pronounces, "The trains are all right, but the buses are a joke" – can become the occasion for an entire article by a local journalist celebrating the absurd, "jokey" things that happen on Trinidadian buses.[6] Conversely, when a travel writer uses a line from Keats's "Ode to Autumn" – "barrèd clouds bloom the soft-dying day" – to describe a tropical sunset, the competing clichés impose new associations on Keats's words.[7] The images thus produced are even more striking because they are so mismatched, like the fresh associations the stranger's child brings to Tennyson's landscape in the first of my "epitaphs".

From this perspective, to read someone else's world is always to distort, and to see one's reflection distorted is to see oneself anew, to re-imagine the frameworks of one's life. Thus, although he makes the surgeon criticize Raleigh's version of the story of the Negro, Naipaul goes on to use it as the opening image in his penultimate chapter, which he describes as an unrealizable screenplay about the explorer. The camera's sweep across the silent pre-dawn river "is broken by the sound of a heavy splash. A man has jumped overboard. After a while there are shouts from the decks of the ship, and the sound of running feet."⁸ The motif of the Negro who jumps to his certain death thus embeds a critique of Naipaul's narrative strategy in his novel, even as the author uses it to undermine Raleigh's credibility. Its clichés and distortions facilitate a fresh reading of the divergent meanings that Naipaul and Raleigh bring to the landscape they share.

By positioning Raleigh's story immediately after the chapter on Lebrun, Naipaul calls attention to how he represents "Negroes" in his fictions. Like Hawkins, Naipaul is more careful than Raleigh about where and how he locates his black characters, even when he transposes them from the New World to the Old. Such characters – the West Indian educator whom the narrator meets in French Africa; Phyllis, the relocated Antillaise; even Lebrun – all are presented with painstaking attention to gesture and idiom that enhance their authenticity, even when the stories told about them strain our credibility. But Naipaul, like Raleigh and Hawkins (as well as the directors of countless action movies), also needs a Negro whom he can throw to the crocodiles, a sympathetically drawn black character whose fate is dictated by the demands of the plot rather than the limitations of historical fact, whose function within the text is to carry the burden of its angst, and whose untimely death can stand in for that of the protagonist.⁹ Such a figure is the character Blair, whom we first meet briefly in chapter two, where Naipaul's narrator describes the first job he held in the registrar general's department after leaving school. Blair returns at the end of the novel to embody the contradictions Naipaul wants to explore in his own experience, before the plot throws him – literally and metaphorically – to the crocodiles.

In "The Crocodiles of Yamoussoukro", Naipaul uses the image of crocodiles in the moat around Bokassa's palace to represent the atavistic forces that he imagines are always lurking just below the civilized surface in the modern African state.¹⁰ These forces also destroy Blair when he is ambushed on a model banana farm by military personnel from the very African government that has hired him as a consultant on economic reform. Like Hawkins's Negro, Blair stumbles accidentally into the ambush; like Raleigh's Negro, his resurfacing at this point in the narrative, after having been introduced only briefly, seems pretty arbitrary, given the symbolic importance that Naipaul proceeds to attach to him.

Like Lebrun and the narrator, Blair has rewritten himself. He has used the educational and political opportunities that decolonization offers to transform himself, from an uncomfortably formal clerk in a circumscribed colonial bureaucracy into an urbane, cosmopolitan professional whose career is furthered by postcolonial nationalist agendas. He travels to Africa as a well-paid independent consultant, a man of extensive practical knowledge and impressive international experience. Moreover, he uses his new authority to lay claim to a subjectivity that transcends ethnic or political loyalties. When the narrator meets Blair in Africa, decades after their time as fellow workers in the office of the registrar general in Trinidad, he perceives this self-made man as dominating his environment rather than being dominated by it. His laugh is "bigger than I remembered"; he seems "less neat in his movements, more assertive, to be taking up more room".[11] Blair's new-found assurance results from his having realized, at about the same time as the narrator, "that the character he had been presenting to the world – the self-made man, still striving, looked up to by all, correct, with the manners of his special community – was in some essential way false to himself".[12] The narrator speculates that this self-knowledge might have granted him "another vision of his isolated community living in the debris of old estates; he might have taken their story back and back, to unmentionable times. And he might have decided then – like me as a writer – to remake himself."[13]

Blair's self-assurance allows him to accept the limitations of his specific history. But it also allows him to claim the right to criticize racialism and tribalism wherever he finds it, even within the race-based political movements that have created lucrative professional opportunities for men like him in the twentieth century. Rather than suggesting that he has betrayed his race, the narrative presents Blair's openness as a sign of insight and maturity. In the stories Blair tells against himself about his own petty racist responses in unguarded moments, and about the limitations of the governments that employ him, he assumes that all his listeners, including the white African De Groot and the Indo-Trinidadian narrator, will extend to him the same acceptance he offers them and that most of us expect of our friends: the freedom to name one's personal biases without apology or explanation. Moreover, from the narrator's perspective, Blair, unlike Lebrun, can acknowledge his racial origins without reifying them. He celebrates the political process of decolonization that has enabled his new status, without overlooking the excesses that many nationalist regimes have perpetrated in the name of racial solidarity or international socialism.

In this text of echoes and ventriloquist effects, Naipaul's use of Blair to model the relationship with his Afro-Trinidadian readers that he wishes he could take for granted signals another significant appropriation of a voice. Blair shares biographical details with a number of Naipaul's black Trinidadian associates, including William Demas, a fellow graduate of Queen's Royal College who became an internationally eminent economist, and the lawyer Selby Wooding, whom Patrick French describes as a long-time trusted friend of both Naipaul and his first wife, Pat.[14] Naipaul makes it clear that he does not share the ambition for "the Race" that drives both Blair and the black Trinidadian lawyer Evander. However, in the passage quoted in this chapter's epigraph, he goes to great lengths to insert a series of parenthetical statements directing the reader's attention to the explicit parallels between the differently complicated pasts both he and Blair trail behind them, including their ambition and their optimism about their power to reshape the meanings of their lives through hard work and imagination.

The fact that Blair is black also allows Naipaul to respond to black readers who accuse his work of racism. The narrator describes an Afro-Trinidadian typist at the Red House, where he worked as a teenager, who dismisses his first short story, which satirizes the master of ceremonies at a black beauty contest, on the grounds that, as an Indian, he is incapable of identifying with a black character. The typist's bald assumption – "If it was an Indian man, you wouldn't have written like that" – unleashes upon the narrator a flood of doubts about his right as an artist to represent the entire world he can see: "I grew to feel after some weeks there was something wrong with the writing. What was the basis of the writer's attitude? What other world did he know, what other experience did he bring to his way of looking? How could a writer write about this world, if it was the only world he knew? I never formulated the questions like that; the doubts were just with me."[15] The narrator's reflections do not identify which condition he considers more disabling – to write about worlds beyond one's immediate experience or to write from within the only world one knows. He sees the writer's relationship to his subject as a form of dialogue that assumes the writer's intimacy with his subject, even as he positions himself beyond the frame that he imposes on the observed image.

Like the local subjects and readers of travel-book clichés who have learned to interpret their sunsets through captions borrowed from Keats, both the Caribbean writer and his Caribbean reader must learn to see what they think they know from unfamiliar perspectives, even if that shift may on occasion distort a familiar image.

Speaking through his narrator, Naipaul claims to have laid to rest his doubts about his authorial prerogative after writing *Miguel Street*, "the first true book that came to me . . . prompted by my discovery of Port of Spain before the war, my delight in the city".[16] But many of his readers over the years have not been as willing to let go of the typist's point of view. Almost every critical position Naipaul has taken in writing about black characters has been interpreted at one point or another as evidence of his inherent inability, as an ethnic outsider, to represent black characters fairly, even though some of his harshest fictional representations have been of European characters, as well as of his own Indo-Trinidadian community. Naipaul uses Blair's response to the story the typist critiques to reverse the charges of racism levelled at him. He suggests that if a black writer had said the things Naipaul's narrator does about black characters, he would have been read differently. Moreover, Naipaul challenges his critics to utilize supposed authorial biases as opportunities for new insights. After all, such biases may provide the reader with fresh ways of apprehending absurdity in the everyday, of registering cruelty in the mundane.

In order to support his counterargument, Naipaul must do more here than simply appropriate the voice of a black character. He also has to demonstrate that he too is capable of empathy. Thus Blair must be given a historical specificity as uncompromising as Naipaul's. Early in the novel the narrator notes that the small all-black village that bequeathed Blair his formal manners and strict work ethic is as unfathomable to him as his orthodox Hindu community must seem to Blair. At the same time, he locates Blair's village in northeast Trinidad, among the debris of the same abandoned cocoa estates that his narrator inhabited as a child. In this way Blair's world and the narrator's are represented as occupying the same physical space, so that both characters are equally linked to and separated from all the other historical communities that have occupied this landscape. From this perspective, it does not matter that neither he nor Blair can ever understand fully the origins of the values that each brings to his public life at the registrar general's office and to his sojourn in Africa. They perceive each other and the worlds they share from different angles, but they accept that their different perspectives may in fact converge upon the same object. Years later, when they meet again, Blair accepts the narrator's satirical vision of black Trinidad society, not by arguing politically for Naipaul's right to satirize black people but by affirming the imaginative achievement of the narrator's first story – the way it keeps faith with a world they both know, although they know it in different ways. As Blair puts it to De Groot while describing the reception of the story about the black beauty contest, "one of the typists . . . didn't like it. She thought he mocked the black M.C. too much. . . . As soon as I began to hear about it I recognized the fellow."[17]

    Had Naipaul simply claimed Blair's accolade for his narrator as a means of propping up his own arguments, he would in fact have achieved little more than Raleigh does when he appropriates Hawkins's Negro. But Naipaul offers Blair a degree of reciprocal understanding here that often has been missing, or at least obscured, in his earlier writing about black characters. For instance, he makes a point of allowing his narrator to register, without cynicism, the enthusiasm for the politics of racial advancement that Blair shares with his lawyer friend Evander. Such political shifts have facilitated Blair's career, as well as those of postcolonial writers like Naipaul, even though, from Naipaul's perspective, some of the political alliances those shifts shaped in Trinidad had the effect of alienating, and at times disenfranchising, the Indo-Trinidadian community. Naipaul has often written about how excluded he felt from the Caribbean nationalist movement by its racially inflected rhetoric. He builds *The Enigma of Arrival*, another semi-autobiographical fiction, around the crippling sense of loss he experienced in the aftermath of these changes. The psychic disorientation of not fully belonging anywhere forces his narrator in *Enigma* to reassess his relationship to the landscape of his British exile. In such novels as *The Mimic Men* and *Guerrillas*, Naipaul has also savaged the worst excesses of what he reads as the politics of race. In *A Way in the World* he recounts once more the trauma of his return to an ultra-nationalist Trinidad in which the black Trinidadians with whom he grew up have become consumed by a new racial assertiveness, one that shuts him out of the circle of camaraderie he once imagined he might share with them.

Naipaul does not alter his estimation of the effect these changes have had on him, and on his narrator in *A Way in the World*, but he acknowledges through his presentation of Blair that his view of events is not the only one that matters; that other, contradictory aspirations and world-views are part of the landscape he once considered his own; that whatever its limitations and worst excesses, the wave of racial affirmation that transformed his world and Blair's, like every other important historical event, has been both enabling and exclusionary. He seems almost to concede after all that men like Blair have succeeded in writing themselves into history in a part of the world that, at an earlier time and from a brasher perspective, he would have dismissed as a place in which nothing was made. Although his plot ultimately throws Blair to the crocodiles of atavism and nationalist excess, it nonetheless affirms this black character's achievement:

> In the version of his death I carried in my imagination I saw Blair alive in that banana plantation, a big man floundering about in silence in his big, shiny-soled leather shoes in the soft mulch, between his sure-footed attackers. There would have been a moment in that great silence when he would have known that he was being destroyed, that his attackers intended to go to the limit; and he would have known why. And I feel that if, as in some Edgar Allan Poe story, at the moment of death, while the brain still sparked, a question could have been lodged in that brain – "Does this betrayal mock your life?" – the answer immediately after death would have been "No! No! No!"[18]

Once again, at the moment of crisis Naipaul uses the subjunctive to emphasize the fictive nature of the scene he describes. Although he claims to intuit Blair's thoughts, he stresses that they arise in his imagination and are fuelled by the stylized conventions of the horror stories associated with Edgar Allan Poe, another consummate storyteller. So we are not entirely sure if we should read Blair's dying words as an affirmation or as a form of self-delusion – a final cruel irony that the narrator imposes on his hapless Negro. It is as if, to return to Raleigh, Naipaul is insisting that Blair's gold is a mirage of sand, even as he urges his reader to believe in that gold, in the authenticity of Blair's voice.

Yet Blair has taken a stand in a way that Naipaul's first-person narrators seldom do. I am thinking, for instance, of Ralph Singh, the narrator in *The Mimic Men*. Singh's spiritual shipwreck washes him up in a rundown London hotel, evading commitment or ultimate pronouncements as he watches the man eating next to him painstakingly reduce the food on his plate to precisely defined piles of garbage. And even in *A Way in the World*, Naipaul's autobiographical narrator never quite shares Blair's steady, if somewhat melodramatic, conviction that "the world I will be leaving is better than the one I came into".[19] He distrusts the claims of Blair's racial politics in the abstract, but he understands at a deeper level that they enable the new man Blair has become. They allow Blair to conceive of his new freedoms as containing an assumption that his racially fuelled passion will be accepted by others without having to be explained or defended. And Blair's assumptions are not that different from Naipaul's estimation of his own position. Naipaul claims the freedom to be taken at his word. To be argued with or contradicted, yes, but not to be dismissed or accommodated on purely racial grounds, or to be subjected to a race-based test of his political correctness, before he is allowed to enter the debate. In a world that claims to have empowered both a Naipaul and a Blair, it should be possible for both men to rewrite themselves, to make their way in the world in terms of their specific histories and individual ambitions without constantly having to justify their right to do so.

Through his presentation of Blair, Naipaul underwrites the terms of the bargain he hopes his literary legacy can strike with his readers. One might well ask whether his literary record extends to all his characters the generosity and insight that he demands for himself and he bestows here on Blair. In later publications Naipaul presents himself as having become mature enough as a writer and an intellectual to re-evaluate his relationship to the Trinidadian society he once felt had wounded him deeply. By comparison with *An Area of Darkness* (1964), the Naipaul of *India: A Million Mutinies Now* (1990) seems detached and self-assured enough to reconsider his first, terrified response to the Indian subcontinent. At the time he wrote *A Way in the World*, however, it still remained to be seen whether Naipaul would acknowledge that any good could come out of Africa, even as he declared himself willing to think afresh about the "lost community in the blighted cocoa woods" that might have produced both his Indo-Trinidadian narrator and his black Trinidadian character Blair.[20] However, Naipaul could reasonably claim that, in subjecting his work to such scrutiny, we hold him to a higher standard than we would a black writer.

It is easy for an author to love a character that he creates in his own image and destroys in the service of his tale; it is more difficult, however, for him to accept or interpret public figures or historical events that challenge his view of the world. Naipaul acknowledges these difficulties by insisting on the incompleteness of the historical stories he inserts into his narrative, and by documenting his own contradictory responses to the meaning of C.L.R. James's legacy. In the end he concedes that, just as his vision will never be impartial or exhaustive, he cannot expect to control the meaning of his literary legacy for future generations. Conversely, Naipaul argues, the reader can demand that Caribbean writers construct credible fictions that do not patronize their characters or their readers. But that is not the same as insisting that a writer's vision support the reader's specific ideological position. As he puts it in his final reflections on Phyllis, the displaced Antillaise, "We all inhabit 'constructs' of a world. Ancient peoples had their own. Our grandparents had their own; we cannot absolutely enter into their constructs. Every culture has its own: men are infinitely malleable."[21] With that caveat in mind, *A Way in the World* challenges us to engage with Naipaul's vision, whatever its distortions, and to use its insights, however incomplete, in order to reconsider the delineation of the social landscapes we think we inhabit.

4

LAST W/RITES

> The truth would have been simpler. The body would have been in a box, and it would have been placed in a refrigerated part of the aircraft's hold. The body would have been embalmed in Africa; that meant the internal organs would have been removed. At the airport in Trinidad the flaps of the hold would have opened, and when the time came the box would have been transferred to a low trailer, and perhaps in some way hidden or covered. There would have been formalities. Would the embalmed body in its box then have been transferred to a hearse? The hearse didn't seem right. I made enquiries. I was told that the box would have been taken away in an ambulance to Port of Spain, and then the shell of the man would have been laid out in Parry's chapel of rest.[1]

What are the implications for our understanding of Naipaul's literary project if we accept the preceding readings as establishing that Naipaul's fantasy of his ideal reader – the reader of his posterity, the one by whom he most hoped and feared he would be (mis)understood when he wrote *A Way in the World* – is a black Trinidadian? Perhaps that ideal reader might be C.L.R. James, the theoretician and activist at the opposite end of the political spectrum, who nevertheless shares with Naipaul a thorough colonial education at one of the island's leading high schools. Or perhaps Naipaul imagines that his ideal reader will be a self-made technocrat like Blair, who comes from the same corner of Trinidad as Naipaul and has made his career in many of the same places around the world that Naipaul has visited. The latter reader would be the type of person who has little truck with esoteric art, even though he might have a few native art objects mounted on the walls of his smart townhouse in Washington or Geneva. He would enjoy these objects not merely for their anthropological significance but also because they captured for him memories of Africa – such as when his car broke down and he had to walk through the debris of an abandoned cocoa estate, like the one near his grandmother's house in the foothills of Trinidad's Northern Range – or the time in Asia when he saw, framed in the space between his windshield wipers, a child who reminded him of the half-forgotten Chinese or Indian Trinidadian schoolmate standing next to him in an old class picture. He would read Naipaul's novels not for their politics or their pronouncements on development – for, after all, as a development consultant he would know a lot more about the putrid underbelly of such things than Naipaul – but because, in a hotel room at the end of a long day, with his jet-lagged internal clock completely out of whack, he would encounter in a Naipaul story the master of ceremonies at the black beauty contest. Laughing heartily, he would "recognize the fellow" from his memories of a place made simpler by the distilling properties of art, or perhaps more vivid on account of his uncharitable thoughts about the Third World bureaucrats at the meeting he had just left.

Or maybe the ideal reader in Naipaul's imagination is that bright, nervous small-island scholarship boy now cramming for exams at Queen's Royal College, Naipaul's and James's alma mater. The child eats Kentucky Fried Chicken now, rather than ground provisions cooked in a pitch-oil tin, and because he has so much to lose if he does not win a scholarship to university, he snatches his readings of a Naipaul novel like a guilty secret between cramming for chemistry and math exams. Or maybe the boy returns the book, unread, to its shelf at the back of the school library, next to James's *Beyond a Boundary*, before stealing out to watch the popular boys play cricket, barely registering that both volumes were written by men who as youths might once have sat at his desk. This boy's childhood, like Naipaul's, and like the childhood of the small-island children he describes in *The Middle Passage*, would be encompassed by small, private humiliations delivered by people who laughed at his food and his accent while exploiting his relatives to weed their gardens and mind their children. For him, Naipaul's novels – if and when he eventually read them – would take the place of the handful of local stories Naipaul remembers from his own childhood as having brought order to a "dry haphazardness" and having given him the beginnings of an appreciation for the "distorting, distilling power of the writer's art".[2]

Naipaul's distance from and identification with these readers is almost palpable in *A Way in the World*. It is as if his encounters with fame and death have made him yearn all the more for that narrow island world that he vowed as a schoolboy to leave behind for good.[3] My discussion of *A Way in the World* demonstrates how this writer's understanding of what constitutes the self and how that self is constructed through writing has shifted over time. Rarely in this semi-autobiographical later work is Naipaul the supercilious, distanced observer of some of the journalistic pieces of his middle period. He no longer describes writing itself as a menace or a burden. Unfinished manuscripts are pulled out, shaken free of dust and pondered in their incompletion without inducing hysteria. Acts that he formerly would have perceived as violations become opportunities for personal redefinition. In the pages of his fictions, the people he imagines himself seeking out for leisurely conversation are other Caribbean transients, adrift like himself, men and women "on the run" in a postcolonial world where everything and nothing has become accessible.

Derek Walcott divines this possibility as early as his review of Naipaul's *The Enigma of Arrival*, where he quotes this passage from that work: "It was odd: the place itself, the little island and its people, could no longer hold me. But the island – with the curiosity it had awakened in me for the larger world, the idea of civilization, and the idea of antiquity; and all the anxieties it had quickened in me – the island had given me the world as a writer."[4] Walcott points out that another way of reading Naipaul's syntax in the last part of the passage is that the island had given *Naipaul* to the world as a writer. He goes on to affirm, "Despite his horror of being claimed, we West Indians are proud of Naipaul, and that is his enigmatic fate as well, that he should be so cherished by those he despises."[5] But Walcott's review also points out that, far from being exceptional, Naipaul's story – the story of a bright, lonely West Indian child who breaks through the isolation and provinciality and obscurity of his origins to become a writer of international renown – has been repeated ad infinitum over the years by generations of Caribbean writers, from C.L.R. James to Jamaica Kincaid. So, in approaching a reckoning with his literary posterity, Naipaul must first understand himself within a literary tradition of Caribbean writers and readers that contextualizes what at first might seem an achievement without precedent. Naipaul's petulant defence against Walcott's critique of *The Enigma of Arrival*, which he puts into the mouth of Miranda in

A Way in the World, reveals how vulnerable he remains to Caribbean readers' attacks on his work. Nevertheless, in responding so directly to such criticism through his fictionalized characters, Naipaul seems to inch closer towards dialogue, and perhaps even rapprochement, with those very readers.

Naipaul's critics may argue that his fantasies about an ideal Trinidadian reader might place his ego above the line – in the space that "White" usually occupies, according to Fanon's paradigm – and his unacknowledged black Trinidadian readers below the line, in the space reserved for "Ego different from 'the Other'", in relation to which the racially dominant subject asserts his humanity. That construction of the subject supports a reading of Naipaul's novel as manipulating blackness in order to set himself apart, racially, from some of his fellow Trinidadians. And certainly there is an element of this, as Naipaul himself points out in the parallels he draws between his story about Blair's death and Raleigh's story about the Negro who obligingly jumps to his death in the service of the white author's self-aggrandizement. But my readings also argue that, through his descriptions of the two meals he associates with Lebrun, Naipaul ultimately identifies himself as a subaltern subject who, like James, remains vulnerable to appropriation as well as to erasure. That provisional solidarity rotates Fanon's figure so that its dividing line runs vertically instead of horizontally, demarcating equivalent rather than hierarchically defined spaces between Naipaul and his black Trinidadian alter egos. Naipaul's novel invites this reading when it presents both its narrator and the character Blair as occupying communities whose separate histories have been superimposed at different junctures on the same landscape of blighted cocoa woods. From this perspective, we can conceptualize the relationship between them as moving across time rather than across space.

Fanon's figure rotated allows us to read Naipaul's later works as approaching an understanding of being in the world that moves beyond self-evident configurations of dominance and subordination, towards something more slippery, less bounded. Like Derrida's concept of "being-thrownness", it presents the shuddering mass of untouched coo-coo on his plate – against which Naipaul's narrator seeks so desperately to define himself – as both an unassimilated foreign body and a profoundly intimate facet of his interior life. Naipaul tells us that his childhood discovery of a creole world, and his later discovery of a handful of stories written about it by black and Portuguese

Trinidadians, first gave him the distance from which to examine his own Hindu community, to approach it as a community rather than as a random collection of improbable relatives. Like the act of writing itself, Trinidad's African-based creole culture provided him with a frame of reference through which to define his relationship to his family and the variously raced communities among which he grew up. That framework precedes and accompanies his attempts to write a grammar of the self. It thus partakes in a landscape whose forms, in Derrida's language, "are not yet those of the *subject* or the *project*".[6] If *A Way in the World* seems to project that world as an unassimilable object, it also reveals the superfluity of its author's consuming something that is already an inalienable aspect of his consciousness. His narrator's gagging response to the coo-coo may mark an attempt either to forestall ingestion or to expel what already has been consumed, in much the same way that Naipaul's writing resists incorporating blackness into his imagined self, where it always has resided.

Naipaul's bizarre closing fantasy about how Blair's corpse might have returned to Trinidad is a good example of how he superimposes the Indian and creole aspects of his imaginary identifications by interring them in the same narrative space. On the one hand it represents a complete "othering" of Blair. Naipaul's Hindu background, after all, dictates that bodies be cremated, so the whole messy business in the novel about Parry's funeral home and Leonard Side's traffic in embalmed bodies and wedding cakes is one of the ways by which Naipaul marks the distinctions between himself and other, more creolized Trinidadians – in this case, the Muslim Indo-Trinidadian mortician who embalms Christian bodies. On the other hand, in placing his description of Blair's embalmment at the end of *A Way in the World*, Naipaul explicitly recapitulates the way he ends *Enigma of Arrival* with a description of his sister's cremation. Naipaul thus inters Blair's coffin in the space he reserved for his sister's ashes in his previous semi-autobiographical work. The cannibalizing details of his image draw the eviscerated shell of the black character into the ambit of the Hindu family, as it were, reversing the presumed direction of black–Indian assimilation in the Trinidadian imaginary. Thus, even though the burial that Naipaul imagines for Blair invokes alien cultural traditions, it can stand in, like his sister's cremation, for the writer's own demise. Naipaul handles the substitution with all the bizarre excess and solicitous attention to detail that one imagines he would want to see expended on his own last rites – the ones that no writer can hope to render on the page.

The vagaries of Trinidad's racial politics add another dimension to these palimpsestic identifications. Relationships between Trinidadians of African and Indian descent – both varieties of the subaltern at different historic moments – could never have corresponded to the stratified hierarchies of Fanon's paradigm. Over the years each group has occupied, often uncomfortably, the space assigned to the Other in their respective imaginary identifications. As the Indo-Trinidadian population has moved, both demographically and politically, to claim a position equivalent to that of the black population, the tensions between the two groups have become much more explicit than the hysteria and unease Naipaul recalls feeling on the edges of the political rallies he witnessed in the 1960s and 1970s. Those historical changes have drawn and redrawn the lines of ethnic demarcation, social rivalry and economic mistrust between the two groups, to the point where their shared national identity seems undergirded by nothing more substantive than the accident of a shared landscape. And yet, amidst the constant wrangling over cultural histories and loyalties, members of both groups increasingly sound more like one another, eat one another's foods and recognize the same fellow in one another's stories.

In acknowledging his relationship with Trinidad society, Naipaul does not attempt resolution where a lived contradiction remains. His projected black Trinidadian readers include both the admiring Blair and the offended typist whose dismissal of his first story clearly still rankles, decades later. Indeed, the work of identification rarely produces complacency or erasure of difference. To imagine oneself occupying a space occupied by another is to fantasize both that one is unified with the other and that one has obliterated the other. Like the meals of coo-coo and gefilte fish, this fantasy cannibalizes while ultimately acknowledging the impossibility of self-possession. This is heady, transgressive stuff in a discursive space shaped by notions of bounded identities. At the time of writing *A Way in the World*, Naipaul's actual relationships with Trinidadians of all races probably remained as embattled as they always had been.[7] Nevertheless, I read this novel as confirming that the imaginative landscape Naipaul shares with Trinidadian readers of all races, and with his Caribbean readers more generally, makes them, for better or worse, his most intimate readers. Their passions, insecurities and fantasies suffuse his writing. Through them, he must take his chances with posterity. Naipaul's novel reminds us that all promises of remembrance are provisional and ambiguous. Ultimately he concedes that, like the landscapes that so insistently haunt his narrators, his literary legacy will have to surrender to the fresh associations of a stranger's child.

PART 2

EKB

5

FOR KAMAU

> *You have to be concerned with the sources of a poet's life a people's inspiration and try to protect care for as best you can, those sources. . .* **We** *have to be concerned with the poet's health well-being comfort. yes; but above all there are the* **archives** *– that written memorialized recorded record of his/her life/hope/history/art. Because if you can applaud him/ her ('clap a likkle') as he/ she stands before you, if, as I assume, you feel that he/she has something important to say,then you've got to be concerned with the* **whole thing**. *Don't wait until you hear that so-and-so dying of whatever, that so-an-so aint got no dunny, cast away in him garret or ghetto. . . Don't wait until you hear that fire or flood destroy Bratwaite house to say that you sorry an start runnin arounn about what to do what to do how we can help etc etc etc*[1]

In this passage from "Saving the Word", appendix V of *Barabajan Poems*, Kamau Brathwaite frames his own words from an earlier essay in two ways: between the black lines within which his extravagant "video style" layout allows him to box his citation, as if it were a wedding announcement or the epitaph on a gravestone, and in the frame of novelist and critic Carolivia Herron's voice as she cites Brathwaite in her introductory remarks to a lecture he gave at Harvard University in September 1988. Herron's citation of Brathwaite predates by two years the publication in *Savacou* of the essay/prose poem *Shar*, from which Brathwaite lifts this passage.[2] The time lag suggests that a completed version of Brathwaite's essay must have been in circulation well before it finally appeared in *Savacou*, the chronically underfunded oneman publishing enterprise that Brathwaite used after 1970 to disseminate some of his most important essays, as well as to produce *Barabajan Poems*.

These kinds of inefficiencies around the distribution and preservation of the written word in the Caribbean contribute to the frustration so evident in Brathwaite's words. For Brathwaite is a historian as well as a poet, the kind of writer (like Naipaul's revolutionary Miranda) who understands the value of keeping everything – invitations, drafts, letters, invoices, manuscripts, bibliographies, journals – which later generations will need to reconstruct the achievement of a public figure. The fact that he first self-published some of his most important works, and that he feels he must have recourse to citing himself via an American critic to affirm the importance of his writerly legacy for the Caribbean, underlines his bitterness at the way in which he perceives his region's neglect of its artists has perpetuated the collective cultural amnesia his work tries so hard to counteract.

The near destruction of Brathwaite's archives in 1988 by Hurricane Gilbert, to which Brathwaite alludes in Herron's citation, was one in a series of devastating personal losses the poet suffered in midlife.[3] The worst of these was the death in 1986 of his first wife, Doris, who for decades had been the poet's chief source of spiritual support, as well as his archivist and research partner. In 1990 Brathwaite's post-Gilbert Kingston apartment was invaded by robbers, who held the poet at gunpoint while they stripped him of all valuables, including his wedding ring. Their violation of his person severed the poet's last, tenuous imaginative links to his adopted Jamaican landscape, which appears thereafter in the grimly disconsolate vision of *Trench Town Rock* as "a city smouldering [sic] in garbage. & men & woman plundering that monstrous HELL of stench & detritus & death. dead rat. live rat. for bread. bone. dead rotting flesh. dead rotting fish. the decomposing contexts of yr kitchen sink & toilet bowl & latrine & what you sweep off from yr floor & doormat tabletop in greasy paper plastic bags".[4] Gordon Rohlehr writes perceptively in his introduction to *DreamStories* (1994) about how each of these crises informed Brathwaite's subsequent publications. He sees Brathwaite as transforming his personal trauma into meditations on guilt and loss, allegories of the dark night of the soul that announce a new severity in the poet's vision. This vision is hinted at in the earlier *The Arrivants* (1967) and more clearly enunciated in *X/self* (1987), but only fully articulated in the more recent prose poem/journal such pieces as *Shar*, *Trench Town Rock* and *The Zea Mexican Diary* (1993). These texts write from within "the silent howl and scream of the straitened man", while his *DreamStories* chronicle "the events of an interior journey; to divine directions from the signposts of the dark valley: broken tree stumps, frowning rocks, thorns of the dark wood".[5]

For me the most searing of these documents is *The Zea Mexican Diary*, the poet's journal account of his wife's death and the changes her passing produced in his work and in his relationships with family and friends. The *Diary* is brutally autobiographical, in an unmediated way that makes me want to lower my gaze, as one instinctively does when forced to stand eyeball to eyeball in a crowded train with a person one does not know. Until the publication of the *Diary*, I considered Brathwaite a very formal writer, that is, a writer whose most important effects depended on his ability to work through formal masks, through poetic personae whose appearance and perspectives were "obviously" not those of Brathwaite the individual.[6] Like the absent white father with whom the poet often competes in his work, Kamau Brathwaite was the man who possessed them all – Uncle Tom in *Rights of Passage*; Ogun, the carpenter in *Islands*; Esse, the "forward" country girl in *Sun Poem*. Paradoxically transcendent and transparent, Brathwaite's public persona was that of a vessel; he was the shaman or mouthpiece through whom his audience heard the submerged voices of Africa, of the island, of history.

In *The Zea Mexican Diary* this mask is ripped off, taking with it the first layer of skin on the public orator's face. We are forced to look directly at the raw exposed flesh of Kamau Brathwaite the man – a frightened man at times, incapable of providing to the wife who supported him for decades the support she now needs as she lies dying, and at times a wise man, capable of naming and writing this failure of will. Bereft of his reflection in Zea's gaze, incapable in the first terrifying months after her death of even retrieving his words from the womb of her computer, Brathwaite presents himself in *The Zea Mexican Diary* and in essays like *Shar* that followed as overwhelmed by the fear of extinction. He seems suddenly aware that no one may actually have known or heard him – the man behind the mask, rather than the masquerade through whose orifices the voices of the collective issued.

Barabajan Poems is the most exhaustive of these confessional texts, torn out of the poet's consciousness in the aftermath of loss. In it, Brathwaite attempts to place himself and his message more securely within the reach of his readers. He does so by drawing together the explicitly biographical material from across his oeuvre, especially the poems rooted in the private Barbadian landscape of his childhood, as opposed to the public Jamaican landscape of the shaman/orator or the reconstructed African landscape of the historian. He then embeds these "Barabajan" poems in the historical and intellectual apparatus he imagines will best facilitate their reading. I like to think of *Barabajan Poems* as a piece of virtual sculpture, a plastic artefact that enacts the process of creating an archive through its innovative form. The "video style" layout of the project quotes the stylistic conventions of computer hypertext. It produces for its readers the illusion that they can consume with Brathwaite's words all the ramifications of the multiple landscapes that have produced his poet's sensibility: his family networks, his aesthetic influences, his place within Barbadian society and his relationship to the Barbadian landscape – and his position within a Barbadian literary history that extends chronologically back to Matthew J. Chapman's nineteenth-century poem "Barbadoes" and outward to embrace other, contemporaneous poets and makers of Barbadian culture.

The text is set up to be read via the click of a mouse rather than the turn of a page. Its only concession to linear progression is a long, unfurling essay that runs through the entire document. Part memoir, part scholarly dissertation, the essay section was first presented as a Sir Winston Scott Memorial Lecture in Barbados in 1987.[7] Into this prose banner Brathwaite threads what he considers his most significant Barbadian poems from previously published collections, as well as snippets of poems, memoirs and interviews written by a range of other Barbadian scholars, athletes and artists. Beyond the body of this narrative collage, the volume expands to include more than fifty endnotes, as polymorphously perverse in their content and form as the main corpus of the text itself. There are also seven appendices. They include a listing of Shango train songs – secular and religious music from Africa and the African diaspora that makes use of the metallic effects and driving rhythms Brathwaite associates with the Yoruba god Shango – and a chronological checklist of poetry by Barbadians since the eighteenth century. "Finally finally finally", as the narrator puts it, there is "a brief vertical interview" – the *I and I* trope par excellence – in which the author creates a whimsical conversation between himself as critic and himself as poet on the "meaning" of his work.[8] Even then the text is not complete, as Brathwaite adds an index, cross-referencing every person, concept and place-name mentioned in his virtual archive. The text's interactive format allows the reader to scan it in a variety of ways: from cover to cover, like a conventional book; from text to endnotes, like a scholarly treatise; from poem to personal narrative, like listening to a poetry reading; and from icon to text, like a computer multimedia installation.

Brathwaite also produces dramatic visual effects on the page by making use of the full range of typefaces to which his earliest computers gave him access. His "video style" layout, as he names it, calls to mind the way in which reggae and hip hop musicians have foregrounded the technology of the studio in their music, by exploiting the acoustic possibilities of dubbing, mixing and scratching, as well as electronic distortion of the sound itself. Like these musicians, Brathwaite is interested in breaking through the illusion of verisimilitude offered by more conventional forms of production. The technical details of representation are no longer transparent to the reader. Instead, like the no-longer-invisible poetic persona Kamau, they deliver the effects the artist desires by calling attention to themselves. Brathwaite constantly shifts the layout patterns of his text so that we are forced to register how and why they affect the words on the page. Thus, as the poet moves between commentary, bibliography, anecdote, chant, lyric and endnote, the typeface of the poem expands and contracts to demarcate or blur the boundaries between different genres, as well as to indicate a range of emotions.

Some of Brathwaite's visual effects are predictable. For example, in part VII, which brings together poems that explore the metaphor of religious possession as a form of cultural affirmation, the poet interweaves a scholarly commentary on the process of possession, as well as his subjective response to such phenomena. The heavy typeface of his commentary on "Angel/Engine" – a sequence he imports from *Mother Poem* (1977) – mimics the heavy-handedness of an academic presentation. It even highlights words like *loneliness*, *disappointment* and *dispossession* in oversized black lettering, just as a lecturer working with PowerPoint might highlight the main ideas he expects students to glean. The first section of the poem, describing the mother's life, is rendered in small italics that seem to run together like the mundane details of the grinding poverty and dispossession that characterize her experience:

> *The yard around which the smoke circles*
> >   *is bounded by kitchen, latrine & the wall*
> >   *of the house where her aunt died, where*
>
> *her godma brought her up, where she was jumped*
> >   *upon by her copperskin cousin*
> >   *driving canemen to work during crop*
>
> *time, smelling of rum and saltfish*
> >   *who give she two children when, so she say,*
> >   *she back was turn to the man, when she wasn't*
>
> *lookin*[9]

Each new act of violence that encloses the woman pushes the words away from the margins as if, over time, her horizons have contracted to the point where, in the last line cited, there is nothing to look forward to beyond emptiness.

Brathwaite also uses empty space and esoteric symbols to make his reader "see" the extra-textual powers at work in the poem. The passage from "Angel/Engine" cited above is prefaced by a grid that suggests prison bars or the closed gate of a cattle pen. Further on, the conventional typeface of the scholarly treatise on possession is interrupted by irregular runes – a circle, an arrow, a spiral. Like the *vèvès* chalked at crossroads in Haitian Vodun rituals, they announce the presence of symbolic elements drawn from beyond the boundaries of language. As the description of the woman's possession approaches the arrival of the gods Shango, Damballah and Erzulie, the scholarly typeface contracts and recedes until it is crowded against the margins, mimicking the way the researcher now cowers on the periphery of the ritual he is describing, overwhelmed by the unseen forces released through the possessed woman's body:

> . . . that was the night PROFESS-
> OR ?slumming w/ us from the UNI-
> VERSITY - recorder tape the camer
> (a) the lot - becames embarrassed fr
> ightened - *Erzulie too xtreme?* wh-
> en he meant 'obscene' - K/Ka/

Kam/Kama/Kama
Kamau/ too sacred = scared

He switched the light of the 'Niag ara'(Nagra) off - xcuse? - *don't want invade the privacy. . .*¹⁰

Here the layout allows us to make a direct connection between the frightened, embarrassed professor and the poet K/Ka/Kam/Kama/Kama/Kamau as we later glimpse him, confronting Africa's spiritual forces in the "Limuru" section of part XII, where he recounts his ambivalent response to the traditional African ceremony at which he received the Kikuyu name Kamau. Consulting the entry "Kamau" in the index, the reader can "click" forward to the Limuru passage in order to develop the connection the poet is making. This cross-referencing allows Brathwaite to indicate his complicity in the professor's discomfort with the folk culture and to acknowledge in himself – the hitherto omnipotent creator of "Angel/Engine" – the same human limitations that assail his dramatis personae.

When the text returns to the poem "Angel/Engine" after a detour through "Stone Sermon" – an earlier poem from *The Arrivants* that describes a similar moment of religious transformation, but in terms of Christian imagery – the italic font is thicker and more assertive than in the earlier stanzas. The voice of the scholar/narrator also re-emerges, intermittently, tentatively, each line stretching a little longer. Once Shango, the Yoruba god associated with machines and lightning, and Damballah, the snake god, enter the circle of worshippers, the words spread themselves with confidence across the page in huge oversized lettering. In the final downhill rush of the woman's possession, her signature italic font straightens up. The short lines beat out in squat, upright boldface the rhythm of the woman's breathing, to which her entire body, stretched taut like a drum, moves, while the sibilant swish of the departing spirits continues to be registered in italics.

sh

praaaaze be to
praaaaze be to
praaaaze be to

> *shang*
>
> **praaaaze be to**
>
> *sh*
>
> **praaaaze be to**
>
> *gg*
>
> **praaaaze be to**
> **praaaaze be to**
> **praaaaze be to**
>
> *sssssssssssssssssssssssssssssssss*hhhhhhhhhhhhhhhhhhhhhhhhh
>
> # an de train comin in wid de rain[11]

The association of computer visual effects with extra-textual spiritual powers in *Barabajan Poems* is no accident. In this period of self-revelation, Brathwaite's first computer ("Sycorax") and second computer ("Stark") became named symbolic presences in the poet's private iconography. Brathwaite has written about how his inability to retrieve his manuscripts from his late wife's computer seemed to portend the creative desolation that he dreaded would overwhelm him in the aftermath of her death.[12] His subsequent mastery of computer technology constituted a point of cathexis within the mourning process. It gave him new access to the qualities of nurture and preservation that he associated with his wife's support of his artistic project.

Brathwaite's new-found understanding of the possibilities associated with "writing in light", as he has called it, and with electronic memory also enabled an illusion of total recall: a fantasy that his reader could attain unmediated access to his imagination and could move beyond language to the remembered wholeness of the womb. Not surprisingly, the symbol of that access is unmistakably gendered. Sycorax, Brathwaite's first anthropomorphized computer, takes its name from Caliban's mother in *The Tempest*, one of the images for the submerged maternal principle in *Mother Poem*. In "Hex" from *Mother Poem*, for example, the poet invokes Sycorax to accomplish a shift in his presentation of the mother from sufferer to avenging force, through a series of images that move from the domestic to the elemental:

> so she sits, bandana ikon
>
> stool in the corner
> that cool stone in the backyard
> that flat rock underneath the cotton tree
> that rocking chair on the enslaved verandah
> black sycorax my mother
>
> she is as young as the pouis
> as ancient as dead leaves
> she will outlast the present season's thunder
> the ovens of august
>
> and the september's breath of hurricanes;
> and when the wind from the east brings dust,
> brings crack, brings flowers,
> she will begin to creak and give the dry rot meaning[13]

The progression of images here – from the domestic (bandana, rocking chair, verandah) to the vegetative (cotton tree, pouis, dead leaves) to the brutally elemental (season's thunder, ovens of august, breath of hurricanes) – mirrors and anticipates a similar series of shifts in the associations that accrue to Zea in *The Zea Mexican Diary*. Zea's impending death precipitates the poet's (and the computers') abandonment to the elements, in images that make it increasingly unclear whether she is a protective muse or an embodiment of the vengeful elements to which the poet feels abandoned:

> For it was she who handled the French & Spanish & all the hazards of all the foreign travel Who navigated the car across Europe & into New York & Chicago & Edinburgh & from Massachusetts to the Miami shoreline & sometimes took over the wh/eel after midnight on those long crazy drives back from Accra on Nkrumah's new lonely highways when possessed by the red firefly eyes of *sasabonsam* I was dreaming the MinX up a tree or over th/(e) black redge of ravines . . . dealt w/ people . . . from marketwomen to workmen to editors professor/(s) madpeople & specialists . . . Whatever else may be fall me now after 26 years can only be cola or coda/appendices - can only be luck/ if a lucky/ if a don't get ill/ if a don't meet mi dessert or deserts w/ an asp or an adder or a boa-constrictor or gorgon O poor little helpless What will happen to Savacou & the computers Who will love you so **total/ly**, friend[14]

The images in this passage present Zea as a bulwark of strength so fixed, so impervious to the assaults of the elements that her absence, like Sycorax's presence in "Hex", is the equivalent of a natural disaster: the ripping away of a headland by an earthquake or volcano, the violence of a hurricane that tears open the roof to let the forces of destruction into the home. In calling his first computer – her computer, really – Sycorax, Brathwaite brings together the nurture and violence he associates with Zea and with electronic memory more generally. In the face of death his dependency becomes a terrible curse, as he realizes that he does not know – has never known – the command that will allow him to retrieve the part of himself that has been stored in it by her.

Brathwaite's second computer, however, whose programs allowed him to create his new video layouts, he calls Stark. The meanings that accrue to Stark's name derive from both the English word *stark*, meaning "spare" or "bold" ("in your face"? "womanish"?), and its Germanic root, connoting indefatigable strength. Stark is also the name the poet gives to Caliban's sisters in the private iconography laid out in endnote 43 of *Barabajan Poems*, where he discusses plantation personality types:

> **Stark**/Sister Stark, Caliban's sister . . . did not walk clearly away from me until the October evening 1991 at NYU when I spoke of Paule Marshall's then new book, **Daughters** and recognized Stark in what Marshall was doing - the first time that the Plantation has a black woman w/ firm feet, sensitive/ aggressive breasts and a space & plan if not always a room of her own She begins in James Carnegie's Mary **(Wages Paid)** and now makes her way in & through the wonderful efflorescence of STARK WRITING since Mary Prince since Mary Seacole since Walker since Morrison since Brodber since Kincaid since Condé since Warner since Carolivia Heron since Cynthia James/ to name only a few[15]

This is how Brathwaite imagines the personality of his second computer, the one he acquired not as a terrified, sightless child searching vainly for the lost words he has entrusted to Sycorax, the submerged mother, but as a man in control of his technological world, who can work with its creative possibilities rather than being overwhelmed by them. It is also the collective term he uses to describe the emergent cohort of black women writers in the 1980s and 1990s whose successes he could have read from a more paranoid perspective, as having eclipsed his own. Whereas the supportive, submerged, subversive Sycorax communicates loved and feared Medusa-like magical powers that, if not contained or understood, can reduce the poet's gift of language from Prospero to silence and stone, Stark is the poet's comrade and creative equal. The emphasis is on kinship and solidarity rather than on a generational or erotic opposition. Stark's femininity is also contained, however, by the interchangeability of the names of the women writers and Brathwaite's computer. Through the exchange, the poet inadvertently figures feminine creativity as synonymous with a technological resource available to the male writer. From this perspective, the poet's invocation of Carolivia Herron's voice in "Saving the Word" to frame his own words renders her silent. Rather than speaking her own lines as an independent source of creative possibility, she becomes a mechanical recording device, returning the poet's own words to him and preserving them, like an archive or a faithful computer, from the corrosive indifference of the Caribbean community and the economic vagaries of indigenous publishing.

There is nothing inherently invidious about this utopian image of woman as supportive cyborg.[16] It arises out of Brathwaite's conceptual preoccupation with images of wholeness and complementarity, his search for a history that "will not always bleed on other people's edges".[17] Where Naipaul sees first a landscape wiped clean of past associations, and then a past so overwhelming in its ramifications that it defies representation and threatens to engulf the writer's subjectivity, Brathwaite sees his subjectivity as tied up with a submerged cultural landscape that the power of the word – associated with the feminine principle, the voice or the computer – can help him raise intact to the surface. For him, the blank page *can* be filled. The problem is not the excess of infinite ramifications but the threat of sabotage, an anxiety that somehow the page will remain blank because of indifference, denial, repression or the violence of technical and economic constraints.

The artist in this scenario is always in search of allies. Rather than capitulating to the ravages of history, he combs the landscape for clues to the meaning of his community's past. He enlists the creative powers and voices of his sister writers not as a form of self-aggrandizement but as part of what he imagines is their joint project and duty in relation to the plantation cultures that have produced them both. It is in this spirit of solidarity and communal retrieval that Brathwaite ends the main body of his text with a selection of Barbadian proverbs collected by another woman, Margot Blackman. Conversely, in his penultimate endnote he presents himself as the archival conduit through which one of his NYU students of Barbadian descent discovers Blackman's proverb collection in *Bim*. He reports that through her work for his class on *"Bim and the development of Caribbean Literature through Bim*, she began to learn & understand thi/ngs that she didn't know or rather things that she had SUBMERGED".[18] Like the community's archives and the personal computer, the creative and critical contributions of both male and female writers thus become the mediums (or media) through which the submerged memories of the Caribbean folk will possess (or become accessible to) a new generation of Caribbean initiates in search of their history.

But Brathwaite in this text, like Naipaul in *A Way in the World*, is also in search of personal affirmation. The words he places in Carolivia Herron's mouth, about the community's responsibility to preserve its cultural legacy, represent the poet's life and personal well-being – as well as his reputation and the critical apparatus that maintains it – as part of that legacy. For if it is true, as he says in his essay "The New West Indian Novelists: Part II", that "for a [writer's] mind to be truly itself, it cannot only be self-regarding, introspective and selfish, it must be out-going: aware of its responsibilities to others in society",[19] it is also true that society has a responsibility to "care if i-man never write another word another poem".[20] For Brathwaite, the individual artist is incomplete if he cannot see himself reflected in the gaze of his community. However, in order to be whole and able to see the artist, the community must remake itself in the image that the artist lays out in his work. Thus Brathwaite sees himself and his text as incomplete until both can come back to him through the understanding and appreciation of his listeners. The black woman writer Carolivia Herron must first internalize the meaning of Brathwaite's text in order to return it to him as tribute or epitaph.

"One haan cyaan clap!" the poet remonstrates in a letter to the editor of the *Barbados Advocate*, reproduced in bristling oversized calligraphy in appendix I of *Barabajan Poems*.[21] The letter takes to task the Barbadian community for neglecting the contribution of other Barbadian writers in the course of the Barbados Archive's hundredth-anniversary celebrations of the life and work of Frank Collymore, the founding father of *Bim*. Brathwaite was particularly distressed that his own contributions to *Bim* was not mentioned at any point in the anniversary exhibition. His letter invokes his services to the magazine as Collymore's associate editor for more than thirteen years, and his publications in the journal of some sixty poems and twenty critical articles, as entitling him to recognition. Moreover, he notes, "what is most dismaying is that I - **myself a Bajan** - should have to make this point to **Barabados** at this stage of our development".[22]

Brathwaite uses the Jamaican saying "One haan cyaan clap" (You can't clap with one hand) to suggest that Collymore's editorial legacy is diminished when it is viewed in isolation from the contributions other Barbadians made to the achievement of *Bim*. Nevertheless, it is difficult to avoid the implication that Brathwaite too is clapping with one hand. However necessary may be the acknowledgement he demands for his work and that of other Barbadian writers alongside the celebration of Collymore, it is impossible for the poet to eulogize himself, to be both the grammatical subject and object of his own speech act – the transcendent *I and I* of Dread Talk, which, in its uncompromising appropriation of all subject positions, negates the possibility of an object/interlocutor, and therefore of dialogue.[23] Brathwaite attempts to circumvent this problem by citing himself through the words of other writers and through deployment of his anthropomorphic computers. But without the unsolicited support of his community, the poet's virtual archive runs the risk of becoming an echoing hall of mirrors, giving back to the writer only the images of himself that he has brought to the text.

And yet the act of naming oneself, of claiming and establishing one's own worth, is often represented by writers – and accepted by their readers – as the superlative act of literary instantiation. As critics we affirm the creative possibility of this tautology every time we distinguish between the poet and the poetic persona of a text; every time we allow the artist to be the agent of representation as well as the object represented; every time we refer to the act of writing as a process of self-creation. We see the paradoxically tautological and creative possibilities of the dramatic monologue the poet performs, in the absence of communal dialogue, in the closing sections of the main text of *Barabajan Poems*. Section XII brings together a number of "endings" from previous long poems by Brathwaite, as well as a new autobiographical sequence describing the ceremony in Limuru, Kenya, where the poet was given the Kikuyu name Kamau by the writer Ngũgĩ wa Thiong'o's mother. The Limuru sequence is the linchpin of section XII, as it is here that Brathwaite identifies himself most clearly as sharing the denials and repressions that produce the collective cultural amnesia he attributes to "the eternal victim of 'The Man Who Possesses us all'".[24] He notes that, especially in the postcolonial Caribbean, this victim is "also increasingly victim of himself (like Prof, like Redman, like the Father of **Mother Poem**)", and in the Limuru section he places himself briefly within this catalogue of self-imposed victimology.[25]

Brathwaite surrounds the description of his naming ceremony with other stories about the giving and claiming of names. He cites his use of the concept of "nam", or inner name, in *Mother Poem* and *Sun Poem*, as well as biblical and Shakespearean precedents for the importance of names. He recounts the battles he has fought to get others to call him Kamau rather than Edward, and he quotes from a transcript of the television version of Alex Haley's *Roots*, where the overseer beats Kunta Kinte into accepting that his name is Toby. He then offers the reader an explication of each syllable of his new name, spelled forward – K/Ka/Kam/Kama – and backward – U/au/mau/amau/ama.[26] Section XII ends with a re-rendering of the poem "Nametracks", from *Mother Poem*, in which a deadly game of O'Grady ("Simon says") between the mother and "The Man Who Possesses us all" takes place. As "O'Grady makes a last desperate effort to dictate/nominate/re/name **eat** Mandingo", we hear the child begin to sing in his mother tongue, "to unsubmerge, to begin the come/ the come/ the come back up assertion/reassertion of the **nam**".[27]

There is a point in his description of these heroic struggles, however, where Brathwaite stumbles in parenthesis: when he allows his reader to see him as more fallible than his mythologized alter egos. It comes during the description of his surprise naming ceremony when, in tiny script enclosed in parentheses, he glosses (over?) the emotions he felt:

> kneeling on the ground with the wind on my face & the great sky of Eden all around me in fro/nt of these old women who like ripped open my shirt & like spat upon my chest (the water of baptism/though I was very much alarmed to say the least at first) & began chanting deep deep down inside their chests & deeper down into their very bellies searching for my **nam** so they cd find my name[28]

There is a vertigo about the language in this passage, produced by the effect of the parentheses, the diminution of the type and the use of slashes and ampersands to connect words. It approximates the feeling of "being-throwness" that Derrida invokes to describe the space before/beyond subjectivity. It is as if in this passage the poet is hurtling through the space between two modes of potential subjectivity – the incompletion of *Edward* and the aspiration of *Kamau*. The force of his destinerrance may throw off either outcome at any moment, just as in the process of birth the foetus/child must pass through a hypothetical moment when its connection to life's breath comes neither through the lungs nor via the umbilical cord. Moreover, the understated neutrality of *alarmed*, which Brathwaite places within parentheses, isolated from the rest of the sentence and written in extra-tiny script, recalls the professor's euphemistic usage of *extreme* at the possession ritual discussed earlier:

> wh/en he meant 'obscene' - K/Ka/
> **Kam/Kama/Kama**
> **Kamau**/ too sacred = scared[29]

Brathwaite's linkage of these two passages, through the insertion of his African name in the first one, draws attention to the poet's embarrassment and vulnerability in the face of the primitive, almost obscene elements of this naming ritual. The word *like*, reiterated before *ripped* and *spat*, registers, without naming, the poet's fear, like that of a rapist's victim or a woman in childbirth, that his body will be exposed and violated.

The use of parentheses and understatement to sequester the poet's admission of shame and fear calls to mind the stories of cultural refusal and repression inserted into the earlier "Legba" section: the embarrassment of the Garifuna in Belize, who tell outsiders they know of no African survivals in their culture while hiding and hoarding their drums, and the stubborn insistence with which the hired help at the poet's sister's home in St Vincent denies her agency, refusing even to acknowledge the sound of drumming in the hills when asked about its message:

> **she didn't hear anything** - *me nevva hear nothin - me na hear nuttn - mwen na rien, msieu*[30]

All these stories demonstrate how people of African descent in the Caribbean "bracket" memories and associations they are not ready to deal with, repressing their cultural connection to Africa through slavery as a way of circumventing its attendant shame and pain. Brathwaite, in announcing his new name and describing the entire naming ceremony, as well as the meanings he imputes to each syllable, forces onto the page a series of associations that even he concedes he once found "alarming". In the process, our sense that the poet is pushing it – overdoing the narcissism, being embarrassingly personal, clapping with one hand the syllables of his own name – pushes us as readers through the whole messy, self-absorbed, introspective, exhibitionist, shameful business of watching someone (ourselves?) giving birth, or being pushed into existence. It draws us into those self-confessional moments when we are forced to look too closely at the poet, skin peeled away, without the mask of aesthetic distance, and find in his eyes our own reflections, repressions and unnamed fears.

In closing the poem, the poet begins to rewrite his opening acknowledgements to the sponsors of the Sir Winston Scott Memorial Lectures, as he wishes he might have been able to articulate them. It hardly comes as a surprise that the symbol that he fantasizes this virtual archive will now have made possible turns out to be a plaque with the poet's new name, placed over the door to his dressing room:

> 𝔉𝔦𝔯𝔰𝔱 𝔬𝔣 𝔞𝔩𝔩 Mr Chairman, I must thank the Central Bank of Barbados for bringing me here at this time and for promoting me to labour what I have hear this out over all these years. Never befo/re in this island (and I am still standing to yr attention) have I been treated so royally. [There was even, I remember, The Artist's Dressing Room with NAME
>
>
>
> on the legba door (remember?) and large photos all over the palace] It is something I never χpected but which, I can assure you, I am enjoying. It is good to feel that your own island and your own people have somehow... understood what you have been trying to do[31]

Here the undersized script of the words in the brackets within brackets serve to frame the oversized <KAMAU> that the poet longs to see inscribed in his community's imagination. It is the kind of detail, he contends, that a loved and respected artist should be able to expect without having to clap for it – *"Because if you can applaud him/ her ('clap a likkle') as he/ she stands before you, if, as I assume, you feel that he/she has something important to say,then you've got to be concerned with the **whole thing**."*[32]

Brathwaite's project by this point seems at risk of being undone by its very success. For if his fantasy were indeed to come true and the talk he was giving could have started in the manner he now imagines, there would have been no talk. Certainly there would not have been this prose poem whose whole purpose has been to educate a reluctant audience into accepting the poet's right to name himself, to be loved and respected on account of the image of himself he has created through his work for his community. In such a scenario, the consciousness that would have stood before that imagined audience, secure in its expectation of respect and applause, could not have produced that painfully elegiac plea for lost community and submerged self that propels *Barabajan Poems* at its finest. Nor could a society that no longer needed such an elegy have produced the artist Brathwaite presents himself as having become. Like the biblical paradise where "I shall know as I am known", such a society would recognize and honour its own prophets without prompting. And the fear of rejection, the mourning of loss, the necessity of grammar and, thus, the possibility of poetry would be no more.

All writers play a version of this game whereby the object desired is precisely the one whose presence would disable the possibility of narrative. What makes the strategy so fraught in Brathwaite's case is the inescapability of the autobiographical presence – our sense that for Brathwaite this is no mere game of words and that he genuinely feels that an artist *should* be able to expect this kind of unconditional love from his community – and that his writing will be the better for it.[33] His predicament dramatizes the Sisyphean extremity of the postcolonial writer who, in the absence of an established literary tradition, has only himself or herself as literary subject and pre-text. Even as Brathwaite's virtual archive invents a literary tradition for Barbados through his painstaking appendices, drawing attention to the way his own achievement has been part of a wider moment of cultural possibility, the poet remains trapped. He is unable to write from outside the castle of his skin, the only literary subject position available to him in a community whose histories remain submerged.

And so the *Barabajan Poems* drift erratically between the tidal pulls of autobiography and the anchor of art, creating a society for the poet as well as a poet for the society it attempts to represent, talking at times in circles to itself. Its insistence that the value of the poet's person be inseparable from the achievement of the poet's work seems wistful at times, but there is no question – as I will show in the readings of two further epitaphs – that the poems this virtual archive allows Brathwaite to re-present from other collections gain depth and texture as a consequence of their insertion into the framework of his autobiographical hypertext.

6

FOR SON/SUN

an inn yu gwine screw/off de bonnick yu thay yu is man yu is man
& crank up de fan wid dat handle yu hand/le an pump/it she
laughed him & then as wind like a cloud brings a sudden
change to the canefields breathing grey where there once had been

green/ esse say

yu theee/yu theee/yu theee what uh thell yuh! dah is all yu ramgoats
wantin wid we
pump gath up de tank an is not even tanks
like muh mutha say
an aftha yu finish drive bout like yu like
ooona gone back to town when yu dun & fuhget bout de bill when a
accident happen & de lorry dey pun de dump/heap

but lithen to
me mith/ter john belly guts
no
body int drive thith lil lorry yet
showing him where it was
in the tree
an no
body inn gethin no chance to-rit needa
unleth they kin show me thuh lithunse

her lips curled & curved drinking shade & the shadow &
she spat out a dunck seed *thoo* through the air & hit him hard on the forehead

Brathwaite lifts this wonderful stream of invective and innuendo into *Barabajan Poems* from *Sun Poem*, in which Esse, the country girl of the heavy lisp, is the first to excite the lust of the boy at the artistic centre of the poem. Even in *Sun Poem* Esse's language was outrageous, but here, among the solemn pieties of the poet's search for dignity and respect, her irreverence attains the full force of a hurricane, deluging the narrator with its free-ranging mechanical metaphors. Where the poet bestows on his sister writers the accolade of equality with his computers, Esse seems to choose her own cyborg identity as one of the powerful new motorized trucks that replaced horse-drawn carts in the Barbados of the poet's childhood – an image still redolent today with associations of speed, sexual danger and independence.

Esse represents these qualities and more in *Barabajan Poems*, but to assemble all the images associated with her, the reader has to push the resources of the virtual archive to their limit. Apart from the heavily glossed excerpts from *Sun Poem* cited in the epitaph above, Esse appears in a number of endnotes and authorial asides, notably note 42, where Brathwaite claims her as his actual first love, and in note 47, which elaborates upon a parenthetical remark explaining the inspiration for the poem "Legba".[2] Esse's relatives are identified as the women who provide the chorus of voices in the poem from *The Arrivants* called "The Dust".[3]

On the surface, the details of Esse's background are predictable: a country girl of a lower class than the poet's petit-petit-bourgeois family, who are shop-owners in the Mile and a Quarter country district he visits as wa boy. Under the surveillance of the Aunts, the (mostly?) chaste relationship between these star-crossed lovers is doomed to failure, but Brathwaite claims that Esse's love letters to him were his first encounter with the erotic possibilities of written Barbadian language: "you cd FEEL, the passion 'crude' and clear, confessional, sy/ mbolic, very vivid & concise - the lack of CENSORSHIP or rather freedom from it & rooted in her WORLD; with assignations/ rendezvous conveyed sometimes by hurried folded notes delivered with spy-like circumspection by my little cousin Fillmore".[4]

In Brathwaite's account of their actual relationship, Esse seems to have all the power. She writes to him; she curses him; she even grabs his balls on his aunts' half-lit front verandah, where she and the other pubescent village girls have been corralled to participate in a church choir practice:

Out of all that dark & chaos, I remember, in all that dark & shakshak whisper, this Esse reach out, I remember, TOUCH me . Not just a touch of tentative - it was a touch of search - of CLAIM - of jasmine - a quick attempt - believe you me - *these country girls*! - to FEEL ME UP. It was as if out there that night on Bob'ob's muse/ical verandah . I hear the muse/ic of the spheres[5]

It's all there in this passage: male hysteria in the face of the threat of castration; the swooning possibility of more pleasure or more pain; the poet's tongue-in-cheek class-inflected displacement of responsibility for his arousal onto "these country girls", echoing the deepest prejudices of "The Aunts". All in an endnote to a parenthetical comment inserted into a vision of the poet, decades later, standing on the same verandah, searching for a personal connection to a submerged culture he fears he may never find. Esse is shak-shak sibilance, the dispersed menace and promise of Damballah, the snake god who haunts the body of the possessed woman in "Angel/Engine". Esse is the music of the spheres, as well as the poet's first muse who guides his pen/is into the rhythms of her island's language. Esse is the vehicle of metaphor, the lorry she dares him to drive without a licence. If *jouissance* had not been discovered by the French feminist critics, Esse would have invented it.

For all the rhetorical force of the invective she delivers from her superior vantage point up the duncks tree, however, Esse harbours few illusions about the power dynamic in her relationship with the son/sun. She knows he can go "back to town when [he] dun & fuhget bout de bill when a / accident happen & de lorry dey pun de dump/heap". The sociological statistics on cross-class encounters in the Caribbean like this one are seldom as benign as the poet's rose-coloured memory of his relationship with Esse suggests. Boys like the poet gain their manhood and their access to the folk, as well as their first intimations of social power, through their sexual encounters with girls like Esse. Girls like Esse gain babies and broken dreams. Brathwaite registers all these nuances in the reflections with which he surrounds Esse's dramatic monologue. He acknowledges that usually a young man like himself, from a "good" family, could expect to have the run of the plantation girls, who were "keen on brown-skin fathers. / for them plantation wreck / and ruin still meant pride & prejudice and / certain in- // grained customs & a relationship & attitude / & distance".[6]

Esse's actions recognize and reject these familiar clichéd roles. She takes what she wants from the poet's pants while remaining beyond his grasp. Yet even the significance of these actions is not straightforward, as Esse establishes her discursive and physical dominance at the tremendous cost of rigid sexual repression. If her speech is any indication of what she writes, then the "'crude' and clear" passion of her text, "confessional, symbolic very vivid and precise", arises precisely from its representation of her body as tantalizingly forbidden, and sexual ardour as a weakness the speaker herself can ill afford to indulge. Thus the text with which Esse surrounds her body, rather than articulating her sexual independence, delivers to the poet a transgressive fantasy of "absence of censorship", the possibility of his forced entry into a world where for him, at least, there will be no consequences for having broken the rules.

All the more puzzling, therefore, is Esse's absence from the list of female plantation archetypes that Brathwaite elaborates in note 43, directly after his extended description of this forward plantation girl. Brathwaite takes the names for the archetypes – Antoinette, Sylvia and Fola – from works by other Caribbean writers. Antoinette is the name of Jean Rhys's white creole heroine in *Wide Sargasso Sea*, whose English stepfather and English husband are both types of Prospero in Brathwaite's iconography. Their hostility and lack of understanding of her creole origins ultimately destroy her. Edgar Mittelholzer's novel *Sylvia* follows the doomed career of a tragic mulatto girl who is reduced to madness after her white father dies and her black mother is unable to provide her with the social and economic protection she needs to function in Guyanese society. Fola, the heroine of Lamming's *Season of Adventure*, identifies as black, although her father's race is shrouded in uncertainty. She avoids the fates of Antoinette and Sylvia by surrendering herself to the experience of possession within the folk culture.

Apart from the names Brathwaite borrows from other Caribbean writers for his plantation typology, he invents one of his own – Stark – discussed in the previous chapter. But Esse is not Rhys's Antoinette, creole wife of Prospero, nor Mittelholzer's Sylvia, "the daughter schizophrene in love w/ Father Prospero".[7] Nor is she Lamming's Fola, the Legba woman on the threshold between two worlds who must be taught how to lose herself in the culture of the folk. Esse, the only actual plantation girl Brathwaite may have known intimately in his youth, cannot be subsumed into any of his plantation types. For a start, although her father is (almost) white, it is difficult to equate him with "The / Man Who Possesses Us All".[8] At best he is a Prospero bereft of his magic, fallen on hard times. Brathwaite describes him as a typical "'red man' who, under 'normal' plantation circumstances or in an earlier time, wd have been a busha (overseer) but instead became a washed-up lorry driver and like too many of his 'type' in M&Q & elsewhere, too given up to drink".[9] He curses his daughter's seducer softly and incomprehensibly under his breath whenever their paths cross, but he does not have the kind of social power wielded by the Aunts to intervene on behalf of his daughter's honour. Esse's mother, who looks straight through the interloper, disdaining dialogue, is described as a dougla woman – half Indian, half African – who works in the cane fields and wears a felt hat over her untidy plaits.

Judging from her parentage, however, in Caribbean terms Esse probably looked "more white" than the poet and most of his family, who, as respectable brown-skinned Barbadians, probably were a little further removed from the great house in terms of colour and illegitimate origins than this mulatto girl. So, although she lacks the pure racial pedigree of the frail white creole of the Antoinette or Miranda variety, within the local context she would have been light-skinned enough to be a symbol of the whiteness the boy desires – "a beautiful & desirable (on many levels) young female", as Brathwaite puts it in one of his cryptic parentheses.[10] However, her mother's hostile silence and strength ensure that Esse, unlike Mittelholzer's tragic mulatto Sylvia, is not doomed to waste away without the support of her white father. Nor will she make common cause with the supportive sisters Stark, the strong black women with firm feet and aggressive breasts who come tramping out of the October evening into Brathwaite's computer. In a word, Esse will not fit into the careful shade and race hierarchies of Brathwaite's plantation iconography. For although her light skin ensures that for the poet she embodies the erotic pull of whiteness and power, she is also black enough culturally to possess the folk language he aspires to master. She can spit her dunck seeds into the poet's face – "thoo!" – from her vantage point above him in the tree while indicating to him what is under the bonnet of the lorry she says he will never drive.

Esse is thus the daughter of both Prospero and Sycorax. Perhaps this is why the poet gives her the distorting "tie-tongue" lisp that he reveals (in another parenthesis!) she did not have in "real" life.[11] In its original context in *Sun Poem*, Esse's lisp was primarily a technical device that helped the reader distinguish between the voice of the son/sun and that of the girl in their extended repartee. It may also have been deployed as a visual marker to suggest the fantasies of lasciviousness associated in the Caribbean imagination with a pronounced space between a girl's front teeth.[12] However, sandwiched between the visually exaggerated representations of the swishing sound of the departing spirits in the "Angel/Engine" sequence and the alliterative names of Brathwaite's plantation types in the endnotes of *Barabajan Poems*, Esse's lisp has the effect of both masking and calling attention to the sibilance that connects her to Stark, Sylvia and Shango. It brackets her otherwise uncontainable signification outside the boundaries of the poet's private iconography.

M.M. Bakhtin, in *The Dialogic Imagination*, makes the point that "language is not a neutral medium that passes freely and easily into the private property of the speaker's intentions; it is populated – overpopulated – with the intentions of others. Expropriating it, forcing it to submit to one's own intentions and accents, is a difficult and complicated process."[13] This is as true of Prospero's language as it is of Caliban's, which, to the extent that it realizes its subaltern aspirations to mastery, becomes in turn vulnerable to subversion from below, next door or up a tree. Thus, even as the poet sets out to wrest from the English literary tradition a Barabajan language for his poetry, that aspiration in its turn is challenged by the voices it sets free. The writer who resists this dialogic imperative, who imagines that his monologic system can contain and account for all possible meaning, is likely to truncate the full range of communicative possibilities. Again Bakhtin says it most succinctly, this time in *Problems of Dostoyevsky's Poetics*:

> Monologism, at its extreme, denies the existence outside itself of another consciousness with equal rights and equal responsibilities, another *I* with equal rights (*thou*) . . . *another person* remains wholly and merely an *object* of consciousness, and not another consciousness. No response is expected from it that could change everything in the world of my consciousness. Monologue is finalized and deaf to the other's response, does not expect it and does not acknowledge in it any *decisive* force. . . . Monologue pretends to be the *ultimate word*. It closes down the represented world and represented persons.[14]

Without the dialogic structure of *Barabajan Poems* that embeds Esse's dramatic monologue in Brathwaite's autobiographical essay, the figure of Esse would have run the risk of becoming, in Bakhtin's terms, no more than an extension of the author's consciousness, an object to be manipulated in his grand scheme of things. So although Brathwaite ultimately creates both her voice and his own in this new text, the two voices have the effect of qualifying and contradicting each other's claims.

Esse's dialogic intervention brings into Brathwaite's first-person reverie elements of the community that he claims to represent but is forced to concede that his text does not fully control. In *Sun Poem* the dialogue was between the son/sun and this "tie-tongue" girl, and it was easy to imagine Esse, given her lisp, as a completely untutored black country girl who unwittingly delivers to the protagonist a dose of naïve folk wisdom that he proceeds to untie. Framed in the text and endnotes of *Barabajan Poems* by Brathwaite's cryptic confessions and evasions about the nature of their relationship, Esse's status and the implications of her invective become a lot more complicated. This new layer of heteroglossia extends the dialogue in ways that allow Esse to engage the poem's boy protagonist as well as the poet himself. Thus the epic simile – "then as wind like a cloud brings a sudden / change to the canefields breathing grey where there once had been // green/ *esse say*" – that interrupts Esse's diatribe becomes more than an editorializing stage direction. Instead, in the autobiographical context of *Barabajan Poems*, it places Brathwaite, the poet with a formal literary education at his disposal, on the verandah watching the face-off between Esse and his younger self, as well as under the tree, squinting up Esse's skirt. The poet deploys all his literary prowess to capture and define Esse's essence in classical metaphors that invoke Homer and the elements and the cane fields and the clouds, but all this still leaves him tantalizingly unable to see or touch what lies concealed beneath the bonnet of her lorry. When Esse spits her dunck seed into the boy's face, she enacts her resistance to the poet's narcissistic need to fill her with his words and his seed, as he previously had filled his computer and the sisters Stark or as he ingests the body of the lost mother/Sycorax/Zea. Yet Esse is also daring the poet to take her – her body, her language, her cultural space, her signification as both the daughter of Sycorax and Prospero's heir – even as she warns him in no uncertain terms that his pleasure will always be considered stolen unless it is taken with her informed consent. The folk are not an inert vehicle that the poet can marshal as he wishes in his private battle against Prospero. It is Esse – not Prospero or this petit bourgeois Caliban – who will issue the licence to drive her lorry.

Esse's simultaneous tropes of seduction and resistance confront the poet with the dreaded charge of appropriation that haunts all Caribbean writers who have attempted to claim the folk as their subject. Walcott thus accuses himself, in speaking of his reliance on Homer to render Helen in *Omeros*:

> "You tried to render
> their lives as you could, but that is never enough;
> now in the sulphur's stench ask yourself this question,
>
> whether a love of poverty helped you
> to use other eyes, like those of that sightless stone?"[15]

Brathwaite, in his role of conduit for the submerged voices of his islands, has seldom seemed exercised by this charge, since the poet as shaman is only ever a vessel of the gods, not a player in his own right. By introducing a confessional element into his virtual archive, however, Brathwaite forces himself to examine the interactions of his semi-autobiographical poetic persona with the other subjects to whom he has given voices. And indeed, from this new subject position, the poet may hear Esse as implying that she does not need his ministrations; she can write her own language and pleasure her own orifices as she reveals and conceals them from her vantage point above him in the duncks tree.[16] And maybe Esse is also telling the poet that his desire for her language, his claim to Prospero's island, is already implicated in his desire for her status as Prospero's child, even a broken-down, rum-soaked Redman of a Prospero. After all, as another authorial gloss explains, the very status of lorry driver that marks the depths to which Esse's father, Redman, has fallen is the status to which Caliban – in the person of the poet's uncles and the "better class" of ambitious brown men of their generation – aspires.[17]

Conversely, Esse's presence allows Brathwaite to acknowledge the limitations of the symbolic order that his narrator in *Barabajan Poems* may otherwise have tempted us to impose on all aspects of his project. Brathwaite's conceptual paradigms – the ones he uses to imagine Sylvia and Stark, Antoinette and Fola – arise from his experiences of Barbados and Jamaican society – two of the most homogeneous and hierarchical plantation societies among the former British colonies. Hilary Beckles, in his study of rebellion in Barbados, has described the effect that the very early introduction of slavery and the plantation system had on social relationships and strategies of resistance. Although he makes an argument for the survival of traditions of resistance in Barbados, he nevertheless concedes that this resistance had to accommodate itself to an assumption of social order established through violence in the sixteenth century and maintained by force and custom ever since.[18] Jamaica's colonial history contains more heterogeneous sources of hegemony and resistance than that of Barbados, which was an English colony from the beginning. Nevertheless, as Brathwaite describes in his study *The Development of Creole Society in Jamaica*, it was also a society in which certain racial hierarchies were perceived as unshakeable early in its colonial history. Even today, in both islands, a fairly fixed system of class and racial hierarchies remains unchallenged, with poor black people at the bottom, middle-class brown people in the middle and white and near-white people at the very top of the social structure. Religious affiliations run a similar gamut: the Church of England is associated with status and educational clout at one end, nonconformist Protestant sects are in the middle, and African-derived religious practices lie at the other end. In such societies it is easy to imagine hierarchies as fixed and to assign each person a place in that order. It is therefore also easy to fantasize that this order is reversible. The apocalyptic language of Rastafarian Dread Talk articulates just such an inversion, as do the more deeply submerged African religious practices in the Barbados Zion Church that provide the context for Brathwaite's poem "Angel/Engine".

The cosmopolitan jumble of a place like Trinidad has difficulty supporting such tightly structured racial hierarchies. The island's hybridity reflects its tangled history as a Spanish colony settled by the French and Irish, an English colony whose lingua franca was French Creole, and a black society that now has more people of Chinese and East Indian descent than African. Even its elite white stratum has barely contained its rival French creole, English, Lebanese and Portuguese elements, and colour has not always been a guarantee of status. In a culture where Shango may have a Hindu or Roman Catholic double, a person's name or physical appearance is not always a reliable indicator of his or her social status, religion, racial origins or cultural orientation. Although the broad continuum from black to white still structures social difference, it is harder to represent the gamut of social types in terms of this simple binary.

In worlds such as Barbados and Jamaica, by contrast, it is tempting to represent difference in terms of bounded racial identities like those Brathwaite isolates in his list of plantation types in note 43. That illusion of the possibility of order – some might say the inevitability of order – has created in the work of these islands' best-known writers an association between order and control, expressed through utopian fantasies of a stable, affirming postcolonial order, as well as a fear of and fascination with destructive apocalyptic images.[19] Such writing dreads upheaval even as it presents subversion, in Fanonian terms, as necessary for the evolution of authentically stable identities. Brathwaite's fear of and desire for change, and his utopian belief in the affirming possibilities of order and control in the hands of a newly empowered Caribbean community, bears witness to his preoccupation with the project of constructing a stable communal identity that is different from the slipperiness and incompleteness – the elusiveness – of the individual speaking subject in the work of Walcott and Naipaul.

The distinction between these writers should not be exaggerated, however. I see the Caribbean writers I am discussing as sharing many of the qualities that supposedly define their difference. Brathwaite is often as slippery as Walcott, as incomplete as Naipaul, while Naipaul is as invested in stability as Brathwaite. Walcott constantly borrows from them both. The difference lies less in how they represent the present than in how their works imagine the future. Brathwaite, writing from the centre of a social construct like "Little Englan" – so firm, so fixed as to seem indestructible – sees the erasure and dispossession this world inflicts on black Caribbean subjectivity as an absence, an emptiness that can and must be filled. His work seeks to enable this process of self-affirmation rather than to offer a new set of ready-made symbols and cultural tokens. Like Naipaul's narrators, his autobiographical persona is fascinated and frightened by the emptiness and infinite ramification of the past. However, he is determined to see the future beyond himself and his writing as offering a possibility of emergence rather than the inevitability of erasure. The poet's place within this future must also be assured.

His work must remain accessible through publication, through preservation, through dissemination and, above all, through its recognition and acclaim by the society it has helped to build.

Naipaul tutors us to read for absences, while Brathwaite instructs as to how submerged presences might be rehabilitated. The problem, of course, is that this process, like the aesthetic project of the virtual archive, can never be exhaustive. All the hypertexts, all the cross-references, all the background material and documentation, even the resetting of familiar poems in enriching new contexts and spatial arrangements, cannot ultimately retrieve or stabilize all the meanings of Brathwaite's text. Moreover, it is a moot point whether such retrieval or stabilization is even desirable. The popular stereotypes of "Little Englan" are, after all, just that. To be white in Barbados has never automatically meant empowerment, as the constant attempts to explain the anomalous position of poor whites in the island (such as Esse's father, Redman) should warn us.[20] Nor, as I demonstrate in chapter 7 ("For Edward"), does being brown make one automatically black. Esse's multiracial background and the disjuncture between her "near white" appearance and her black peasant status call into question the son/sun's originary claim of blackness as his natural heritage. The social markers that matter in the Caribbean – his class, his erudition, his brown complexion, his command of Standard English – all signal his elite (read "white") status from the perspective of a (black?) country girl like Esse. Perhaps that dissonance is part of the reason why the poet's Bajan community has had such difficulty seeing Brathwaite's subjectivity as co-extensive with that of Kamau.

"Yu thay yu is man yu is man!" Esse's challenge allows the poet to acknowledge the possibility of rupture and dissonance in his carefully calibrated symbolic order. Through her subversion of his overdetermined categories – black, brown and white; rich, middling and poor; high church, low church and Zion church; Standard written and Creole oral – she performs an identity that cannot be reduced to Stark, Sylvia or Antoinette. Moreover, her blurring of the boundaries between Prospero's legitimate and illegitimate heirs keeps the poet honest, fallible, open to the possibility of new meanings and audiences for his work, beyond those he can imagine at this point. By challenging his manhood and his need for ultimate control, she salvages his humanity and forces him into dialogue with all the Barabajan worlds he claims to represent, beyond the Collymore Auditorium of the Central Bank. In these new worlds, other subjects, other audiences may be equally agnostic about his claims to speak on their behalf, on account of agendas that cannot be subsumed under the rubrics the poet blames for hampering his recognition within the cultured circles of the postcolonial bourgeoisie. Ultimately Esse allows Brathwaite to envision a less predictably ordered future, one in which another potential audience will manhandle his work with all the impropriety and casual sense of proprietorship that this forward country girl brings to her exploration of his body and her challenge to his appropriation of her texts.

7

FOR EDWARD

> But heroes were in books
> and few of our fathers were heroes
>
> and we their sons learnt mainly to survive
> although a few went out and fought
> or spoke brave words from pulpits
>
> and when they died
> (the few who fought or spoke brave words from pulpits)
> only their mothers treasured them
> their helpless fathers looked away ashamed they could not do it
>
> leaves leaves leaves   of a forest gone silent
> leaves leaves leaves   without tongue without eyes
> leaves leaves leaves   sun glut and gold and roten[1]

I

There is no epitaph for Edward in *Barabajan Poems*. Although Brathwaite dedicates an earlier volume, *Sun Poem*, to five generations of Brathwaite men, including himself,[2] few passages about the other men make their way into his virtual archive, and this chapter's epigraph is not among them. Moreover, of the three writers discussed in this study, Brathwaite is the only one whose self-representation in his later work evades a direct reckoning with the figure of his father. Whereas both Naipaul and Walcott have written at length about their fathers as aesthetic and moral influences, we know very little from the literary record about the relationship between Kamau (Lawson Edward) and

Edward Hilton Brathwaite. Instead, in *Barabajan Poems* the poet's male progenitors are represented mainly by absence and silence.

It is difficult to account for this omission on thematic grounds, since a central preoccupation in *Barabajan Poems*, as I have discussed in chapter 5 ("For Kamau"), is its attack on Caribbean communities that fail to sustain a record of the achievements of their forebears. But Brathwaite's silence about his father and his repeated attempts to distance himself from their shared name Edward suggest a far more complex relationship to the anxiety of influence (both hereditary and literary) than his anti-colonial challenge to the Caribbean community can accommodate. His evasions help us gauge the extent of the genealogical anxieties with which all three of the writers considered in this book must grapple as they struggle to establish their literary legacies. Apart from affecting the way the poet represents his biological father, Brathwaite's suppression of Edward as name and subject also has consequences for the way he acknowledges his literary mentor, Frank Collymore. In addition, it influences his attempts to manage the subterranean presence in his work of techniques, motifs and allegiances absorbed from the British literary tradition, from which he has maintained a critical distance in his public pronouncements.

Even the biographical facts are scarce. We know from the notes in *Barabajan Poems* about the poems "Ancestors" and "Ogun" (both lifted from *The Arrivants*) that Brathwaite's father, Edward Hilton, was the son of a shopkeeper and that one of his uncles, Bobby O'Neale, was a carpenter and woodcarver.[3] Also in *Barabajan Poems* we are told that Edward Hilton's brothers, Carlisle and Lawson, "both dr/ove Bedford lorries, like most of the stronger, somewhat better off, more ?educated, more progressive (or aggressive) young men in the District".[4] However, there is no indication of what Edward Hilton did for a living and no entries for any Edwards in the lengthy bibliography Brathwaite appends to his virtual archive – although there are plenty of entries for *Kamau, EKB, Brathwaite* and *mother*.[5] This does not mean that elements of Edward *père*'s biography are not present in his son's poems, or, for that matter, that the poet should be expected to signal the presence of such biographical allusions for his readers. The silence becomes an issue only because the structure of *Barabajan Poems* depends so crucially on the prose scaffolding the poet erects to establish connections between significant individuals in his personal history and figures in his poems – such as Esse, Ogun and the women in the poem "The Dust" – whom critics had formerly taken pains to read as allegorical. Because none of the earlier references to Edward Hilton survive the crossing into the virtual archive, Brathwaite effectively sidesteps the task of distinguishing between the allegorical traits in his poems that he takes from his own father and those he develops from other intimately observed instances of failed Caribbean men or unacknowledged Caribbean heroes – not, however, without piquing the reader's curiosity about the deafening silence surrounding this seminal figure.

"Noom", the section in *Sun Poem* from which the epigraph to this chapter is taken, suggests one way of understanding the silence in *Barabajan Poems*. "Noom" comes just after *Sun Poem*'s midpoint: a poem called "The Crossing", which describes the perilous ascent of a busload of children to the top of Hearse Hill, the highest point in Barbados, and their precipitous descent to the rugged Bathsheba coast. In "Noom" both the sun and the son, having reached the zenith of their powers, begin parallel journeys towards geological extinction and death. The son's fantasies of mastery and immortality come up against the history of slavery and the limits placed on black manhood in colonial societies.

Brathwaite demarcates those limits in the passage cited in the epigraph to this chapter, by setting up a tension between iambic pentameter and other, less predictable rhythms, which frustrates the poem's formal progress towards metrical resolution. The iambic trimeter "But heroes were in books" begs for the natural cadence of a full five feet that might have enabled a more definitive claim, such as "But heroes were in books *and we had none*". Instead the iamb's conventional certainties are nudged aside by the vacillating incomplete dactyls in the second line: "and few of our fathers were heroes". The metrical tension between the two lines, as well as the fact that the alliteration that begins with *few* is not sustained, manages to almost rule out the possibility of heroes and of representing fathers on the page. At his public readings, Brathwaite has often commented on traditional English metre's inadequacy for the task of representing Caribbean speech rhythms, so it is worth noting that the triads in the line I am characterizing as "incomplete dactyls" do indeed have a consistent metrical pattern, known as an amphibrach – one stressed syllable flanked on either side by an unstressed syllable

– "and féw of / our fáthers / were héroes". Read with this emphasis, the relationship between the poem's first two lines is one of call and response, as in a jazz performance, where the straightforward annunciation of the opening beat or melody is broken up and thrown back at the lead instrument by the next player without compromising the length of the bar. Whichever way we scan that second line, however, its effect on the first line is to destabilize the conventional certainties of the iamb.

Another line begins by trying to pull the rhythm back into the ambit of iambic pentameter by its use of an alliterative *f* sound. It reads: "the féw who fóught or spóke bràve wórds from púlpits". But once again the poet undermines that aspiration by modulating from *f* to *p* sounds and insisting on the superfluous unstressed final syllable in *pulpits*. That extra syllable renders the effort of the sons flailing rather than firm, and ties their irresolution to the meandering metrical excess of the next long line – "their hélpless fáthers lóoked awáy ashámed and cóuld nòt dó it" – through the weak feminine rhyme between *pulpits* and *do it*. Ironically, the only line in the passage quoted that contains exactly five feet and achieves near metrical perfection expresses the most damaging constraint: "and wé their sóns leàrnt mérely to survíve". But here the extra stress on *learnt* almost drags the line to a halt. The emphasis is on the failure of language – especially conventional poetic diction – to transcend mortality, to offer the sons (or the reader, for that matter) something more meaningful than mere physical survival.

Farther along in this same poem, Brathwaite explicitly addresses the absence of epitaphs for Caribbean men in their own communities, when he points out that "there is still no memorial epigraph" to those failed fathers. He characterizes them through images associated with such mundane figures as cane cutters, lorry drivers, blacksmiths, sailors, carpenters, cricket groundsmen, elementary school teachers and sanitary inspectors: "men who could mend roofs climb trees haul up the fishnets of their all-night silver home".[6] He contrasts their missing monuments to

> those stammaments in stone
> that smile
>
> are fat or romanesque, athletic like good traffic
> cops

piercing or blind to the world but never look
ing like us.⁷

In the 2001 reissue of *Sun Poem* in the *Ancestors* trilogy, that last sentence fragment – rendered as "but nvva look. in like us" – is given its own page and followed by a computer-generated approximation of a human figure, hands clasped as if in prayer, that seems to inhabit the blank space left by this absence.⁸ But it is difficult to decide whether the genially grimacing cartoon is meant to represent the missing Caribbean fathers or the "stammaments" of colonial iconography.

None of these passages about fathers from *Sun Poem* make it into *Barabajan Poems*. Instead, the virtual archive draws on earlier images from *The Arrivants*, of Brathwaite's grandfather in "Ancestors" and of his great-uncle in "Ogun".⁹ In both cases the new video-style layout stresses absence and desecration rather than lived achievement. The short excerpt from "Ogun", in tiny, squat print, is nearly overwhelmed by three pages of prose commentary that compulsively reiterates the highlighted word *neglected*.¹⁰ The video style mutilates the layout of "Ancestors" in an even more savage fashion. It reproduces the first part of the poem, describing the grandfather's farm, butcher shop, riding trap and Edwardian haberdashery, in minuscule script, surrounded once again by busy prose commentary. But the text of the second part of the poem, describing the destruction of the grandfather's property after his death, takes on the nightmare proportions of banner headlines announcing a cataclysmic disaster:

**NOW HE IS DEAD* THE
MEAT SHOP BURNED*
HIS PROPERTY
DIVIDED* A DOCTOR
BOUGHT THE HORSE*
HIS MAD ALSATIANS
KILLED IT***

**THE WOODEN TRAP
WAS CHIPPED &
CHOPPED**¹¹

Altogether, the original seven lines that Brathwaite excerpts from the second section of the poem "Ancestors" take up nineteen lines in *Barabajan Poems*, spread over two full pages. The truncated lines of stark black lettering set against the desolate white of the page suggest a vivid scar that transforms what in the original poem was a quietly elegiac statement of loss into a furious catalogue of abandonment and abuse. Moreover, Brathwaite cuts off the excerpt he includes in *Barabajan Poems* just before this description of the grandson's engagement with the grandfather's legacy that follows in the original version in *The Arrivants*:

> Only his hat is left. I 'borrowed' it.
> I used to try it on and hear the night wind
> man go battering through the canes, cocks waking up and thinking
> it was dawn throughout the clinking country night.[12]

Clearly this omission, the bitter commentary, and the shifts in typeface are meant to ratchet up the assault on the reader/listener, whom Brathwaite addresses directly when he ends the prose tirade that follows the "Ogun" extract with a barbed parenthetical acknowledgement of his audience's largesse: "and I say this even though you have just accorded Ellice & Cynthia & George & Freddie Forde & me such signal public honour".[13] But the assault is perpetrated at a cost to the integrity of the original poems, as well as to the dignity and multifaceted nature of the father figures whose lives they originally celebrated.

Brathwaite's most direct engagement with the figure of his biological father before *Barabajan Poems* occurs in a poem called "Fleches", which elucidates the cover photograph of *Sun Poem*'s first edition. The photo shows a tall, conventionally suited man whose face, obscured by shadow, is inclined towards a toddler standing on a cane-bottomed chair. The child too is partially obscured, but the camera's angle manages to catch the way in which the sun's rays illuminate the child's eyes, as well as his tiny penis. Thus the viewer's gaze, like that of the adult figure in the photo, is directed towards these twin sources of light and power emanating from the boy's body. The poem identifies this photo as a portrait of Brathwaite and his father, but not before invoking in its opening lines an earlier image of Edward Hilton:

> Still i suppose he married well: the wedding picture shows a quiet con-
> fidence: tight grip on the icing cake bri-
> dle bold look into the few-
>
> ture: the close shaved well brushed head
> the dark framed glasses. there were,
> unless i'm wrong, no other family pic-
>
> tures: except the one with me i found already faded
> framed among the cuff links and the round hard collar leather boxes
> in his dresser in the bedroom with the simmons bed with springs[14]

The father's description conveys an uncharacteristic degree of ambivalence, since Brathwaite usually deploys family figures in his poems to dramatize a single distinctive moral characteristic or frame of mind – creativity in the case of his carpenter great-uncle in "Ogun", and dignity in the case of his grandfather in "Ancestors". It is hard to know, for instance, how to inflect the parenthetical "i suppose" in the poem's first line, especially as it is qualified by the preceding word, *still*. The reader feels dragged involuntarily into an internalized family squabble; the poet seems to want either to convince himself that his father's decision to marry was a good one or to satirize the petit bourgeois values that would privilege such an assertion in the first place. Similar ambiguities haunt the line made up of the single syllable *con-* and the splitting across lines and stanzas of the pun on *future* ("few- // ture"). Is the father a con artist or is he being quietly conned by life? Does his tight grip on the icing cake bridle portend a bold engagement with the future, or does it betray a spasm of fear as he intuits a "few-ture" of diminishment and betrayal?

No matter, because in the next breath the poet nudges the father out of the spotlight, replacing the wedding portrait with the cover photo of father and son in which the father's face has become indistinguishable from the inanimate backdrop:

> ... this pic-
> ture shows him always suited dressed for work hat
> on his head no light between his him and me

> looking out into the cameras of glass with the same quiet wedding pic-
>
> ture confidence and me just three
>
> my mother say is almost tall as he[15]

Here the enjambment that links the first two stanzas allows the pronoun *me* to function as both indirect object – in the phrase "no light between his him and me" – and the subject of a new sentence that starts "and me // looking out into the cameras of glass" and ends "is almost tall as he". With this deft stroke the son unmans the father, usurping his "quiet wedding pic- / ture confidence", the light in his eyes and his place in the heart of the mother/wife in whose gaze the diminutive toddler is now elevated to "almost tall as" his father. Moreover, the child's unruly hair and "naked doggie pee/ping out between my bandy legs / for all the world to see" throw into relief the limitations of the father's body. The once virile bridegroom is now "always suited dressed for work". His "close shaved well brushed head" remains perpetually shrouded in the shadow of his hat.[16] For the rest of the poem the father appears only in "fleches", which the poem's glossary describes as "flashes of sunlight" or "Amerindian rainbow feather crests" – as arbitrary and ephemeral as the angle of the sun in a camera's lens that transfixes one figure in light, the other in shadow; as ornamental and superfluous as the brittle bundled letters, the cufflinks and the "round hard collar leather / boxes" in his father's dresser among which the boy forages for photos and forbidden sixpences.[17]

More unsettling than these visual ephemera, however, is the father's silence, broken only to suggest the possibility of an even more final absence:

> we listened in the dark to how our mother quarreled all night long like surf lines on the other shore: he never angered we could hear
>
> though sometimes coughed and sometimes terrible to fear: what would become of us: said
>
> he would go back out and *stay* back out: our mojer bawled
>
> then silence[18]

Here Brathwaite uses silence to represent the fear of abandonment that grips both mother and son, and to foreshadow his own later abandonment of the name Edward. The father's cryptic utterance, in which the son can barely detect an emotion, is surrounded by his silence, just as the line "then silence" on the page is surrounded by blank space. Its veiled threat betrays none of the vulnerability of the mother's querulous nagging, which the poet associates by contrast with the reassuringly predictable sound of the surf. Suspended in an emotional void, the father's words, like his cough, resist the poet's demands of language – that it nurture, connect and memorialize.

Brathwaite elides the oedipal tensions in "Fleches" by way of two strategies. In the first place, he deflects attention away from the son's complicity in the symbolic death of the father (enacted in the composition of the cover portrait) by relegating the circumstances of the image's production to a time and space beyond the child's memory, where he cannot be held responsible for its immanent violence:

> this photograph was taken at a man-
>
> sion house my mother said she'd borned me in:
>
> a place i didn't know a time i can't remember
> how could they take a memory of time i can't remember
> how could i have been there and yet forget[19]

The syntax of the sentence on either side of the colon works best if the son's failure of memory occludes the time and place of his birth as well as his intention at the moment when the photo was taken.[20] That occlusion produces a particularly intractable quandary for a poet who also considers himself both archivist and historian, as it forces him to concede that he cannot control every aspect of his own history and consciousness. In order to remain untainted by the charge of complicity in his father's erasure, the chronicler must consent to be represented through someone else's gaze: he must forget him*self*. Like Oedipus in the presence of the blind seer Tiresias, the poet situates himself on the threshold between evasion and accountability, self-deception and lost innocence, as he confronts the tragic paradox that innocence can be preserved only at the cost of self-knowledge. The poet revisits this threshold obsessively in the pages of *Barabajan Poems*.

Brathwaite uses a related strategy to manage the complicated anxieties his poetic persona associates with fear of abandonment. Throughout Brathwaite's oeuvre, the image of the father is bound up with the poet's representation of both the yearning to possess an authentic personal past and his refusal of colonial subordination to "The Man Who Possesses us all". The symbolic thrust of "Fleches" constantly recalibrates its trajectory in response to these differently remote horizons of yearning and refusal, so that its language never fully disentangles the metaphors related to these two kinds of father figures. Thus the son's snapshot memories in "Fleches" align his father with images of colonial assimilation – "canadian english apples red- / der than the holly on our x- / mas cards" and "purple grapes / cold with the ice house vapour / on them with their own light // within them"[21] – as well as with the cultural nationalist values invoked when the son insists that his father "bought bajan too":

> brown purity bakery bread still breathing from the oven and ihs holy name
> *amen*
> in great brown paper bags we tried to run
> sack races in and fruit as precious as those six-
>
> pences: star apple sugar
> apple akee pawpaw pa-oui lakatan
> fat pork and soursop and sapodilla eyes[22]

But even within these binaries there are no simple oppositions. The Christmas apples and grapes, symbols of the colonized subject's alienation from his native landscape, inform some of the child's most treasured, albeit fleeting, memories of filial belonging. Conversely, the exotic catalogue of local foods, familiar from so many of Walcott's St Lucian poems, would be unremarkable were it not for the way in which the colonial legacy insinuates itself into even this proto-nationalist catechism. In describing the warm, breathing local bread, the poem reconfigures *his* as *ihs*, a monogram for Jesus Christ familiar within colonial high-church iconography.[23] Moreover, the off-rhyme that links *ihs* to *six* a few lines later connects the precious sixpences to which the fruit are compared with another image of transubstantiation earlier in the poem. In the earlier image – of stolen sixpences – the poet uses the idea of transubstantiation to convey the exquisite sensation the boy experiences when he touches the coins' "milled edges oaktreeleaf britannia / as beautiful and light as wafers that the priest put on miss sissies tongue / on certain saddened sundays".[24] Thus, even at their most intimate, their most benign and their most uncorruptedly Bajan, the images associated with Brathwaite's biological father in this poem seem suffused with the texture and breath of the colonizing patriarch.

Brathwaite finesses these contradictions with consummate grace by setting up a shell game involving three Edwards: Edward *père*, Edward *fils* and Edward VII, whose head should have been stamped on the reverse of all the "oaktreeleafed" silver sixpences in circulation in the late 1930s.[25] Glistening and forbidden, the silver sixpences tutor the boy in the meaning of desire. As his fascination turns into lust, the child moves from observing the coins in his father's drawer to taking them:

>   . . . one by one first
> just to borrow then to keep help
> me to buy brown bus stand nuts and sugar-
> cakes and cockies[26]

But it is never clear to him – or perhaps, more accurately, the poet does not clarify for the reader – whether the father is complicit in his son's purloining of the coins: "he never said he knew and never / said he missed them: perhaps he never missed / them".[27] One can hear the boy in these lines almost willing his father to take responsibility for the theft. Indeed, he seems generally impatient with the older man's passivity, criticizing him implicitly for never having made use of the treasured sixpences hoarded in his dresser, just as he faults him for never claiming the patriarchal prerogative of wearing the ceremonial "tie or shirt or pearl white cuff / link from in there or even check[ing] his papers".[28] Like the unfaithful steward in the biblical parable who is punished for burying his lone talent, the father, from the son's perspective, deserves to be deprived of those shiny tokens of imperial agency. Ironically, it is this same failure of will, this servile impulse to hoard without using, that robs the boy of his stolen sixpences. They disappear from his secret cache under a stone, leaving the boy's guilt to grow "like crab grass trails along the borders of our yard".[29]

Each explanation the boy offers for his action reframes our vision of the father. Each intention that the poet imputes to the father recontextualizes the meanings of those sixpences for his son. Perhaps the father is enamoured with the colonial power and privilege the shiny tokens symbolize, and by allowing the child to steal them, he inculcates in him reverence for the symbols of empire and an abiding guilt about a status he can never legitimately attain. Perhaps the father does not care for what the sixpences represent, and it is the son who invests them with fetishistic powers. More likely, the father too once stole shiny sixpences from his shopkeeper father; he understands his son's obsession with the miracle of transubstantiation, whereby the wafer-thin image of the imperial monarch becomes native body and blood through the mediation of "bus stand nuts and sugar- / cakes and cockies". The father's silence about the missing sixpences allows the boy's imagination and that of the reader free rein to reformulate ad infinitum the father's relationship to empire, without actually defining whether his silence should be read as complicity or abandonment vis-à-vis the empire or the son. It accommodates both the native's primal fantasy of consuming the colonizer and the son's ancient desire to (dis)possess the father. But Brathwaite can sustain this series of displacements only by rendering the father in his poem mute, thus relegating him to a space outside the symbolic order in which he remains interred, sequestered and fragmented, for most of *Barabajan Poems*.

> leaves leaves leaves   of a forest gone silent
> leaves leaves leaves   without tongue without eyes
> leaves leaves leaves   sun glut and gold and roten[30]

II

The gaps between the fleches/flashes Edward *fils* retains of his biological father and the law of the Father that the poet Kamau Brathwaite excoriates in his later work corrugate the poetry and prose of *Barabajan Poems*. They help explain, in my reading, the extent to which Edward, as name and subject, remains under erasure even as Brathwaite attempts to provide his readers with a comprehensive history of his past. Brathwaite's suppression of the name Edward in his virtual archive thus becomes more than a politically expedient move to reorient himself towards his African heritage. It blurs the distinction between the poet's attempts to erase the traces of the literary legacy of "The Man Who Possesses us all" in his work, begun as far back as his first poem about snow, and the son's usurpation of his father's place and subjectivity, begun in the space where he was born, at a time beyond his conscious memory. The two patricides – one political, willed, literary; the other intimate, involuntary, unarticulated – are intertwined in a series of displacements in *Barabajan Poems*. They are kept in circulation by the currency of the figure of Frank Collymore, who stands in for both the unnamed Edward Hilton and the abdicated Edward on the lost sixpences, on account of his multiple significations as a "white man", as a father figure and as Brathwaite's first literary mentor.[31]

Brathwaite pours a libation at the beginning of *Barabajan Poems* to

> My Mother, Beryl Emmeline; my wife, Zea Mexican, who died only a few months ago (she so loved this i-land); and my literary godfather, Frank Appleton Collymore
>
> I pause for them. . . for those who have gone before. . . *'once you were here . . .hoed the earth. . . and left it for me. . . green rich ready/ with yam shoot, the . . . tuberous smooth of cassava, , ,'* that may I attempt here. . . that may I have strength to attempt here. . . strength enough to attempt here. . . *trying to play like myself* - no matter how idiosyncr/atic. . . *'eat/ and be happy. . . drink/may you rest. . . '* that we may welcome you into the tonnelle[32]

Brathwaite's three-way dedication creates multiple hierarchies: Beryl, Zea and Frank stand for Nurture, Love and Art in one series of three, and for the natural world, the virtual space of computerized production, and the symbolic world of language and metaphor in another series of three. Poets are fond of such trinities. Walcott constructs his share of them in the autobiographical poem *Another Life*, in which he invests the figures of "Harry, Dunstan, [and] Andreuille" with the representative virtues of mentorship, brotherhood and romance in one triptych and Death, Art and Love in another.[33] And it is in the nature of such trinities, like the shell game of interchangeable Edwards, that they are always asymmetrical in ways that make it difficult to stabilize the hierarchies they enunciate: two females and a male in one triad become one elder and two youth in another, and two blacks and one white in a third. The constant redistribution of attributes and status along multiple axes keeps all these meanings in circulation. Thus we know that Zea, the poet's wife, like Beryl, the poet's mother, symbolizes nurture in the poet's private iconography, but that her world of the computer is also contiguous in Brathwaite's symbolism with the space of metaphor he associates with Collymore. Moreover, in the language of Brathwaite's libation, all three figures partake in the images of fertility, cultivation and poetic inspiration that support the author in his attempt – to use his own curious formulation – at *"trying to play like myself"*.[34] The effect of such mutually overlapping significations can be both expansive and diminishing. In one reading, for example, Brathwaite's triptych starts out by naming a sequence of biological and social relations (mother, wife) but enriches that pattern when it introduces the concept of spiritual and aesthetic affinity in the person of his "literary godfather". From another perspective, however, the same pattern runs the risk of impoverishing the writer's representation of the black community by eliding the roles of black males as parents, loved ones or mentors. To compensate for the limitations of Brathwaite's triumvirate, therefore, the body of Collymore must bear the significance of all the aspects of masculinity, black and white, even as the bodies of mother and wife must carry the burden of blackness, both masculine and feminine.

One example of how this kind of displacement functions in *Barabajan Poems* occurs in Brathwaite's description of Collymore's use of silence to protect his literary protégé. In an image that recalls the comparison in "Fleches" of the mother's querulous nagging to the night-long wash of "surf / lines on the other shore", Brathwaite describes the wave of ridicule he feels crashing over him when one of his aunts (his godmother's sister) attacks him, in the presence of Collymore and others, for attempting to popularize jazz music on the local radio station.[35] The commentary momentarily indulges the comic hyperbole of adolescent narcissism as Brathwaite recalls his younger self: first dissolving with embarrassment like the ice cube in his drink, then awash in humiliation as the undertow of mockery in his aunt's laughter sucks away his creative resolve, *"like the Titanic wrecking on the canefields of Atlantis & all my future publication drowning in the cold & fish & fly-gone flash of the afternoon"*.[36] Collymore's silence rescues him:

> **but it didnt happen like that though it could so easily have been written into that kind of scenario had Colly not failed - or rather *refus/ed* - to catch the gleam in the dragon-aunt's voice & the towline of laughter on her scoffs & simply by remaining**

silent at that momen/(t) & walking into the kitchen for more iceberg, as if he had not heard, he allowed the incident to interpret itself in its own wash, shall we say, so that it was washed away in what became the silence of the room[37]

Where in this kind of scenario, one wonders, would Brathwaite's biological father have been? Absent? Dead? Uninterested? Asleep after an exhausting day of dehumanizing labour? Present but excluded from the literary patter? Warwick Walcott died when Derek was not quite two years old, and Seepersad Naipaul died while Vidia was an undergraduate at Oxford, so neither man was physically present at most of the important junctures in his son's literary development. Nevertheless, their memories are still very much part of these kinds of moments in the work of their sons. The difficulty here is not so much that Edward Hilton is absent but that his absence remains unrepresented. But perhaps this hardly matters. By substituting the figure of "Colly" for that of Edward Hilton in *Barabajan Poems*, the poet makes the silence he imputes to the father in "Fleches" work on behalf of the son. Instead of the child feeling stranded with the mother by the ebbing tide of his biological father's silent withdrawal, the son in this passage is swept along in the wake of his literary godfather's silent authority. The threat of Colly's silence authorizes a space-clearing gesture in this claustrophobic world of female conventionality that makes room for the Word – the heroic (white?) masculine prerogative to name, to innovate and to risk.

Brathwaite first introduces the notion of Collymore's nurturing silence in the tribute that precedes his anecdote about the ribald aunt. In an earlier passage from that tribute cited below, he explicitly allows his literary godfather to stand in for his biological father: Collymore's "easy & quiet & certain sense of what it meant to be Bajan to be West Indian to be Caribbean to be New World to be craftperson & un-self-centred Man in the World/New World. It was he & my Mother who taught me about & kept me in touch with Ba/rbados all the years I was away".[38]

Here Collymore takes pride of place next to Brathwaite's mother as the young poet's role model and connection to manhood, to Barbados and even to blackness, signified in the commentary's deployment of such terms as

Bajan, West Indian and *Caribbean*, and especially in its reference to the "Man in the World/New World", which resonates with Brathwaite's more familiar formulation "New World Negro" elsewhere in his prose.[39]

Like the father in the stanzas from "Fleches" about the missing sixpences, the figure of Collymore can contain its contradictory significations because Brathwaite never allows his mentor to speak. All the meanings the mentor takes on are imputed to him by his protégé. Thus Brathwaite's prose can distil the essence of the man as he wishes Colly to be remembered, precipitating out of this remembrance any circumstantial details of appearance, manner or personal history that might otherwise have bound his mentor to whiteness, to privilege or to the role of the oppressor. From this perspective, Colly's silence within Brathwaite's prose signifies solidarity rather than abandonment. It becomes the medium through which the father nurtures and communes with his son and in which the son memorializes the father.

In the symbolic economy of *Barabajan Poems*, Brathwaite can assign the role of literary father to Collymore despite his mentor's race, because the actual historical figure Frank Collymore is so widely recognized as the founding father of Caribbean writing in general as to be unassailable in this role from any racialized perspective. Moreover – unlike Naipaul, who enjoys flirting with the charge of xenophobia on the page – Brathwaite, both as a private person and in his political espousal of a cultural nationalist position, has always been much more racially inclusive than some of his critics have been willing to concede.[40] But that inclusivity does not obviate the symbolic difficulties for Brathwaite *as a poet* of rendering a paternalistic white figure sympathetically without in some way compromising his larger cultural project. So it should come as no surprise when, in the very next breath, Brathwaite reveals that he remains unable to represent the significance of his mentor in his poetry: "it is one of my regrets that I have no/(t) yet been able to write a poem about or for him, as Sam & George & Derek & Pragnell & Harold Marshall & Monica Skeete & Karl Broodhagen have done".[41] In fact he offers the "likkle anecdote" in *Barabajan Poems* about Collymore's silent support as a gesture of reparation for the poetic tribute he remains unable to speak.[42]

"Derek", in Brathwaite's list of artists who have paid tribute to Collymore in their work, refers to Derek Walcott. In order to understand Brathwaite's poetic reticence, it may be instructive to look at how Walcott represents whiteness in

"Che", an abbreviated sonnet about the death of Che Guevara, another racially white hero in the pantheon of the oppressed:

> In this dark-grained news photograph, whose glare
> is rigidly composed as Caravaggio's,
> the corpse glows candle-white on its cold altar—
>
> its stone Bolivian Indian butcher's slab-
> stare till its waxen flesh begins to harden
> to marble, to veined, white Andean iron;
> from your own fear, *cabrón*, its pallor grows;
>
> it stumbled from your doubt, and for your pardon
> burnt in brown trash, far from the embalming snows.[43]

Although he has been apotheosized in popular lore for his role in the liberation struggle of colonized and indigenous peoples in Latin America, Che Guevara was a white man, and his assassins were brown Bolivians. In the poem "Che", Walcott deliberately plays up this paradox, invoking all the associations of white with purity and light and of darkness with moral turpitude, to honour the martyred hero and to castigate those who betrayed him. Drawing on Caravaggio's monumental painting *The Entombment of Christ*, which depicts a group of Christ's followers placing his lifeless body on a slab of stone, Walcott makes explicit the connection between Che's death and the Crucifixion. He invigorates the figures in the well-known grainy black-and-white newspaper photograph of Che's corpse by invoking Caravaggio's chiaroscuro technique: bathing the naked human body in light emanating from a single source, so that the contrast between its glowing whiteness and the dark hues of surrounding objects is heightened.[44] In Walcott's poem, Che's white body is further associated with the marble used to create enduring public memorials to heroes, the strong white veins of iron in Andean rock, and the "embalming snow" of the mountains in Che's Argentinean homeland. Che's brown betrayers, like the shadowy, unsaintly looking background figures in Caravaggio's paintings, are depicted as swarthy, low-browed types – irresolute men, unable to bear the consequences of their dark deeds, delivered up to their servile fate by their own complicity in their continuing oppression. In order to establish these connections, Walcott highlights the messianic properties evident in popular images of Che. Moreover, he foregrounds their origin in Renaissance art and Christian iconography, even as he acknowledges the political imperialism of the cultures that first generated these images.

Also following Caravaggio, however, who refused to portray his bent, cowering or reclining figures as heroic, Walcott resists the urge to represent any aspect of the human experience as sublime.[45] His poem seems less interested in condemning the shadowy assassins than in capturing the pathos of their all too human fallibility. Moreover, there is more than a hint in its references to doubt and pardon that the poem wants us to see a parallel between the actions of Che's Bolivian butchers and those of Christ's disciples Thomas and Peter, who, in spite of initial denial and doubt, eventually championed their leader's sacrifice and took his message out into the world. That parallel recuperates Che's martyrdom as redemptive and his peasant assassins as redeemable, but it does not invert the valencies of Walcott's imagery. *White* remains associated symbolically with the sublime, and its opposite – here, brown – although inescapably human, with abjection, betrayal and trash.

Walcott can use these racially freighted images because he acknowledges no allegiance to a rhetoric of racial affirmation. He considers it his right as an artist to exploit any aspect of any culture or language he needs to if it can convey something of meaning to his readers, however apposite to his own sensibilities or offensive to those of his readers the racial stereotypes that have accreted around such cultural signifiers may have become. Moreover, he presents historical epochs in his poetry as simultaneous rather than sequential; the passions and values of the world inhabited by Che can commune metaphorically with the passions and values that produced the worlds of Christ and Caravaggio, rather than being overdetermined by them. For Walcott, the attempts of other postcolonial writers to anchor the imagination by aligning themselves with a teleological interpretation of history or politics can only be debilitating. As he puts it in his essay "The Muse of History", "The truly tough aesthetic of the New World neither explains nor forgives history. It refuses to recognize it as a creative or culpable force. This shame and awe of history possess poets of the Third World who think of language as enslavement and who, in a rage for identity, respect only incoherence or nostalgia."[46]

For Brathwaite, by contrast, the recourse to history is a necessary component of cultural coherence. Both as a historian and as a creative writer, he has a great deal more than Walcott invested in a Caribbean history and a black cultural project that "will not always bleed on other people's edges".[47] He sees the reluctance of many Caribbean artists of his generation to acknowledge the primacy of their historical relationship to African cultures as one of the vitiating consequences of their attachment to European aesthetic values. Indeed, for Brathwaite an underlying attachment to European aesthetics contributes as much to the profound sense of alienation and cultural superfluity in these artists' work as the philistinism of their audiences or their neglect by the metropolitan literary machine.[48] He makes this point most eloquently in the essay "Roots", in which he argues that Naipaul's novel *A House for Mr Biswas* is about one man's attempt to join a community rather than to isolate himself from it:

> In this tribal/communal world, individual love may or may not find itself, but it can do/not do so only after the communal agreements have been observed. Biswas' note to Shama was a "creole" act, that is, outside the ancestral tradition. If it was a black household, he might have got away with it, probably got the girl pregnant and got away with that too, without burden of responsability: that being a (black) creole norm. But in Hanuman House, Mr Biswas' creole tendencies are still regarded as eccentric, because the community of the household represents something larger and more enduring than any individual. It represents a (cultural) base. It represents the tenacious traditional socio-cultural matrix that Biswas, the "modern", wants to escape from; and having "succeeded", wishes to relate back to. His "freedom" in fact leads only to uncertainty, fear of the future, and madness.[49]

In Brathwaite's estimate, the way in which Naipaul's novel takes for granted the centrality of traditional Trinidad Hindu values through its agonistic engagement with them becomes the essence of Naipaul's paradoxical "message" and achievement: "the perception that art and coherence can come only out of a coherent pattern of traditional values, no matter what kind of variations the individual may choose to play upon them".[50] There is an investment here in order and continuity that goes beyond what Walcott seems so quick to dismiss as nostalgia or remorse in the postcolonial writers' romance with history: a conviction that for a writer's work to *matter,* it must function within an explicit tradition that is recognizable to a community more corporeal than the writer's imagination. Such work achieves greatness when its meanings are recuperable through social and political intercourse and responsive to specific material conditions, even when this stipulation places limits on the range of aesthetic choices available to the writer for his subjects. In Brathwaite's radically conservative vision, the greatest accomplishment an artist can hope for is not consummate expression of his individual virtuosity but the creation of an artefact that succeeds in articulating for his community a shared understanding of their world. From this perspective, Afro-Caribbean culture has only just begun to name its cultural values in writing – to think, in the words of *Sun Poem*'s "Noom", about the relationship between its heroes and its books. By affirming the racial memory and shared cultural values of his people, the Caribbean writer of African descent accepts his responsibility to organize the region's incoherent fragments of culture and shards of history in the service of a literary tradition that can resist the ravages of Euro-American cultural imperialism.

All this has consequences for Brathwaite's representation of Collymore and the other father figures in his poetic repertoire. Within his project of cultural resistance and racial affirmation, the meanings Brathwaite associates with the signifier *white* tend to cohere around two poles: that of the colonial sycophant – most memorably represented in *Mother Poem* by the figure of Chalkstick, the colonized schoolmaster – and that of the overbearing white man "Who Possesses Us All".[51] In the case of Chalkstick, *white* comes to stand for draining away of the vitality of black culture. It is associated with Barbados's porous limestone rock that sucks all the water out of the land, with the "white" values insinuated into the native's consciousness by the colonial education system, and with brittle, broken sticks of chalk that suggest male sexual impotence. Chalkstick's task is "to build a nation of forked sticks / to kill the blade in those dark mahoe bodies // to iron the devil out of their pants".[52] At the other extreme, whiteness in Brathwaite's private iconography is associated with Prospero's manipulative magic, with the cold distance of the Alps, the suffocating omnipresence of sugar and the clinical cruelties of technological progress:

> God is glass with his type-
> writer teeth, gospel

jumps and pings off the white
paper, higher and higher[53]

To make Collymore white in any of these ways would be anathema. Although he was a schoolmaster, he is never represented as a purveyor of colonial values or as a leech on black vitality like Chalkstick. Although he was phenotypically white, Brathwaite distances him explicitly from all forms of technology, censorship or cruelty. Although he is represented as silent, that silence is never a mark of alienation or contempt. In fact, if we take Brathwaite's prose statements at face value, the connotations of whiteness that best represented Collymore in a poetic tribute would probably be very similar to those used by Walcott in his poem about Che: whiteness as a symbol of integrity, as synonymous with endurance, as an aspect of silent, redemptive suffering. And these are qualities that Brathwaite is more interested in affirming for black culture than for a white man at this historical moment.

To complicate the matter even further, there is a curious echo and inversion of one of Walcott's images in "Che" in Brathwaite's description of Collymore's silent withdrawal to the kitchen in the face of his aunt's challenge. An underlying biblical allusion in both scenarios is the denial of Christ after the Crucifixion, when Peter turns away from the challenge of identifying himself as a disciple and melts into the group of Pontius Pilate's retainers to warm himself at their fire. Colly's withdrawal into the kitchen to replenish the ice in his drink suggests a similar denial, but from Brathwaite's perspective, the allegiance thus repudiated is to the cultural hegemony of empire, and Brathwaite has no desire to prevent that defection. However, if we read Collymore's silent turning away in tandem with the passive complicity of Che's Bolivian peasants, the action can be perceived as a denial of Brathwaite himself – the messiah of a new black culture – a reading that would align Colly's silence more closely with that of Peter in the biblical story, as well as that of the father in "Fleches". Brathwaite chooses to interpret his silence as an act of solidarity rather than betrayal – refusal rather than failure, as he puts it – because of the effect he imagines it has on his ribald aunt. And Collymore's silence offers the reader no way to divine any other intent. Nevertheless, Brathwaite would have had a much more difficult time managing the well-established associations of the biblical allusion if this had been a poem rather than a prose anecdote, the form of which allows the author more editorial control over the meanings that accrue to his language.

White literary forebears, such as Collymore and the English poet Chapman, who wrote heroic couplets about the "Barbadoes" landscape in the eighteenth century, are among those whom Brathwaite summons in *Barabajan Poems* to construct a Barbadian belletristic tradition into which he can insert his own literary legacy. He pays generous tribute to these heroes in his book. On the other hand, given the tremendous signifying power of the racial archetypes he is up against, the communally accessible cultural landscape that Brathwaite strives to nurture in *Barabajan Poems* (and which he insists Collymore gave him the space to cultivate) cannot fully accommodate a white man in its racial topography without compromising the poet's political project of affirming an alternative hierarchy of black cultural values. Like the obscured face of the father in the photo on the cover of *Sun Poem*, certain aspects of Collymore's legacy are destined to be nudged into the shadows by his literary offspring, even though Brathwaite finds himself unable to articulate in his poetry his own complicity in this act of erasure.

Something similar happens in "Ancestors", Brathwaite's poem about his grandfather. As we have seen, the poet presents the grandfather of his original poem in *The Arrivants* as a black man of substance and dignity. But all the visible markers associated with these qualities are derived from his grandfather's attempts to approximate the figure of a perfect Edwardian gentleman. In *Barabajan Poems* Brathwaite confines these attributes to the tiny, undersized print that precedes the oversized record of destruction of his grandfather's legacy, already cited:

> ... **He was a butcher.**
> **Six foot three and very neat: high collar,**
> **winged, a grey cravat, a waistcoat, watch-**
> **chain just above the belt, thin narrow-**
> **bottomed trousers, and the shoes his wife**
> **would polish every night. He drove the trap**
> **himself: slap of the leather reins**
> **along the horse's back and he'd be off**
> **with a top-hearted homburg on his head:**
> **black English country gentleman**[54]

In a series of vignettes of failed fathers in *Sun Poem* that he calls "Clips", Brathwaite savages the mimicry and hypocrisy of this kind of "secular bourgeois family man".[55] Although most of the fathers in "Clips" seem to belong to a generation more contemporaneous with Brathwaite himself, or at least with his father, Edward Hilton, it is difficult to overlook how many of the aspersions Brathwaite casts on their borrowed symbols of respectability could have been directed at figures such as the grandfather in "Ancestors". Moreover, even if we are meant to assume that the grandfather in "Ancestors" was indeed a dignified authority figure, all the images in the poem that establish him as a pillar of the community are tied up in his self-presentation as an English country gentleman.

Whether we read such images as depicting integrity as "white" or black dignity as mimicry, it is clear that the poet needs to dismantle them in his Barabajan landscape. From this perspective, the savage destruction of the material objects around which the grandfather constructed his subjectivity – perpetrated in the oversized script cited earlier – is as much an aspect of the revisionist project of Brathwaite's cultural nationalism as it is the consequence of the community's neglect or the violence of the doctor's Alsatians. When Brathwaite in *Barabajan Poems* suppresses the stanza from *The Arrivants* in which the boy appropriates his grandfather's homburg hat – an appropriation that either anoints him the inheritor of his grandfather's black English legacy or implicates him in its desecration – the poet sidesteps an oedipal threshold between evasion and accountability, self-deception and lost innocence, not unlike the oedipal moment in "Fleches" when the son forgets himself in order to suppress his complicity in his father's erasure. The boy who "borrows" his grandfather's hat may have no conscious memory of dismantling the man's legacy, but the poet who omits from *Barabajan Poems* the stanza describing this action must be aware that the ideal of Caribbean masculinity he now seeks to establish retains few niches for an icon of black Englishness like his grandfather. Again, imaginatively, we are in the kitchen of the English great house that Naipaul describes in *A Way in the World*, facing, with the revolutionary black intellectual Lebrun, the impossible choice of accepting the white patronage of his great-uncle as a mark of recognition of the black man's equality or savaging the fragile dignity of his forebear because its foundations seem so risible.

III

Over and over in his virtual archive, Brathwaite brings the reader to the brink of this crucial oedipal threshold, forcing us to consider with him the consequences for the writer of this splitting of the subject in the service of cultural resistance and racial affirmation. At one point in *Barabajan Poems* he splits apart the first and last stanzas of an early poem titled "The Day the First Snow Fell", by substituting six pages of prose commentary for its two short middle quatrains. Brathwaite uses the lengthy commentary to argue against the assumption that an elite colonial education was all he needed to escape the limitations of race and become a "citizen of the world". In order to dismantle this assumption, he encourages the readers of *Barabajan Poems* to interpret his early poem about snow as recording a moment of disillusionment rather than one of delight. In its original form, the poem's skipping rhythm and uncomplicated end rhymes appear to offer a straightforward celebration of the poet's pleasure at his first sight of snow:

> The day the first snow fell I floated to my birth
> of feathers falling by my window; touched earth
> and melted, touched again and left a little touch of light
> and everywhere we touched till earth was white[56]

The commentary in *Barabajan Poems* explains that this was the first of his poems Brathwaite published while at Cambridge to capture the attention of the literary establishment. It is not hard to divine why the poem's English readers may have seen in these deceptively simple rhythms a naïve optimism that went well with their notion of what a young poet from the colonies should sound like. Brathwaite does not dispute the validity of that first reading. Indeed, by giving the stanza a new layout in *Barabajan Poems* he demonstrates what he tells us, by way of introduction, the Cambridge critics liked about the poem: "the sense of **touch** . . . mimicking, they said, the actual fall (and what I called in another poem, 'the slow salaam') of sn o w".[57] The new layout conveys the unexpected buoyancy of the snow, the manner in which it seems to resist the forces of gravity – in much the same way that the youthful Brathwaite assumes his intellectual aspirations can overcome the limitations of race. As in the images associated with the coveted sixpences in "Fleches", the emphasis here is tactile:

> The day the first snow fell I floated to my
> birth
> of feathers falling by my window **touched**
> earth
> and melted, **touched** again and left a little
> **touch** of light
> and everywhere we **touched** till earth was
> white[58]

In this new layout, the boldfaced words form a spiral like a snowflake twisting through the air. The placement of the rhyming words on separate lines make the end rhymes seem internal to the lines while emphasizing the family resemblance between the *th* sounds in *birth* and *earth* and the *ch* sound in the bolded word *touch*. The connections soften the *t* sounds at the beginning of *touch(ed)* so that the effect is one of delicacy and soft delight.

Brathwaite's emphasis on touch in this new format supports an optimistic reading of his initial response to England and the snow. But his retrospective comments on the poem's two middle stanzas downplay the poem's appeal to the senses, focusing instead on the poet's memory of his frame of mind when he wrote the poem:

> What they didn't perhaps catch was the symbolism of pain & separation & χile loneliness (my first Christmas away from home) of the two middle stanzas & the χpression of the stark (black/white) racial prejudice I was χperiencing in the dark wood of the winter carved into the two white swans of a literary Cambridge of among others Thom Gunn, Peter Re/dgrove, Frederick Raphael, Alistair Reed (& with me at Pembroke) Ted Hu/ghes, Arthur Ravenscroft (later to become editor of the *Journal of Commonwealth Literature*), Alisdair Aston, Tony Dyson & Brian Cox (later founder-editors of the *Critical Quarterly*), an American with very thick glasses named Bob Gottlieb. Despite the circumnambient prejudice, though, (they didn/(t) seem to find my poetry 'good' enough or ?modish enough to publish) I became quite friendly with Redgrove, and from my own College, w/ Aston, Dyson & Cox - and Ted Hughes (now Poet Laureate of England if not Great Britain) who I remember spent much of my last day in Cambridge chatting in my room[59]

This "who's who" of fledgling Cambridge poets and critics who have since become famous – and with whom Brathwaite seems to have had cordial, if not intimate, relations – feels awkwardly self-important next to the revelations of homesickness, as well as of the colonial's feelings of abandonment and cultural isolation. It is hard to be sure who *they* are in the parenthetical "they didn/(t) seem to find my poetry 'good' enough or ?modish enough to publish". Were Brathwaite's fellow students also his editors and, therefore, his censors, or were all these young writers trying to get their work published and meeting varying degrees of acceptance and rejection from an unnamed editorial *them*? Brathwaite's prose captures that achingly familiar balancing act between awkwardness, uncertainty, real and imagined slights and the desire to please that is familiar to generations of minority students at predominantly white institutions. But it does so without directly presenting the reader with the middle stanzas it purports to explicate, so we have only the poet's word for the presence of these emotions in his poem.

And, in fact, the commentary's claims do not quite convey all the sentiments we see and hear in the stanzas they replace:

> wood was now black or white
> white world was bright at night
> and water was black wood
> carved into two white swans
>
> birth was black water
> where the white swans bend
> death was black water
> where the white wood ends[60]

There is a palpable gloominess here, a clear indication of the depression with which the poet tells us he was struggling at the time. But there is also unmistakable delight in the metaphysical play of the poem's language: the mirroring effects of the chiasms that arrange words such as *wood* and *white* at opposite ends of successive lines, and the almost geometric patterning that both heightens and blurs the distinctions between black and white, light and dark, birth and death. Moreover, the words themselves suggest an eager engagement with the paradoxes of Enlightenment ideas about the limits of vision, the desirability of knowledge and the inevitable suffering involved in its pursuit. Only an undergraduate infatuated with the Tennyson of "The Lady of Shalott" and consumed by the Romantics' quest for truth, love and beauty could come up with the melodrama of lines like "death was black water / where the white wood ends". Brathwaite in these stanzas can still find solace in the Enlightenment freedoms he assumes will come to him as a "citizen of the world" – the same freedoms, he tells us decades later in this six-page prose commentary, that all educated young colonials dreamt they would inherit once they arrived in England. However, there is an important distinction between Brathwaite's telling us in prose that this was an illusion, entertained by colonials like him and Naipaul, and the passionate idealism of those excised stanzas. That idealism animates the delight the poem takes in the snow, as well as the linguistic arabesques of Romantic and metaphysical poetry, even as it registers the young colonial's distress at finding himself alone in the imagined landscape of his literary godfathers, insecure and homesick and cold.

The extended prose commentary that interrupts the poem takes us on a protracted detour through the isolation of Brathwaite's college years, the racial ironies and injuries he encountered in his attempts to find a job after graduation, and his reflections on the similarities between his difficulties in England and the difficulties of less privileged West Indians back home:

> Some people doin well
> while oth. ers are catch. in
> hell[61]

Thus, by the time we return to the poem, there is not much wiggle room left for interpreting its final stanza as anything other than the tombstone epitaph it now resembles:

> **The day the first**
> **snow fell**
> **I floated to my death**
> **of feathers falling by**
> **my window**
> **left love and melted**

> **loved**
> **again to touch the little**
> **left**
> **of light**
> **and all the world was**
> **dark while**
> **earth was white**[62]

The ornate, heavy type and the shorter lines give the stanza a much more sombre air of finality than is the case in the original. It chips away at the playfulness, the celebration of possibility still there in the stanza's repeated references to love and light, so that we are left with only the poet's death wish rather than a moment of simultaneous ecstasy and pain. In his attempt to inoculate his present self from his youthful enamourment with all that Cambridge represented – the influence of seventeenth-century English poetic form and nineteenth-century English poetic angst, those tentative student friendships with aspiring white writers at the university, and his naïve first delight in snow – Brathwaite goes so far as to consign his alienated younger self to the level of Naipaul, repeating the latter's gloomy recollection of nightmares of being back in the Caribbean when he fell asleep in his English bedsit with the electric fire on. Thus, in splitting apart the first and last stanzas of the poem with his commentary and suppressing the two middle stanzas altogether, Brathwaite insists on a reading of his earlier *naïveté* that can align it only with death.

Postcolonial applications of psychoanalytic theories usually locate such splitting of the subject within the psyche of the colonizer. Catherine Hall, in her study of the making of English subjectivity in the late nineteenth century, follows John Barrell's anatomy of the psychopathology of De Quincy's imperialism in defining the splitting of the subject as central to "thinking 'otherness', splitting between good and bad, taking in or identifying with those aspects which are seen as good, projecting the bad on to absolute others".[63] She summarizes Barrell's argument thus: "De Quincy was constantly terrorised by his fear of infection from the East . . . and inoculated himself by splitting, taking in something of the East, projecting whatever he could not acknowledge on to the East beyond the East, the absolute other. But there was always something of the East inside himself, precluding any possibility of a metropolitan identity safe from colonial invasions."[64]

Hall also cites various feminist theorists who have located a similar set of unstable discursive practices in the operation of white feminists' claim of sisterhood as a universalizing category. Homi Bhabha takes this figure in another direction when he examines the effect of destabilizing forms of colonial mimicry – not unlike those I impute here to the figure of Brathwaite's grandfather – on white colonial subjectivity. He makes a distinction between what he calls the "*colonial* articulation of man and his doubles and that which Foucault describes [in *The Order of Things*, vol. 2, chap. 9] as 'thinking the unthought' which, for nineteenth-century Europe, is the ending of man's alienation by reconciling him with his essence".[65] Bhabha uses this distinction to argue that colonial discourse about the nature of the colonized subject articulates the colonizer's desire for an authentic historical consciousness. Furthermore, he insists that the colonial subject can never be fully defined or accounted for in the terms of his master's discourse.[66]

None of these formulations, however, comes at the problem from the perspective of the new nationalist subject announced in the symbolic project of a writer such as Brathwaite. For Brathwaite, as is true in different ways of both Walcott and Naipaul, the discursive universe is no longer the colonial world but rather the imagined community of the postcolonial nation-state. In it the writer is engaged in the project of shoring up the subjectivity of a new dominant class that is male and middle-class and non-white and is competing *within* the state for control of a discursive space that will legitimate its ascendancy. Brathwaite silences fathers and father figures alike, therefore, to underwrite the subjectivity of his own imagined cohort, in much the same way that the colonial Ego, according to Fanon, underwrites its subjectivity through racial differentiation.

Thus, in the Fanonian model discussed in my introduction, the white Ego defines itself over and above an unnamed racialized subaltern:

$$\frac{\text{White}}{\text{Ego different from "the Other"}}$$

In Brathwaite's usage, however, the figure of Kamau defines itself over and above a version of the subaltern:

EKB

Edward

Edward stands for father, imperial monarch, literary godfather, Cambridge literary acquaintances and Romantic and metaphysical poetic influences, but it is also contained inevitably within EKB himself, whose monogram, like the remnants of the Greek spelling of Jesus Christ in the Jesuit monogram IHS, never fully sheds the vestiges of its origins in *Edward*. To paraphrase Hall's reading of Barrell's De Quincy, there is an aspect of Brathwaite's work that remains constantly terrified by his fear of infection by whiteness – the fear that his position in relation to word and text within the Caribbean discursive space continues to align him with the former colonizing power. He inoculates himself against this infection by splitting, taking in something of whiteness from such figures as his grandfather and Collymore, and projecting whatever he cannot acknowledge about his relationship to whiteness onto a more distant horizon of whiteness, a more absolute Other. In the comments on Cambridge discussed above, that Other is named only as *they*. Elsewhere in *Barabajan Poems* it hovers as the faceless white "man who possesses us all". In "Noom" it takes the shape of the missing sixpences. And its presence even contributes to the poet's decision to repress the poems about his father that do not make it into the virtual archive. But there always remains something of whiteness inside the poet himself, precluding any possibility of a Caribbean identity safe from imperial invasions.

This is not a battle that Brathwaite is fighting with Britain or empire per se. Rather, it is a struggle he must engage within the Caribbean community, in which any number of competing discourses on national subjectivity are vying for hegemonic control, and in which the success of the poet's cultural project is by no means guaranteed. In the course of *Barabajan Poems*, the chronic inadequacies of the black Caribbean men for whom Brathwaite speaks are exacerbated by the aunts' vitiating laughter, by Essie's sexualized challenge, by the ambiguities in Colly's silence, by the black English allegiances of the grandfather's homburg, by the competing meanings of Africa, the anomie of Dread and the one hand that cannot clap – all the forces of *noom* that drag the busload of children backwards down Hearse Hill in "The Crossing", only to send them hurtling over its pinnacle towards the black rocks of Bathsheba, towards extinction and the limits of mortality. The authority of each of these discursive projects is undermined when Brathwaite attempts to build upon Edward's legacy while freeing himself from its stranglehold.

From the postcolonial vantage point of *Barabajan Poems*, it is thus no longer a simple act to put on or take off the grandfather's homburg, to include in the virtual archive that excised stanza from the poem "Ancestors":

> Only his hat is left. I 'borrowed' it.
> I used to try it on and hear the night wind
> man go battering through the canes, cocks waking up and thinking
> it was dawn throughout the clinking country night.[67]

The boy in this poem is a man now, nearing the end of a life that has seen the rise of pan-African nationalism, as well as the crises of the postcolonial state. In acknowledging that he has placed his grandfather's hat on his head, he too risks being obscured in the shadows that surround Edward Hilton's shrouded head in "Fleches" and discovering that, after all, there is "no light between his him and me".

Brathwaite's genealogical dilemma is no different from Walcott's or Naipaul's, although it offers us an alternative perspective from which to read their strategies for confronting fame and mortality in a postcolonial setting. Naipaul's gagging inability to take part in the slimy meal of coo-coo with his fellow Caribbean authors does not prevent him from swallowing whole the new international spaces their anti-colonial struggles have made available for him to pursue his attempts to become what Brathwaite has called a "citizen of the world". Because Naipaul can invoke his ethnic difference to shore up the distinction between what he sees as the success of his own literary project and the shortcomings of other Caribbean intellectuals' endeavours, he can evade a reckoning with some of the racial limits of that world citizenship with which Brathwaite struggles. Walcott, by embracing whiteness as a literary trope, can deflect its more vitiating consequences onto his literary personae. But this substitution constantly defers the poet's engagement in the flesh with his human subjects, who, as I will discuss in later chapters, seem always to be mediated by other people's metaphors. Only Brathwaite, because of his insistence on naming his literary project as explicitly political and historical, has no means of renouncing this desire for cultural relevance and, therefore, of keeping the spectre of aesthetic and political failure at bay.

In a world in which heroes and fathers remain unrepresented in books, the poet who chooses to write himself into his community's heroic traditions must give birth to himself. Rather than raising a "stammament in stone" – or sentences – to earlier failed heroes, the poet, like Virgil's Aeneas, erects his new cultural edifice over the silence of those ancestral corpses. Brathwaite's abandonment of his father's name, his dismantling of his grandfather's legacy, the poetic silence to which, despite his effusive prose, he ultimately consigns Collymore, and his disavowal of the earlier, more naïve literary self that gave birth to the poet he has become, are profoundly painful acts of patricide. But the poet considers such space-clearing gestures necessary if he wants to excavate a submerged Afro-Caribbean cultural tradition and commit it to text. The guilt generated by this necessary violence haunts the silent spaces in Brathwaite's virtual archive, occasioning the truncations and omissions that this chapter has delineated. Such patricides make palpable the difficulties inherent in exterminating the racialized subject in Fanon's call for violence, so often romanticized in the work of cultural theorists as if it were nothing more than a theoretical abstraction. It is the true price to be paid for new beginnings. And it offers the poet no guarantee that his legacy too will not in its turn be exterminated:

> leaves leaves leaves of a forest gone silent
> leaves leaves leaves without tongue without eyes
> leaves leaves leaves sun glut and gold and roten[68]

PART 3

DEREK WALCOTT

8

FOR NAIPAUL

> Join, interchangeable phantoms, expected pain
> moves me towards ghosts, through this page's scrim,
> and the ghosts I will make of you with my scratching pen,
>
> like a needle piercing the ring's embroidery
> with a swift's beak, or where, like a nib from the rim
> of an inkwell, a martin flickers a wing dry.[1]

I

In the stanzas preceding these lines, the poet interrupts his description of Maud Plunkett's funeral to explain to his reader why he is "both there and not there.... attending / the funeral of a character [he has] created". He reasons that "the fiction of her life needed a good ending // as much as mine", since both he and she are artists and cultivators – she with her needle and he with his pen.[2] But Walcott also describes how, in the process of inventing Maud's story, he had looked up at her through her husband's eyes "to see light going / from her image", and had known with Plunkett in that moment both that Maud was going to die and that "that image was my mother's, / whose death would be real, real as our knowing".[3] The *our* in the phrase "real as our knowing" connects Walcott to Plunkett, as well as to his mother, blurring the distinction between fiction and autobiography, as well as between the living and the dead. But the phrase also draws attention to what it means to really know a person – to enter, through empathy with another, into their relationship to a particular landscape, person or creative endeavour. That aspiration subtends many of Walcott's metaphors. In the lines cited in this chapter's epitaph, for instance, the poet establishes his connection to Maud by substituting her piercing needle for his scratching pen, and comparing both to the natural grace of a swift's piercing beak or the flicker of a martin's wing. But such serial substitutions can also become reductive; in this case the involuntary movements of the swift's beak and the martin's wing obscure the agency of both writer and embroiderer, by paring down their creative process to the movement of their implements. Similarly, as Walcott's narrator asserts his solidarity with Plunkett on account of their shared experience of loss – Plunkett's of his wife, Walcott's of his mother – it is never really clear if the poet has usurped his character's agency or has been possessed by him.

For the writers in this study, such questions of empathy loom large. Naipaul's attempts to define his relationship to such literary predecessors as Walter Raleigh and C.L.R. James depend on his enlisting support for his literary legacy from readers like his composite figure Blair. Brathwaite's three versions of his persona – Kamau, Sun/son and Edward – measure the varying degrees of empathy the poet imagines between his past and future readers and three versions of himself. By creating fictional alter egos and addressing phantom readers, both men hope to ensure that their ghosts will be honoured. In some ways *Omeros* is similarly self-referential. The poet intervenes in his own voice early in book I, to identify himself as its "phantom narrator" – "since every 'I' is a / fiction finally".[4] He weaves details about his actual life into his epic's plot – a third failed marriage, his movements back and forth between Boston and St Lucia, and his attempt to represent his island's history. He even allows his phantom narrator to interact directly with his fictional protagonists. The sheer scope of *Omeros*, however, demands a different approach to the question of what it means to shape one's literary legacy than my discussions of *A Way in the World* and *Barabajan Poems*. The poem's three-hundred-plus pages reprise every theme in Walcott's poetry of the preceding five decades. Moreover, the poem is all about chasing shadows, ghosts and echoes, including lost African, European and New World histories, as well as the barely discernible outline of a future national culture.

Walcott's preoccupation with phantoms helps elucidate his complex literary relationship to Brathwaite and Naipaul, neither of whom *Omeros* names but both of whom provide Walcott with thematic and technical challenges, through which, he anticipates, his own aesthetic achievement will be judged. The implicit connections among their works trace the outlines of a shared Caribbean literary culture. As Walcott moves through his page's scrim, channelling and challenging his peers, the three writers' individual achievements begin to blur, filling in for posterity a composite legacy that may well survive the wagers with fame and death that fuel their separate ambitions.

The blurred boundaries between fiction and autobiography provide us with a strategy for reading *Omeros*'s phantom discourse with Naipaul's fictionalized memoir, *The Enigma of Arrival*. The Plunketts' attempts to reconcile themselves to life in a community that can guarantee them neither the comforts of privilege nor the solace of acceptance allows Walcott to respond to Naipaul's controversial embrace of England's landscape and history in *Enigma*. Plunkett moves past merely documenting St Lucia's history when he realizes that the island also has shaped his marriage. That realization provides a rich commentary on Walcott's own ambition to write St Lucian epics in *Another Life* and *Omeros*, as well as Naipaul's attempts to do something similar for Trinidad in *The Loss of El Dorado* and *Enigma*.[5] *Omeros* responds directly to Naipaul's claim in *Enigma* that only ruins connect him to the landscapes of his birth and exile, by demonstrating that history does not trump relationships with actual places and living people. The Plunketts' eventual embrace of life in the tropics also helps us read Walcott's ambivalent relationship with the pleasures of his American exile, which, after all, may not have been that different from Naipaul's relationship to England. By stitching the childless Plunketts into his memories of his deceased parents and sharing with them his twin vocations of writing and art, Walcott extends to his protagonists – and through them to Naipaul – a cultural and aesthetic kinship expansive enough to accommodate their shared colonial legacy of loss.

II

After V.S. Naipaul's *Enigma of Arrival* appeared in 1987, Derek Walcott published a review of it in the *New Republican*, in which he took Naipaul to task for finally having gone too far in rejecting the Caribbean. Walcott scolds:

> What is the cost to [Naipaul's] Indianness of loving England (because that is what love of the English countryside means)? To whom does he owe any fealty?

Ancestors? The surroundings that history placed them in, the cane fields of Trinidad, were contemptible, as they themselves would have to be, having lost both shame and pride. Therefore, the only dignity is to be neither master nor servant. . . . The punishment for the choice is the astonishment of gratitude, to be grateful to the vegetation of an English shire. Not to India or the West Indies, but to the sweet itch of an old wound.[6]

When he penned this harsh reckoning, Walcott was working on *Omeros* and grappling with challenges very similar to Naipaul's: how to integrate into his writing – so redolent with the sights, smells and sounds of his Caribbean life – the new sensory burden of the alien American landscape, and how to continue to write about a Caribbean landscape he no longer fully inhabited. In the decade leading up to his winning a MacArthur Foundation "genius grant" in 1981, he had begun to shift his professional base from Trinidad to Boston and the prize established him as a major American poet. Although for the next three decades he divided his time between America and the Caribbean, Walcott was no longer merely a regional phenomenon. Within the metropolitan cultural milieu he was becoming as much a literary celebrity as Seamus Heaney or Joseph Brodsky, or any of the other émigré writers of the twentieth century who lived in America.[7]

Walcott's new situation drew him inexorably into the cultural life and professional politics of America as a permanent resident rather than as an occasional sojourner. Wayne Brown, in a review of *The Arkansas Testament*, notes that this gradual shift had begun to produce a tension between the American and Caribbean landscapes in Walcott's poetry as far back as the *Midsummer* collection of 1984. Brown reads the *Arkansas* poems, which the poet groups under the headings "Here" and "Elsewhere", as a further stage in Walcott's long farewell: a signal to perceptive readers that the "Light of the World is moving away from these islands, is moving on".[8] Walcott, like Naipaul and many other Caribbean writers before him, had begun the insidious drift away from *here*. Henceforth, Brown predicts, the poet's imagination will be dominated by landscapes and experiences "elsewhere".

Brown identifies one aesthetic consequence of Walcott's migration as a "tending towards the incorporeal", both in the way the poet figures self and place and in his experiments with poetic form.[9] Actual Caribbean landscapes become distorted as they lodge themselves in memory; imagined foreign ones recede as the poet moves towards them. Citing the scorn the poet evinces in "Sunday in the Old Republic" for a Martinican aesthete who conjures his nostalgia for Paris wholly from Impressionist paintings –

> Lies. It was never like this. . . .
>
> for peace only exists
> in the leaf-shadowed prose
> of the imaginary republic"[10]

– Brown calls attention to how uncannily Walcott's themes in the *Arkansas* poems echo Naipaul's pronouncements in *The Enigma of Arrival*, which also appeared in 1987:

> By a curious coincidence, around the time that Walcott was writing this, V.S. Naipaul, in London, was also describing the elusiveness of "the perfect world I had striven towards":
>> "As a child in Trinidad I had put this world at a far distance, in London perhaps. In London now I . . . put this perfect world at another time, an earlier time." *The Enigma of Arrival.*
>
> The theme of an ideal landscape subsisting, not in space, but in time, echoes back and forth between these two, very different West Indian writers, widely considered the leading practitioners of their respective genres in the English language today. Compare to Naipaul, above, this, from Walcott's "Storm Figure": *The wrong time. The wrong ground. The Wessex Coast / is in another century.*[11]

Although he highlights the parallels between the two writers, Brown is anxious to distance Walcott from the aesthetic of alienation he attributes to Naipaul. However, given Walcott's harsh criticism of *Enigma*, Gordon Rohlehr's observation – "Whatever [Walcott] warns against, he's on the verge of attempting" – bears repeating.[12] Even if he considered Naipaul's embrace of the English countryside disloyal, Walcott must have been aware that no writer can thrive in a new country without at some level betraying his loyalty to home and without being seduced by the other shore. Indeed, some of Naipaul's most exquisite sentences in *Enigma* – the ones that Walcott's review initially praises as "pious in their tribute, and close to glory" – arise precisely out of the intricate interplay of seduction and resentment, celebration and longing, through which Naipaul reconstructs his process of coming to terms with the landscape of his exile.[13] Walcott's poetry after he relocated to America would have been signally impoverished had it failed to register his burgeoning relationship to a new environment.

Before Walcott published *The Arkansas Testament*, Europe and America were primarily aesthetic presences in his work. His borrowings from Homer, Shakespeare, Donne and Auden were matters of literary influence, not of shared experience, and Walcott's signal virtuosity resided in his ability to transpose those writers' characters and techniques into a Caribbean world. In *Another Life*, for instance, he culls many of the names he assigns to St Lucian street characters from his childhood reading of Nathaniel Hawthorne's *Tanglewood Tales* and Charles Kingsley's *Tales of the Greek Heroes*.[14] The European paintings through which he invites us to see the St Lucian landscape all come from another early favourite: "Craven's book", a compendium of art reprints produced for Allied soldiers that probably found its way into West Indian libraries after the Second World War.[15] In fact, for all its air of erudition, *Another Life* is a schoolboy's text in this respect, the "pseudo-epic" – as Walcott terms it in tender half-jest – of a provincial who insists on magically seeing "autumn in a rusted leaf".[16]

Walcott's early poetic imagination thus inhabited the encyclopaedic minutiae of his colonial education in much the same way that Naipaul remembers colonizing English literature in his imagination as a Trinidadian child:

> To open a book was to make an instant adjustment. Like the medieval sculptor of the North interpreting the Old Testament stories in terms of the life he knew, I needed to be able to adapt. All Dickens's descriptions of London I rejected; and though I might retain Mr Micawber and the others in the clothes the illustrator gave them, I gave them the faces and voices of people I knew and set them in buildings and streets I knew. The process of adaptation was automatic and continuous.[17]

What Walcott remembers as magical transformation, Naipaul describes as a survival strategy. Nevertheless, both writers were nurtured by these alien images, even though in their early work they draw stark lines between what they considered their reality and what they knew was imagination. Walcott uses the paintings in Craven's book to bring his provincial world to life as well as to illuminate a universe beyond the island of St Lucia. Yet even when the Caribbean is dwarfed by such infinite vistas, the imagined world remains securely within the poet's head. There is never a suggestion in *Another Life* that Helen is anyone other than the town's one "clear-complexioned whore", or that Troy exists in any other physical space than the tenements of Castries.[18] As the narrator explains to Homer's ghost when he admits near the end of *Omeros* to not having read all of *The Odyssey*, "Those gods with hyphens, like Hollywood producers . . . // aren't much use to us".[19] As long as Walcott's home base was St Lucia or Trinidad, his professional immersion in Caribbean theatre, art criticism and literary debates, as well as in the sensual power of the Caribbean landscape, furnished a lived counterpoint to such imagined spaces.

In *Omeros*, as in *The Arkansas Testament*, the lines between "here" and "elsewhere", between the real and imagined worlds, are more fluid. Not only does the poet get to speak directly to Homer's ghost on a St Lucian beach; now the imagined spaces reserved for the vistas of a world previously accessible only through art also mediate the poet's memories of the Caribbean. Away from home, the poet re-encounters his islands through works of art in Boston's Museum of Fine Arts, in the smoke on the Trail of Tears, and in the way a Greek girl's enunciation "O-mer-os" embraces within it the French Creole words for mother and sea.[20] The more mediated his access to both the Caribbean and the metropole becomes, the more insistently the poet seeks to render the fictional lives of his characters as interchangeable with his corporeal self.

III

Having read and reviewed Naipaul's *Enigma of Arrival* while writing *Omeros*, Walcott may have perceived parallels between the two projects. *Omeros*, like *Another Life*, is framed by the trajectory of the poet's imaginative development. However, because Walcott, like Naipaul, had become an emigrant, that trajectory risked mapping out a journey of terminal alienation from his islands – the career that Wayne Brown's review predicts but cannot bring itself to name. With the Caribbean receding and a new social landscape still beyond his aesthetic grasp, the only fully realized subject in his work would be the writer himself. Faced with the challenge of responding adequately to both

America and the Caribbean, Walcott may have wondered if the classical imagery and foreign histories that always had fascinated him would now claim him so thoroughly that they would relegate his islands to the evanescence of myth, or to the manufactured nostalgia of a tourist postcard.

Walcott condemns such "mercilessly honest . . . self-centredness" in Naipaul's *Enigma*, which "in its seasonal or eruptive sadnesses" (from Walcott's perspective) becomes "as true as life in the terrible sense that nothing really concerns us".[21] However, the poem "The Light of the World", *Arkansas Testament*'s magnificent homage to St Lucia, already intimates a similar self-centredness. Anticipating the taxi ride in *Omeros* during which the narrator learns of Hector's untimely death at the wheel of his transport, the poem takes as its point of departure a market woman's request that a quickly filling transport, in which the poet and other passengers are seated, wait up for her. The woman uses the Creole expression for "Don't leave me stranded" – *Pas quittez moi à terre* – which the poet translates variously as

> "Don't leave me on earth," or, by a shift of stress:
> "Don't leave me the earth" [for an inheritance];
> "*Pas quittez moi à terre*, Heavenly transport,
> Don't leave me on earth, I've had enough of it."[22]

The woman's eloquence, as well as the beauty of another fellow traveller, move the poet to celebrate the women and their island, just as Plunkett will feel compelled to celebrate Helen and St Lucia in *Omeros*. But even as the poem establishes one woman, through a series of metonymic displacements, as the Light of the World, the words of the other return to him as accusation:

> And I had abandoned them, I knew that there
> sitting in the transport, in the sea-quiet dusk,
> with men hunched in canoes, and the orange lights
> from the Vigie headland, black boats on the water;
> I, who could never solidify my shadow
> to be one of their shadows, had left them their earth[23]

The image of an unsolidified shadow here works differently from that of the interchangeable phantoms cited in the epigraph to this chapter, because its insubstantiality suggests a failed connection rather than a fantasy of consummation. And indeed, the poet begins to realize that nothing he can say or write from his liminal position will do justice to the island or its people.

As he leaves the transport, the other passengers call after the poet to return the pack of cigarettes he has left behind, and he realizes: "There was nothing they wanted, nothing I could give them / but this thing I have called 'The Light of the World' ".[24] The cadence of these final lines holds in place a fragile equilibrium between the "lights" the passengers insist on returning to the poet and the image of the "Light of the World" through which the poet insists on apostrophizing them. However, Walcott concedes that such mutual reciprocity can be consummated only through art. His speaker's interactions with the passengers are remote, even offensive. He stares lasciviously at the woman he calls Beauty, even as he tells us that under such circumstances "any staring at strangers is impolite".[25] He fails to say goodbye to his fellow travellers as he descends from the transport, even though he had remarked earlier on the warmth of "their neighbourliness, / their consideration, and the polite partings // in the light of its headlamps".[26] He turns away without a word of thanks when they give him back his cigarettes.

Of course Walcott's readers know that this churlish exterior belies a deeply felt connection to the passengers in the transport. His speaker tells us that he is so moved by love for them that he fears he may

> ... suddenly start sobbing
> on the public transport with the Marley going,
> and a small boy peering over the shoulders
> of the driver and me at the lights coming[27]

He does not say goodnight because "Good night would be full of inexpressible love".[28] His silent apostrophe "O Beauty, you are the light of the world!"[29] attains a religious intensity, as it alludes to Christ's words in Matthew 5:13, as well as to the pre-Raphaelite William Holman Hunt's famous devotional painting of the same name.[30] Nevertheless, the façade the speaker presents to his fellow travellers makes no allowances for empathy on their part. The poet is enough of an insider to realize that a sentimental attempt to connect across the distance created by his transient's privilege would be patronizing and might be considered intrusive. That refusal of empathy, that "mercilessly honest self-centredness", is part of the burden of exile. Even though he transposes the woman he calls Beauty into Delacroix's painting *Liberty Leading the People*, and fantasizes about the smooth white nightgown she will wear as she prepares for bed by lamplight, the speaker resists speculating whether she has intuited his passion or can picture the worlds he inhabits.

Walcott's liminal position constitutes for Naipaul one of the enigmas of arrival: the moment when the traveller's return to the bosom of the home community is no longer an option, even though he will never be fully at ease in the world beyond. Ralph Singh, Naipaul's protagonist in *The Mimic Men*, faces a similar dilemma on the eve of his retreat into self-imposed exile in England. Deschampneufs, the father of Singh's French creole political collaborator, warns him that he will never succeed in forming fresh attachments to the landscape of his exile:

> [W]here you are born is a funny thing. My great-grandfather and even my grandfather, they always talked about going back for good. They went. But they came back. You know, you are born in a place and you grow up there. You get to know the trees and the plants. You will never know any other trees and plants like that. You grow up watching a guava tree, say. You know that browny-green bark peeling like old paint. You try to climb that tree. You know that after you climb it a few times the bark gets smooth-smooth and so slippery you can't get a grip on it. You get that ticklish feeling in your foot. Nobody has to teach you what the guava is. You go away. You ask, "What is that tree?" Somebody will tell you, "An elm." You see another tree. Somebody will tell you, "That is an oak." Good; you know them. But it isn't the same. Here you wait for the poui to flower one week in the year and you don't even know you are waiting.[31]

The language in this passage achieves the same lyrical purity that Walcott initially praises in his review of Naipaul's *Enigma*. Its image of the poui blossoms, for which we wait each year without realizing it, assails the reader with a melancholy that precisely mimics the longer passage's evocation of the thing lost as the thing not consciously registered, and thus beyond cathexis. Singh resists what he sees as Deschampneufs's attempt to "drag me back into his world, where he walked with security".[32] He understands that this French creole patriarch, who even on the eve of the island's independence still refuses to shake hands with an Indo-Trinidadian, relies on his racial privilege to preserve a refuge for him in the land of his birth – a refuge that Singh can never take for granted. Singh is rightly appalled at the provinciality of Deschampneufs's world view. Yet the old man's prophecy remains poignant. Although exile makes the social gulf between them less relevant, it does not obliterate their reciprocally formative experiences of racism, the shared intonations of their speech (*browny-green, smooth-smooth, going back for good, a funny thing*) or the intuitive associations they both bring to guava trees and poui blossoms. And it cannot domesticate an elm.

Naipaul's *Enigma of Arrival* offers Walcott one way of approaching the conundrum that Deschampneufs names and with which both he and Naipaul have struggled. In it, Naipaul recounts in painful slow motion the incremental steps by which his narrator constructs a relationship to the landscape of his exile through his memories of Trinidad. Like a careful ethnographer, he offers us detailed descriptions of the settlements and customs in the remote corner of Wiltshire to which he retreats: the trees, the barns, the houses, the footpaths, snippets of conversation. Each time he reports a detail about Wiltshire, he inserts a remembered connection to Trinidad: some nuance of scandal; some record of tiny humiliations; some memory of a plant, a ditch, a feeling. These haunting primal identifications extend the process of substituting a remembered Caribbean for England that Naipaul describes in his "Jasmine" essay, cited earlier. They make us feel that we have come to know both the Trinidadian and English landscapes as intimately as the narrator does. So the reader feels doubly betrayed when the narrator reveals how each of these precisely observed details – which the narrator first considered immutable elements of the new landscape, and which we, with him, have worked so hard to internalize – turn out to be ephemeral. Buildings and communities disintegrate beyond recognition over the passage of time, leaving only the soon-to-be-forgotten hurts and habits with which we and the narrator have invested them.[33]

Although his readers participate in constructing and dismantling the landscape of his exile, Naipaul characteristically refuses to allow his narrator to build long-term relationships with the other people who inhabit his corner of Wiltshire. As with Walcott's simultaneous embrace and distancing of his fellow travellers in "The Light of the World", this narrator's struggle to come to terms with Wiltshire and its surroundings remains intensely private. So when, at the end of the story, a stranger comes to his door in search of her childhood home, rather than explaining the changes he has made to the building or sharing his process of domesticating the space, the narrator denies her access to his cottage and to his imagination. Unlike Walcott, however, Naipaul does not editorialize, leaving us to judge the narrator's actions as either callous or kind and to gauge his relationship to the English landscape as colonially obsequious or postcolonially critical.

Walcott's self-reflexive commentary in "The Light of the World" allows us to read the poet's silence as appropriately restrained, while in Naipaul's *Enigma* a similar reticence appears unrelievedly churlish. Yet Naipaul's method suggests that the impossibility of connection is an unavoidable consequence of exile and transience. Absent a location in which the exile feels fully known, gestures of belonging that rely on empathy – even that of one's readers – can seem hollow. We may develop our own responses to the English and Trinidadian landscapes that Naipaul describes, but those responses do not guarantee a sense of kinship with their inhabitants. The spectre of such interminable alienation exasperates Walcott, because, as he points out, its "concentrated selfishness" is tautological: "either every writer is an exile (not only this narrator-Naipaul) or no writer is".[34] Nevertheless, it is hard to miss the undercurrent of hysteria in Walcott's rebuke. Naipaul's alienation is never far away as Walcott struggles with his own demons.

IV

Landscapes were not the only things that remained out of reach. As the Caribbean receded in the 1980s, Walcott may have worried that he would never be able to write with any degree of authenticity about the new communities he inhabited. Naipaul had confessed to a similar anxiety in a 1950s essay as he contemplated the success of his early Trinidadian novels and the length of time and distance that now separated him from home. England was not a place he could imagine writing about. In the tropical spaces he knew best, private dramas played out in public places, providing him with an infinite range of idiosyncratic characters on which to draw for his novels and stories. By contrast, London's insulated walls and closed doors made observing character and emotion difficult. Naipaul predicted, "Unless I am able to refresh myself by travel – to Trinidad, to India – I fear that living here will eventually lead to my own sterility; and I may have to look for another job."[35]

Eventually Naipaul did manage to write about his new social environment, and *Enigma* is one product of that engagement. But at the time Walcott was writing *Omeros* in the 1980s, his position vis-à-vis America was more complex than Naipaul's had been in 1950s England. Boston by plane was a lot closer to Castries than London had been to Port of Spain by steamer three decades earlier. And although Walcott had lived most of his adult life in the Caribbean, he had also travelled widely. When he shifted his residence to America, he was neither the cultural ingénue Naipaul remembers being when he first arrived in England nor the homesick, mildly paranoid visitor we occasionally encounter in the *Castaway* and *Gulf* collections, composed after Walcott's first stays in America in the late 1950s. All this notwithstanding, Walcott still faced significant regional barriers. Although he returned often to St Lucia and Trinidad, by island standards he was now an expatriate. Moreover, the literary circles in which he moved in America during the 1980s may have imposed a form of cultural quarantine as restrictive as the isolation he experienced as a privileged transient in the St Lucian transport. It differentiated him more effectively from working-class Caribbean immigrants in Brooklyn and Boston than Naipaul, as a struggling writer, would have been insulated from other impoverished Caribbean immigrants in London.[36] Moreover, even when Walcott identified with the aspirations of people in America who looked like him, he did not speak like them or subscribe to their cultural and racial norms.[37] Conversely, although he shared an intellectual tradition with the mainstream students and audiences who read his poetry on college campuses and saw his plays in Boston and on Broadway, his lived experiences remained in important respects distinct from theirs.

The different history of race in America, as opposed to Britain or the Caribbean, thus rendered Walcott simultaneously more exposed and more invisible within and beyond multiple American communities, including the African-American community into which he would have been lumped demographically. It may also have heightened that tendency towards the incorporeal in his poems that Wayne Brown notices. The poet's encounters with an unrelievedly racialized subjectivity in America surface in *The Arkansas Testament*: in his fleeting apprehension of a Newark in which "every shadow seems to stagger / under the fiery acids of neon – / wavering like a piss", and in his vision of a toothless black sibyl who arises from a pile of discarded tyres to warn him, "STAY BLACK AND INVISIBLE / TO THE SIRENS OF

ARKANSAS".[38] Notwithstanding his use of uppercase letters, these ethereal presences lack the linguistic particularity of earlier ghosts, such as the spectral calypsonian in "The Spoiler's Return", who can pun "I decompose, but I composing still".[39] The sibyl's warning also suggests that Walcott may have had a choice; that, unlike members of the black underclass, he may have been able to pass culturally in white society – in certain contexts to slip in and out of the fog of racial invisibility without being assaulted by the police sirens of Arkansas.

In "Tomorrow, Tomorrow", Walcott's funerary images address this loss of corporeal specificity occasioned by exile, fame and racial objectification:

> A world's outside the door, but how upsetting
> to stand by your bags on a cold step as dawn
> roses the brickwork and before you start regretting,
> your taxi's coming with one beep of its horn,
> sidling to the curb like a hearse – so you get in.[40]

Bodies and buildings in the American poems become mere tricks of light. Every departure is figured as a movement out of the body or away from the human condition, into coffins, texts or nature. The poet often seems transfixed, like the mourning relatives in the poem "For Adrian", in which only the dead child's ghost retains the capacity to move:

> ... I am part of the muscle
> of a galloping lion, or a bird keeping low over
>
> dark canes; and what, in your sorrow, in our faces
> howling like statues, you call a goodbye
>
> is – I wish you would listen to me – a different welcome[41]

As with the insubstantial shadows in "The Light of the World", the ghosts in these poems are not interchangeable with living bodies. In fact bodies, when referenced at all, are reduced to disassociated parts – frozen faces, extrapolated muscles. Instead of facilitating empathy or solidarity, they exacerbate the speaker's social isolation, producing, both literally and metaphorically, an out-of-body experience.

The opening chapters in Naipaul's *Enigma* catalogue similar moments of torpor and corporeal disintegration. They include the image of the narrator soaking in the bathtub, convinced that his body has become a bloated corpse (cited in my introduction), as well as the haunting description of the narrator's fragmented sense of self that follows the novel's obliterating opening sentence – "For the first four days it rained. I could hardly see where I was."[42] As Naipaul's narrator explains, "That idea of ruin and dereliction, of out-of-placeness, was something I felt about myself, attached to myself. . . . I felt unanchored and strange."[43] Later he succumbs to a recurring nightmare of his head exploding, conjured, as he realizes in retrospect, by the failure of his epic history of Trinidad to win critical acclaim, his disastrous attempt to relocate to Trinidad, and the disturbing effects of the book he was writing about Africa: "All of this, rolled into one, was what lay on the spirit of the man who went on the walks down to Jack's cottage and past it. Not an observer merely, a man removed; but a man played on, worked on, by many things."[44] Reading *Enigma* after the publication of *Arkansas* and in the aftermath of a failed marriage, a number of abortive theatrical productions, and a succession of professional scandals, Walcott would have been hard-pressed not to have seen potential moments of convergence between his experiences and Naipaul's.[45] At this point in their careers, both writers risked becoming disembodied phantoms, cut off from their home communities, their readers and the communities of their exile.

V

Omeros addresses the multiple anxieties that haunt Naipaul's narrator when the elder Walcott's ghost materializes at the end of book IV, just as the poem's phantom narrator is about to launch his tour of European and American literary landmarks. The father cautions his son – as Walcott cautions Naipaul in his review of *Enigma* – to be wary of the seductive powers of imaginary landscapes that remain alive through the mediation of art and history with so much more clarity than the known world:

> Once you have seen everything and gone everywhere,
> cherish our island for its green simplicities,
> enthrone yourself, if your sheet is a barber-chair,
>
> a sail leaving harbour and a sail coming in,

> the shadows of grape-leaves on sunlit verandahs
> made me content. The sea-swift vanishes in rain,
>
> and yet in its travelling all that the sea-swift does
> it does in a circular pattern. Remember that, son."[46]

The elder Walcott's pastoral apostrophes to the island's "green simplicities" are the hymns of hindsight, a reckoning from beyond the grave with the inadequacies he now admits having felt about the provincial limitations of his own efforts at versifying. Only now, when his son is twice his age at death, can the father let go of his longing "for those streets that History had made great" and his sense that his world was "diminished // even by a postcard".[47] He warns his son against such heresies even as his view of the island's harbour, to which the wanderer must return, remains framed by the grape arbour he planted in his St Lucian garden, in emulation of the vineyards of antiquity.

The ghost's reference to "a sail leaving harbour and a sail coming in" echoes Naipaul's description of the associations he brings to the painting by Giorgio de Chirico that provides *The Enigma of Arrival* with its title.[48] As Naipaul remembers it, Chirico's *Enigma* presents "A wharf; in the background, beyond walls and gateways (like cutouts), there is the top of the mast of an antique vessel; on an otherwise deserted street in the foreground there are two figures, both muffled, one perhaps the person who has arrived, the other perhaps a native of the port. The scene is of desolation and mystery: it speaks of the mystery of arrival."[49] Around this image Naipaul weaves a story about a traveller who at first throws himself into the bustling life of an unfamiliar port but then begins to feel disoriented. Swept up in a street ritual, he realizes, with dawning horror, that he has been pressed into service as its sacrificial victim: "At the moment of crisis he would come upon a door, open it, and find himself back on the quayside of arrival. He has been saved; the world is as he remembered it. Only one thing is missing now. Above the cutout walls and buildings there is no mast, no sail. The antique ship has gone. The traveler has lived out his life."[50]

Naipaul's gloss on his novel's title sets up a dilemma at the heart of Walcott's *Omeros* that goes beyond the insecurities about alien landscapes discussed earlier. It marks the insatiable yearning created by loss of the idea of home, the moment when the traveller realizes that the return is no longer simply a question of geography or community but that the return of the imagination to the "green simplicities" of its former confines is impossible. Exiles or not, for each of us the realization that "the traveler has lived out his life" marks a first reckoning with our death. In *The Enigma of Arrival*, after his initial panic and mental breakdown, the narrator, reluctantly at first and then in tentative increments, begins to order the opacity of the histories that surround his Wiltshire cottage into an intimation of his own mortality. That ordering offers him a perverse sense of continuity with other civilizations that have left their marks on this landscape: the ruins of Stonehenge, the remains of an old Roman road, the abandoned glory of the manor house, the way the occasional domestic dramas of his neighbours seem to sink into the ground without leaving a trace. If his life is diminished by their opaque presence, at least death will connect him to their inscrutable absence. Confronted with the news of his sister's death in Trinidad, he finds himself writing fluently, effortlessly about Jack, the deceased gardener of the Wiltshire estate; about the gardens and gardeners that preceded Jack's tenure in the position; about the vegetable gardens of his Trinidad childhood and his instinctive delight then in making things grow.

The narrator now divines that, despite their associations with his local East Indian community, the Trinidad gardens were designed in cheap imitation of their English originals:

> The vegetable fields of Aranguez in Trinidad, on either side of the American highway, had been created by accident, with the debris, the accidental diffusion among laborers, of the learning of the Imperial College of Tropical Agriculture. They looked like the allotments in England, and there was a connection of learning, of science. But the plots of Aranguez at the edge of Port of Spain and the allotments at the edge of English towns spoke of different instincts, needs, different hearts now.[51]

Walcott interprets this description of the Aranguez gardens' mimicry as further evidence of Naipaul's contempt for his forebears. However, by placing *now* at the end of his sentence, Naipaul leaves us wondering whether one plot mimics the other or if the different needs informing the designs of both plots have now ceased to be relevant. From Naipaul's perspective, both statements will ultimately be true. The Aranguez gardens do imitate their English counterparts, but over time, land-use patterns in both contexts will become unmoored from the cultural habits and political events that produced them. The passage of time has already begun to obscure Wiltshire's imbrication in Britain's colonial past, now sinking into the landscape like the ruins of the Roman road and destined to be forgotten like Stonehenge's inscrutable significance.

Naipaul's embrace of mortality disrupts our temporal expectations. Although the English garden is older than its Caribbean echo in historical time, in the narrator's memory the Aranguez garden precedes Jack's garden in autobiographical time. And its existence helps the narrator see with "[a]dult eyes" not only the "magic" but also the "servitude and ugliness" that attach to both landscapes.[52] Indeed, Naipaul takes these inversions even further, sensing in the Aranguez gardens a connection to an earlier "old world, of planting and fertility, the very early world, [which] perhaps existed in the colony, and only for a short time, in the child's heart".[53] As the narrator takes us through these associations, we understand "why the English allotments [touch] something as small and as far away and as vague as [his] memory of planting three seeds of corn in the yard of [his] family house in Port of Spain".[54] Henceforth, every time both the narrator and the reader come upon a garden like Jack's, they will also see the vegetable gardens of Aranguez, and thus re-experience the multiple conflicting emotions that both landscapes trigger in the writer.

Such temporal disruptions help explain why Naipaul seems to take note of his sister's death only as an afterthought, a move that Walcott's review singles out as yet another instance of unbridled narcissism. In fact Naipaul claims he wrote the passages about Jack's garden, to which he circles back obsessively throughout his fictionalized memoir, as a kind of remembrance of his sister. By associating Jack's garden with its Trinidadian imitations and associating those imitations with an earlier innocence, Naipaul finds a way to transpose into the landscape of his exile those early memories of vegetation that Deschampneufs in *The Mimic Men* had warned no exile ever fully recuperates. The gardens the narrator encounters in the desolation of his exile both disturb and comfort him because they seem both unbearably alien and uncannily familiar. They register an absent presence, like the missing sails in his distorted memory of de Chirico's painting, and the loss he experiences at the death of his younger sister, whom he admits he barely knew.

Although he becomes impatient when Naipaul's narrator compares Trinidad to Wiltshire, Walcott uses similar techniques to different effect in *Omeros*, when he describes how the Plunketts come to terms with the landscape of their St Lucian exile. Our early encounters with Plunkett, peering through the streaming windows at the destruction of a storm, recall Naipaul's narrator's first blurry view of Wiltshire. The poet explains: "For Plunkett, despair came with this shitty weather, / from the industrious torrents of mid-July / till the farm was drubbed to a standstill".[55]

Plunkett perceives the rain as "an unshifting thicket" that reinforces his sense of isolation from the men who work for him, making him hate "the separate silence / that settled his labourers when their work was done".[56] Like Naipaul's narrator, Plunkett works hard to understand the history and culture of the place in which he finds himself. He too is periodically ambushed by old insecurities, unforgiving weather and financial angst. And although initially Plunkett feels no connection to the weather or the people, he too eventually establishes a relationship to this alien landscape after an unsatisfying return trip to the country of his birth. Thus, both protagonists eventually find solace in new landscapes.

By making his dislocated subject an English expatriate marooned on a Caribbean island, however, rather than a colonial exiled in the mother country, and by making St Lucia the landscape that facilitates healing rather than the English countryside, Walcott challenges what he sees as Naipaul's conflation of the Caribbean with mimicry and England with authenticity. Naipaul's narrator tells us that the Wiltshire landscape soothed his "rawest stranger's nerves", and that "in the wild garden and orchard beside the water meadows I found a physical beauty perfectly suited to my temperament and answering, besides, every good idea I could have had, as a child in Trinidad, of the physical aspect of England".[57] In language that echoes and reverses these sentiments, *Omeros* ventriloquizes Plunkett's sense of distance from his fellow Britons:

> England seemed to him merely the place of his birth.
> How odd to prefer, over its pastoral sites –
> reasonable leaves shading reasonable earth –
>
> these loud-mouthed forests on their illiterate heights,

> these springs speaking a dialect that cooled his mind
> more than pastures with castles! To prefer the hush
>
> of a hazed Atlantic worried by the salt wind!
> Others could read it as "going back to the bush,"
> but harbour after crescent harbour closed his wound.[58]

Walcott cannot resist taking a swing here at those who, like Naipaul, prefer "reasonable leaves shading reasonable earth". However, in doing so, he reminds us that both loss and recovery are universal aspects of the human condition. Moreover, he insists that the therapeutic properties of landscape – any landscape – are available to anyone who is dislocated, whether he be a Third World exile or an English expatriate. Indeed, the two landscapes described by these literary titans have more in common than might at first appear. Plunkett's "loud-mouthed forests on their illiterate heights" share many of the unkempt attributes of Wiltshire's "wild garden and orchard beside the water meadows".[59] And his open wound is closed by the "hush // of a hazed Atlantic" just as the "reasonable earth" soothes the narrator's "rawest stranger's nerves" in *Enigma*.[60]

Plunkett's decisive embrace of life in the tropics comes after Maud's death, when he resorts to Ma Kilman, in her role as local obeah woman, to help him communicate with his dead wife. Maud's ghostly unstitching of the birds embroidered on her Jubilee quilt hallows her husband's act of faith, binding him "for good to another race".[61] As Plunkett emerges from his séance, he is surrounded by the whirring sound of wings:

> ... The wound in his
> head froze him in the scorched street. Innumerable flocks
>
> of birds screamed from her guidebook over the shacks
> of the village, their shadows like enormous fans,
> all those she had sewn to the silken quilt, with tags
>
> pinned to their spurs, and he knew her transparent hands
> had unstitched them as he watched them flying over
> the grooved roofs till they were simply the shadow of ...
>
> of a cloud on the hills.[62]

The passage echoes one in Walcott's ironically named 1981 collection *The Fortunate Traveller*, where the poet's troubled reckoning with the stress of an increasingly globalized Caribbean achieves resolution in a cathartic final poem, "Season of Phantasmal Peace". The poem begins: Then all the nations of birds lifted together / the huge net of the shadows of this earth / in multitudinous dialects, twittering tongues" and moves towards "the pause / between dusk and darkness, between fury and peace".[63] Those tropical birds, with their gifts of rapture and serenity, now belong equally to Plunkett and the islanders. Stitched into Maud's quilt in honour of the Queen's Golden Jubilee, they originally seemed the ultimate symbol of the colonizer's superiority. Now, in much the same way that Naipaul's Trinidad memories frame his impressions of the Wiltshire landscape, the birds lift off the quilted squares, framing Plunkett's European past within his Caribbean present. They release Plunkett from his numbing survivor's guilt, making palpable both the pain and the joy he has shared with Maud during the life they built together on the island.

Plunkett has no childhood scars from the bark of guava trees to show, but the personal losses he has endured while surrounded by Caribbean fauna and flora legitimate his claims on the landscape. After the epiphany that Maud's unstitched birds make possible, Plunkett learns "how to pause / in the shade of the stone arch watching the bright red / flowers of the immortelle"; how to forget his obsession with the war and to speak with the workmen on his farm, "not as boys who worked with him, till every name // somehow sounded different".[64] The rituals, artefacts and relationships with which Plunkett surrounds Maud's death in their adopted homeland allow Walcott to affirm the possibility of new beginnings. They also resemble those with which Naipaul surrounds his sister's death and his own new life in Wiltshire. As Naipaul's narrator puts it at the end of *Enigma*, "we remade the world for ourselves; every generation does that, as we found when we came together for . . . death. . . . It forced us to look on death. . . . it fitted a real grief where melancholy had created a vacancy."[65]

VI

Walcott's stitching of Major Plunkett into his text, as the main character through whom he represents his personal struggle with the condition of exile, is one of *Omeros*'s most satisfying achievements. In *Another Life*, Walcott presents the historical figure on whom he based Plunkett, but only as a caricature: a choleric red-haired history teacher from his high school days who barks orders at cadets and fires questions at his students – "Boy! Who was Ajax?"[66] But as the poet approaches the age and expatriate condition of his former cadet-master, the differences of race and historical allegiances between them recede. Plunkett's displacement in the tropics becomes a mirror of the poet's own feelings of displacement in Boston. The move is anticipated in an earlier poem, "North and South", in which the poet, travelling in Europe, acknowledges that the wintry landscape in which he feels so alien and alone

> . . . was home to some consul in snow-white ducks
> doing out his service in the African provinces,
> who wrote letters like this one home and feared malaria
> as I mistrust the dark snow[67]

But Walcott's resolutions in *Omeros* do not simply invert Naipaul's. Plunkett's new ability to connect with the men who work for him is as important to his rehabilitation as his new-found appreciation of Caribbean flora and fauna. Indeed, for Walcott a private connection to an alien landscape through its history or aesthetic properties could never be the end of the story. There remains the necessity of empathy, and in his writing he is constantly on the lookout for ways to use personal growth as a vehicle for communal reconciliation.

Two parallel scenes, from *Enigma* and *Omeros* respectively, demonstrate how Walcott confronts Naipaul, through Plunkett, to insist that human connections trump history and art. Near the end of *Enigma*, when Naipaul's narrator has established a predictable set of surface relationships with people in the Wiltshire community, we encounter (with him) the dairyman's son. The youth's alternating stances of bullying and cowardice recapitulate the history of social relations between the working class and the gentry. Defying custom, which dictates that villagers defer to their elders and betters when seats on the bus are scarce, the dairyman's son not only refuses to give up his seat but also continues to place his feet on the seat beside him. Naipaul establishes the scene in a characteristically cryptic fashion, leaving us to fathom its meaning with minimal editorial intervention:

He was embarrassed when I got on the bus – I was a neighbor, I knew his house and his parents. But he was also among his friends, and he couldn't let himself down.

The bus dropped us both off in the shade of the great manor yews, near his house and mine.

I said, "Peter."

He stood to attention, like a cadet or a boy in a reformatory, threw back his head, and said, "Sir!" As though expecting at the very least a slap; and at the same time not truly intending apology or respect. In that reaction, which made me nervous, I felt I had a glimpse of his past, and saw his need for aggression, his only form of self-assertion. I didn't know how to go on with him; I didn't particularly want to. I didn't say any more.[68]

The genius of this exchange can hardly be overstated. At one level Naipaul is reprising historical relationships between oppressor and oppressed, demonstrating as the working-class youth snaps to attention how hardwired the impulses of servility and resentment remain in those whose psyches have been shaped by centuries of degradation. At another level, by allowing his brown immigrant protagonist to gain the upper hand in relation to the white English youth, Naipaul slyly reverses the caste hierarchies of racial domination. However, he refuses to make anything radical or visionary out of this moment. For him, as Walcott accuses, "the only dignity is to be neither master nor servant".[69] As he presents it, nothing has changed in these social relationships except for his narrator's maverick ability to transcend, if only momentarily, the signification of race. And that works only because of what Walcott labels Naipaul's great "farce": "The myth of Naipaul as a phenomenon, as a singular, contradictory genius who survived the cane fields and the bush at great cost."[70] In this case we can assume that the narrator's local reputation as a writer makes the role reversal possible, although we know that his superiority is provisional and that, at other moments in the narrative, he remains terrified of his continued vulnerability to deep-seated feelings of inferiority. Thus, even as the reader takes vicarious pleasure in the way the narrator passively trumps the race card, we are left to conclude that the only escape from such predictable relationships is to absent oneself from all meaningful social intercourse. The narrator elects this refuge when he declines to engage the dairyman's son.

Walcott borrows Naipaul's anecdote for *Omeros* but gives it a different twist. Near the end of the poem, after attending Maud Plunkett's funeral, his semi-autobiographical narrator encounters his former cadet-master, Plunkett, in a bank. Initially the narrator feels sentimentally protective towards the old expatriate who has so recently lost his wife. Nevertheless, he remains uncomfortably aware that the bugle note in the old man's hoarse voice, which had "racked us in line as cadets", can still elicit in him that "shiver / of fear we all knew".[71] When the two men finally accost one another, each slips into the roles that Naipaul maps out for oppressor and oppressed in the description of his narrator's encounter with the dairyman's son:

> "Our wanderer's home, is he?"
>   I said: "For a while, sir,"
> too crisply, mentally snapping to attention,
> thumbs along trousers' seam, picking up his accent[72]

From this point on their exchange tumbles downhill. Plunkett affects an upper-class English accent that both he and the narrator know is fake – "Not real colonial gentry, but spoke like / them from the height of his pig-farm".[73] And despite his contempt for the farce, the poet finds himself mimicking the accent's cadences like an awkward colonial schoolboy shamed by the island lilt of his speech. As the two men play out the script of paternalism and resentment that Naipaul presents as inevitable in such situations, the poet protests inwardly, "I'm tired of their fucking guilt, // and our fucking envy!"[74]

But in the end, they do make fumbling contact. Plunkett tells his former student about Maud's quilt by way of acknowledging the poet's artistic accomplishments, and the narrator lets his cadet-master know that he attended Maud's funeral. Finally, as the encounter ends, Walcott reverses the linguistic protocols in the Naipaul anecdote:

> "Nice to see you, sir," said my old Sergeant Major,
>
> and my eyes blurred. Then he paused at the white glare of
> the street outside, and left, as the guard closed the door,
> the wound of a language I'd no wish to remove.[75]

Rather than passively usurping without subverting the authority of the oppressor, as Naipaul's version of this encounter does, Walcott shows both parties struggling with the legacy of deformed relationships that *sir* establishes between them. Although neither fully escapes its crippling signification, Walcott insists that this term of respect, though hedged in by class and racial snobberies, still preserves a valued human aspect of the Caribbean heritage that he shares with Plunkett. The empathy it facilitates is mutually reinforcing, demonstrating that genuine respect can coexist with petrified authority. Where Naipaul's narrator turns away in moral exhaustion from the memory of brutality embedded in the response of the dairyman's son to his verbal challenge, Walcott's narrator embraces the wound of a language that he has no wish to remove.

VII

Walcott rejects Naipaul's refusal of the possibility of human connection. In *Enigma* the narrator's psychic journey is facilitated almost exclusively by the landscape and its history, even though Naipaul uses these to say important things about his connections to Trinidad and to his family. From Walcott's perspective, however, the landscape's therapeutic properties become attenuated unless they are reinvigorated by ongoing human relationships. As he puts it in his review of *Enigma*, "What keeps plot and excitement alive in *Robinson Crusoe* is not the myth of isolation but the challenge of endurance through ordinary objects, and through the vibrations of such objects the increase of loneliness, the growing scream inside the heart for companionship or, in another word, for love."[76]

We can follow how Walcott establishes such relationships through his depiction of the Plunketts' marriage. Initially the Plunketts respond to the alien landscape by trying to domesticate it through art or sublimate it through intellectual activity. On good days Maud cultivates her garden. She spends the rainy-season evenings sewing or playing Irish airs on the piano. Her husband immerses himself in history books about the Peloponnesian wars and the British empire, which he connects to St Lucia's maritime history. But none of these activities can relieve their ennui; their sense of having been deposited in "The wrong time. The wrong ground."[77] When, one dreary evening, in a raw, sodden rage, Plunkett slams the piano lid shut, barely missing shattering Maud's artist hands, the poem cuts through the intellectualizing crap, so to speak. It dramatizes viscerally how isolation can distort relationships, however creatively we – like Naipaul or Walcott – may mediate that experience through our immersion in artistic or intellectual activity.

In the aftermath of Plunkett's vicious attack, no words are spoken, no explanations offered. As Plunkett recognizes, it would be too simple to blame his outburst on post-traumatic stress from the war: "Rubbish. Easy excuse. He never blamed the war. / It was like original sin."[78] But later, in the privacy of their bedroom, the couple reaches an unspoken truce: "Sorrow dissolved // him, and he sat on the bed, and then both of them wept / the forgiving rain of those who have truly loved".[79] Although his irritability has been caused by racial isolation, financial insecurity, bad weather and boredom, Plunkett is not relieved of his condition because these irritants have been removed. Instead, the catharsis of shared weeping washes away his psychic pain. Such representations of empathy in *Omeros* seldom require explicit rationales. In staging them, the poet seems to reach back to elemental sounds and movements whose semiotic significance depends on our shared human capacity for sorrow, anger and joy. They encompass Ma Kilman's primal howl as she calls upon the healing properties of African herbs whose names she has forgotten, as well as Achille's silent offering of an oar to his dead rival, Hector.

At moments like these, Walcott goes to extraordinary lengths to refute Naipaul's position on the limits of empathy. And yet in the poem as a whole, Plunkett succeeds better than the phantom narrator in making such human connections. At the end of the poem he establishes meaningful relationships with his workers, and Walcott even allows him to idle in the "lion-clawed tub", recapitulating and reversing the bathtub scene in *Enigma* as he converses "in his normal voice" with his deceased wife.[80] By contrast, apart from his encounter with Plunkett in the bank, Walcott's phantom narrator barely interacts with the "living" characters in *Omeros*. He maintains his distance from the loquacious taxi driver who tells him about Hector's fatal crash, in the same way that the speaker in the poem "The Light of the World" shuts out his fellow passengers. This autobiographical narrator can address Achille as "My main man, my nigger!" when he discovers him in Winslow Homer's painting *The Gulf Stream* in the Boston Museum of Fine Arts, but when he actually places himself in Achille's presence, he might as well be Naipaul's narrator observing other people's lives "across a fence, or on the far side of a field".[81]

Walcott's review criticizes Naipaul for "the suppression of those things that advance fiction: whether the narrator lived in total solitude . . . and, if the narrator did, whether he avoided, for the sake of art, the temporary solaces of sex or marriage, whether he cooked for himself", and he notes that Naipaul omits from *Enigma* any account of his actual living circumstances.[82] Yet few scenes of domestic intimacy in America survive in the final draft of *Omeros*.[83] In fact, when we strip out the passages from *Omeros* in which the poet functions as a character rather than as narrator, and look at that character's interactions with others, a somewhat dismal picture emerges. This reclusive, brooding figure is uncomfortable for significant stretches of time in both St Lucia and Boston, and defensively remote from the very subjects the poem writes so fully into existence. His story seems alarmingly close to the one Walcott accuses Naipaul of telling, in which "our own egocentricity absorbs other people's tragedies as interruptions or irritations".[84]

As if to drive the point home, in the canto describing his shipwreck isolation in Boston after his marriage ends, Walcott breaks with the magnificent rolling hexameters that imbue the rhythms of his poem with the variety and power of the Atlantic surf pounding an island beach. Walcott truncates both the length of the lines and the length of his stanzas, replacing the capacious three-line verses of iambic hexameter with four-beat rhyming couplets arranged in jerky Dr Seuss trochees that make it difficult for readers to take too seriously the narrator's maudlin self-pity:

> House of toothbrush, house of sin,
> of branches scratching, "Let me in!"
>
> House whose rooms echo with rain,
> of wrinkled clouds with Onan's stain
>
> House that creaks, age fifty-seven,
> wooden earth and plaster heaven[85]

In lines like these the poet seems to hold up his isolation to ridicule, faulting his fictional alter ego for making such a fuss about private difficulties he has brought upon himself. The incantatory rhythms cut this semi-autobiographical figure down to size, wielding the infantilizing metre like a stern West Indian parent brandishing a belt to warn a peevish child that he will really have something to cry about if he keeps on whining. Eventually the self-flagellating metre pushes the speaker towards an admission that he is responsible for his own isolation: "I do not live in you, I bear / my house inside me, everywhere".[86] That resolution once again refutes the claim that personal unhappiness is caused by the limitations of specific environments or communities. Whereas Naipaul makes the private angst of his dyspeptic narrator the focal point of his fictional memoir, Walcott relegates his narrator's difficult personal odyssey to the margins of his poem. He instead directs our sympathies towards Plunkett, Hector and the rest of his cast of characters, who have committed themselves to building a new island community in the face of a shared history of oppression, fragmentation and loss.

That is all very noble, but it is not clear that Walcott's strategy always makes for better poetry, or that it does much more than repress the unresolved conflicts he has taken with him into alien landscapes. As the poet moves across his meridian into European cities and the American heartland, his St Lucian characters recede into paintings and remembered fragments of song. Since Walcott refuses to indulge the kind of narcissistic brooding that animates Naipaul's landscapes, his narrator has to depend on literary allusions to North American classics – such as Catherine Weldon's captivity narratives and Thoreau's *Walden* – to fill out the contours of the alien landscape. However, these references lack an organic connection to the local intimacies that domesticate such literary allusions in his Caribbean sequences. After a while, the North American references in *Omeros* blur into the roster of European literary capitals the narrator also visits. The poem's hurried scamper through Europe has its function, since the various literary figures we encounter there are meant to blend into each other. However, this narrator lives in America; he is not just passing through. Yet his American cantos begin to feel like academic exercises to be read with history book in hand, uncorrupted by the idiosyncrasies of personal loss.

As Deschampneufs warns in *The Mimic Men*, such indirect apprehension of foreign vistas cannot domesticate an elm. Thus such a simile as "Here too, at Concord, the contagious vermilion / advanced with the maples, like red poinciana / under the fort of that lion-headed island", which Walcott inserts into a canto about his narrator's North American sojourn, feels mechanical.[87] We respond intellectually to the clever juxtaposition of the tropical and temperate trees – maple and poinciana – grafted onto each other through their shared association with the colour vermilion. The verb *advanced* connects both trees with battle and bloodshed. Eventually the reader may even associate the colour of the poincianas with that of the red immortelle trees under which Plunkett learns to pause in the aftermath of Maud's death. However, unlike the reference to the St Lucian fort on the "lion-headed island", which we have visited on many occasions with Plunkett, the allusion to Concord is not enough to create a network of personal relationships that can domesticate New England maples. Plunkett's discovery of his lost ancestor/son in the annals of St Lucian history humanizes his historical research. By contrast, the inner lives of the constantly changing cast of ghostly characters who have lived among the New England maples fade too quickly in and out of focus to engage our empathy. Moreover, we know too little about the personal circumstances of a narrator who would be capable of drawing such comparisons between North American and St Lucian history.

Flashes of fellow-feeling surface during random encounters with characters like the Polish waitress in Canada, who turns towards the narrator "with that nervous / smile of the recent immigrant that borders on tears" and whom he hopes to unnerve with his frank lust.[88] However, by comparison with other moments in Walcott's Caribbean poems, such connections seem superficial. They do not honour the opacity the poet concedes to the woman he calls the "Light of the World" on the St Lucian transport. Unencumbered by the conventional constraints of the lyric mode, this epic narrator has little compunction about entering the waitress's head and imagining how his gaze is affecting her, or what she must have felt in Poland or at the Canadian border. His knowingness unsettles because, though both the narrator and the waitress are immigrants, the poet's immigrant vulnerabilities resonate only at the canto's margins. Such impersonality constrains our empathy for the narrator, as well as for the characters he describes. "There are days", the poet tells us, after his narrator's encounter with the waitress,

> ... when, however simple the future, we do not go
> towards it but leave part of life in a lobby whose elevators
> divide and enclose us, brightening digits that show
>
> exactly where we are headed[89]

One senses in much of the writing in the middle section of *Omeros* both that desire for new vistas and a paradoxical reluctance to let go of old certainties. Walcott endeavours to establish parallels between St Lucia and the worlds that his poetic persona encounters in his travels. However, he hesitates to commit his alter ego to fully inhabiting any landscape beyond the Caribbean. Instead he draws back from confronting his own mortality, which a lost connection to the "green simplicities" of his former Caribbean existence might have entailed.[90] Apart from the mocking trochees that exorcise his personal demons in a lonely Boston house, this phantom narrator remains a transient, rarely presenting himself as having to craft a new life in exile in the way that Naipaul's narrator does. That work he leaves to Plunkett.

VIII

None of these caveats suffices to discount a poem as massive as *Omeros*. Its achievement does not stand or fall on the close reading of a single image or canto. Rather, the poem's effect is cumulative, depending for its final roar on the steadily building rush of all its patterns and images. The rhyming couplets about the lonely Boston house dramatize Walcott's resistance to Naipaul's narcissism while providing a respite from the mesmerizing rhythms of the poem's hexameters. Partially developed references to Catherine Weldon's captivity narrative balance several of the specific details of Plunkett's historical research. And Homer's appearance, in the guise of a dishevelled Dickensian tramp on the steps of St Martin-in-the-Fields, sets up wonderfully his apparition near the end of the poem as a crumpled black plastic bag bobbing on the surf off a St Lucian beach. My concern in this chapter, however, is with the way Walcott's multiple subject positions within his poem's broader canvas allow him to respond to Naipaul's more narrowly focused but equally slippery *I* narrator in his fictionalized memoir.

Walcott complains in his review of *Enigma* that Naipaul's prose abandons the purity of the lyric present in favour of a stultified perfect tense – an accusation I take to mean that Naipaul's writing is too teleological, too bent on representing the superior comforts of Wiltshire as the inevitable goal of Naipaul's terminal isolation. That insistence on lyric fidelity may seem a curious standard to which to hold a work of prose. However, in much of *Enigma*, Naipaul adheres to the conventions of the lyric. As Walcott demonstrates at the start of his review, when he lays out some of Naipaul's sentences as verse, substantial portions of Naipaul's memoir could easily be reformatted as poetry. *Enigma* addresses us through the consciousness of a single, isolated ethical subject who claims no insights beyond those mediated by personal memories and observations in the lyric present. The pacing of its sentences approximates the breath intervals that give many lyric poems their organic shape. Indeed, Walcott finds in Naipaul's prose a "bracing, springing rhythm, as cool, as fresh, as pneumatic as moss underfoot", which he compares to Edward Thomas's poetry and essays.[91] Save for short exchanges like the one with the dairyman's son, which reads like a misanthropic perversion of one of Wordsworth's lyrical ballads, his fictional memoir contains very little dialogue.[92] Naipaul leaves it to his narrator's descriptions of intimately observed details – such as the fat, useless legs of the manor's hereditary owner or the ruts in the ditch alongside the Roman road – to convey insights about history or politics that exceed the narrator's immediate, often contradictory responses. Beyond this, the memoir's plot line delivers no coherent ethical take on the events it narrates, as the narrator eventually undermines his initial claim that he finds solace "in the wild garden and orchard beside the water meadows".[93] Approaching Naipaul's memoir thus – as a long lyric sequence – may mitigate our craving as prose readers for more explicit narrative direction.

As Naipaul retreats from the literary conventions for writing narrative prose, Walcott expands the range of his lyric poetry to encompass epic, narrative and drama. Moving among these modes, in one breath he can editorialize about the wound he has stitched into Plunkett's character – "He has to be wounded, affliction is one theme / of this work" – and then present his narrator in the next breath, as a dramatist would, "snapping to attention" in response to Plunkett's voice.[94] Then again, the cadences and images in a line like "harbour after crescent harbour closed his wound"[95] could have come directly from one of Walcott's shorter lyric poems. The poet thus disperses his personal anxieties about exile and fame, loss and restoration, over the narrative, dramatic and lyric interludes he creates for a veritable pantheon of characters. As we will see in the chapters that follow, he contains this epic sweep by means of his technical prowess with rhyme, sound and metre. In his hands, those formal disciplines are enforced with such grace that after a while we glide through the poem as if it were a novel written in prose, even as the eye and ear respond with elation to the poem's virtuosic effects.[96]

With such inversions and substitutions in mind, we can better appreciate how, in constructing these very different works, Naipaul and Walcott become interchangeable phantoms. Each writer encroaches on the literary domain of the other to put pressure on the boundaries that separate his understanding of experience from that of his readers. Walcott in particular, writing after having read Naipaul's *Enigma*, draws many of Naipaul's concerns and techniques directly into *Omeros*. Although he quarrels with Naipaul's choices, he learns from them. He steers clear of the isolation Naipaul manipulates so ruthlessly in his fictionalized memoir. But he violates many of the same conventions that he accuses Naipaul of ignoring, especially those separating the omniscient narrator from the private speaking subject of lyric poetry or the public *I* of autobiography. And he uses his direct responses to Naipaul in *Omeros* to position his own work as expressing more comprehensively than his rival's the anxieties and aspirations of a Caribbean community of readers.

Walcott ends his excoriating review of Naipaul's *Enigma* by aggressively celebrating his rival. Just as the travellers in "The Light of the World" insist on returning the poet's "lights", Walcott insists on embracing Naipaul:

> Despite his horror of being claimed, we West Indians are proud of Naipaul, and that is his enigmatic fate as well, that he should be so cherished by those he despises. . . . His own island, a generation before, gave the world C.L.R. James (a Negro) and Samuel Selvon, and other islands offered the world George Lamming, Wilson Harris, Roger Mais, Jean Rhys, Edgar Mittelholzer, John Hearne, Shiva Naipaul, Jamaica Kincaid, scores of excellent short stories, the poets Eric Roach, Cecil Herbert, George Campbell, Edward Brathwaite, a few hundred calypsonians, Bob Marley, Sparrow, Kitchener. But how weak Naipaul's struggle would seem if it were communal;[97]

Walcott's *we* here, like the *our* in the epigraph with which this chapter opens, operates on several levels. Although it seems to place Naipaul outside its charmed circle, as a liminal figure who "could never solidify [his] shadow / to be one of their shadows", it nevertheless insists that he belongs to the Caribbean community.[98] To drive that point home, Walcott indulges in a rare roll call of Caribbean writers, including some with whom, as we shall see, he has quarrelled in the past. Since many of the writers he names would have been unknown to the review's first readers in the *New Republic* – a journal that does not circulate beyond a metropolitan intellectual elite – the roll call does more than claim a space for Naipaul within a regional pantheon. It challenges metropolitan readers to acknowledge that the Caribbean writing community is more capacious than their exclusive focus on its two most famous sons might suggest. Paradoxically, it also gives notice that we are overhearing a family quarrel whose arcane details remain appropriately obscured to outsiders. From this perspective, one could argue that Walcott's review does not go after Naipaul in order to drum him out of the family but rather to draw him closer, to hold him accountable to the islands that gave him to the world by giving him the world as a writer.[99]

Finally, Walcott's stern embrace of Naipaul conceals a plea for his own legacy, which, like Naipaul's, has been challenged on many occasions by those who see his work as Eurocentric or as remote from ordinary people in the Caribbean. Walcott makes this plea explicit in the closing pages of *Omeros*, when he pauses to apostrophize Achille:

> ... whose fist of iron
>
> would do me a greater honour if it held on
> to my casket's oarlocks than mine lifting his own
> when both anchors are lowered in the one island[100]

The poet concedes that his poems "will remain unknown // and unread" by men like Hector and Achille, that despite their shared language neither he nor they can ever fully enter each other's imaginations.[101] And yet he holds on to the idea that when his "pirogue / with its brass-handled oarlocks" pushes off, it will sail "Not from // but with them, with Hector, with Maud".[102] By including Maud Plunkett alongside Hector and Achille in his final passage, Walcott speaks to the possibility of new communities forged through lived experiences within shared landscapes, despite divisions of race and class. This affirmation distinguishes his vision from that of Naipaul, who finds solace in the idea that death's inscrutable absences will ultimately obscure all failed attempts at community.

For Walcott, then, the limits of empathy with which both he and Naipaul have had to reckon do not obliterate their shared connection to the landscape that has shaped their primal sympathies and antagonisms. In defending his decision to "waste lines on Achille, a shade on the sea-floor", *Omeros*'s narrator maintains that "strong as self-healing coral, a quiet culture / is branching from the white ribs of each ancestor".[103] The image of coral constructing new shapes around the phantom outlines of disintegrated bones articulates the poem's most enduring refusal of negation. Its optimism relies on the poet's faith in the manifold creative possibilities of the Caribbean's self-healing culture. And it holds fervently to the promise that, long after both Naipaul and Walcott have become as insubstantial as the phantom narrators in their works, their literary legacies will continue to shape the region's culture, even as future generations forget each writer's individual contribution and begin, like the coral, anew.

9

FOR BRATHWAITE

> And this was the prayer that Achille could not utter:
> "The spear that I give you, my friend, is only wood.
>
> Vexation is past. I know how well you treat her.
> You never know my admiration, when you stood
> crossing the sun at the bow of the long canoe
>
> with the plates of your chest like a shield; I would say
> any enemy so was a compliment. 'Cause no
> African ever hurled his wide seine at the bay
>
> by which he was born with such beauty. You hear me? Men
> did not know you like me. All right. Sleep good. Good night."[1]

I

To characterize the relationship between Brathwaite and Walcott as strained would be an understatement. Their many similarities in age, background, schooling and ambition give the smallest differences between the two men the dimensions of unbridgeable chasms. Although by the end of the twentieth century neither probably would have admitted it, they remained warily alert to each other's pronouncements, covert readers of each other's books and passionate rivals for their Caribbean readers' souls. Brathwaite can hardly have been indifferent to the aesthetic validation that such prestigious awards as the Nobel and MacArthur prizes brought to Walcott. But Walcott also remained irascible on the subject of Brathwaite, by turns dismissive of or irritated by the lip service that Brathwaite's cultural nationalist project elicited from ideological pundits who otherwise evinced very little serious interest in poetry.

Such covert animus is the least interesting aspect of this authorial rivalry. Brathwaite's work mattered to Walcott at the time because its popular appeal exposed Walcott's limits, from the perspective of a regional audience that clamoured for accessibility and direct engagement from their writers – qualities that had never come easily to Walcott. The difficulty cannot be rationalized away by making distinctions between the "humanist" and the socially committed "folk" visions of the two poets.[2] Rather, it signals an underlying tension within Walcott's oeuvre between the effects it derives from the "universally" literary and those it derives from the nationalist cultural milieu that both he and Brathwaite helped to inaugurate.

In *Omeros*, Walcott revisits several techniques that Brathwaite first developed, resolving in the process perennial anxieties that have haunted his work. He relies most explicitly on Brathwaite for the images and arguments in book III, where his protagonist, Achille, like the "New World Negro" in the "Masks" section of Brathwaite's *Arrivants* trilogy, makes his way back to Africa in a dream to confront his ancestors and the legacy of slavery.[3] I want to focus, however, on the more nuanced ways in which Brathwaite's influence can be divined. In its reliance on formal elements derived from creole speech, *Omeros* augments a Caribbean epic tradition famously inaugurated in Aimé Césaire's *Cahier d'un retour au pays natal* (1939) and extended in Brathwaite's *Arrivants*. *Cahier* became the manifesto of the *négritude* movement in the Caribbean, Europe and Africa during the 1940s and 1950s, while *The Arrivants* spawned a host of imitators at home and abroad during the Black Power era of the 1960s and 1970s. Such audiences seem remote from the elite circles in which *Omeros* is often championed, but the poem's formal and linguistic virtuosity would not have been possible without these earlier works.

I used *irascible* earlier to characterize Walcott's response to Brathwaite, because Walcott often uses it to describe his own and other Caribbean artists' relationships with local audiences and fellow artists. He uses the term most notably in *Another Life*, where, in response to the suicide of his mentor, Harry Simmons, he lashes out:

> Irascibility, muse of middle age.
> How often you have felt you have wasted your life
> among a people with no moral centre,
> to want to move from the contagion of too many friends,
> the heart congealing into stone[4]

In Walcott's public pronouncements, that irascibility occasions quick jabs directed at rivals or intimates that the poet almost always hopes will cut, but which, one suspects, he almost as quickly regrets when they do. It inspires the *picong* moment (too good to miss) in the BBC's *Caribbean Nights* interview broadcast in October 1986, when he deadpans a parody of the opening lines of Brathwaite's poem "Negus" –

> It
> It
> It
> It is not
> It is not a very good poem

– effectively deflecting the interviewer's pieties about orality's significance for Caribbean poetry.[5] And few readers of Walcott's magnificent essay "What the Twilight Says" can have failed to take note of moments where its unsparing critical insights tip over into the vituperative: "The worst song, the most sincerely sung, is an original, an anthem to the nation. The sentiments are infantile (though children are innocent of patriotism), the words and phrasing execrable. But the passion with which it is sung is its most desolating aspect. Furiously ungrammatical, emphatically crude, but patinaed with grace. It smells as soon as it is aired."[6]

Regrets aside, Walcott is unapologetic about his irascibility. In his poetry and public pronouncements it has become part of his principled refusal of the heroic in Caribbean writing. From Walcott's perspective, the essence of the Caribbean experience is precisely its pettiness: the rhetorical passion the region's inhabitants expend on relatively insignificant events. Caribbean writers must wrestle into art the straitened circumstances of an island existence that reduces even the magnificent battles of the gods – *dies irae* in the classical and liturgical precedents – to plain old irascibility: peevishness, swift spite and a touch of what West Indians would call *ignorance*. Thus, having castigated Naipaul's nihilism in the essay "The Caribbean: Culture or Mimicry", Walcott backtracks to point out: "The embittered despair of a New World writer like Naipaul is also part of that impatience and irascibility at the mere repetition of human error which passes for history, and that irascibility is also a belief in possibility."[7] In a slightly different register, after critiquing in his 1967 *Trinidad Guardian* review what he considers an enervating melancholy in the tone of Brathwaite's *Rights of Passage*, Walcott qualifies: "It is very difficult for foreign readers to understand the vacuum at the core of West Indian sensibility, a kind of deadness that no exhortations about community and achievement can stir, one that is suspicious and uncertain. The wavering, querulous note that 'Rights of Passage' sounds is right for us. . . . The search for our own sadness is the progression of that sensibility towards being named."[8]

Querulous lacks the asperity of *irascibility*, but in this context the source of its negative energy is the same. Thus, even when it exasperates, Walcott divines in the timbre of that irascibility a genuine attempt at articulating the nothingness that remains the bane and possibility of creativity in the New World. Moreover, in the Caribbean that irascibility is often reserved for interactions with one's closest friends. For instance, in *Another Life*, Walcott imagines his painter friend Gregorias as intuitive enough to divine the fierce protectiveness behind his wish that his friend had died in order to spite an unappreciative regional audience. And although he mercilessly harangued members of the Trinidad Theatre Workshop when they worked with him, he says in the closing benediction of "What the Twilight Says": "I am bound within them, neither knowing which is liana or trunk. . . . All their betrayals are quarrels with the self, their pardonable desertions the inevitable problem of all island artists: the choice of home or exile, self-realization or spiritual betrayal of one's country."[9]

Such intimacy among the region's poets is rare. Absent these personal bonds, it is easy to hear Walcott's pronouncements on his fellow writers as patronizing or elitist. In fact, he sounds a bit like the devil in his play *Ti-Jean and His Brothers* – who complains, "It gets dull in that big house. Sometimes I wish I couldn't have everything I wanted" – when he says in an interview with Edward Hirsch, "I yearn for the company of better Caribbean poets, quite frankly. I feel a little lonely. I don't see what I thought might have happened – a stronger energy, a stronger discipline, and a stronger drive in Caribbean poetry."[10] And yet we know that for Walcott, as for each of the other writers discussed in this study, the yearning for a regional literary fraternity was genuine. In *Another Life* and in many of his essays, Walcott recalls with deep nostalgia the bracing combative atmosphere he associates with the nascent artistic communities of his formative years: his raucous rivalries with the other aspiring young artists who gathered around his mentor, Harry Simmons; magical memories of his parents' friends reciting and performing and arguing long into the night about politics and books; the rush of terror and self-important camaraderie engendered by the attacks the Catholic Church mounted against the plays he and his siblings, Pamela and Roderick, produced with the fledgling St Lucian Artists' Guild. These early associations inform Walcott's idealized vision of a vibrant Caribbean literary culture. Its naked competition and shared risk are qualitatively different from the appreciation – tinged with genuine humility – with which Walcott acknowledges the literary friendships he forged later in his life, with such poetic luminaries from outside the region as Robert Lowell, Elizabeth Hardwick and Seamus Heaney.[11] Even the rambunctious Joseph Brodsky, whom Walcott sometimes makes sound like a Russian version of Gregorias, is still the respected master rather than the sparring partner with whom Walcott wishes he could wrangle over Caribbean aesthetics – the way Shabine does in the long narrative poem "The Schooner *Flight*", when he takes out his shipmate Vincie for mocking his poems: "There wasn't much pain, / just plenty blood, and Vincie and me best friend, / but none of them go fuck with my poetry again."[12] Walcott has managed to approach this passionate ideal in his relationships within Caribbean art and theatre circles, but he has rarely achieved it in his interactions with other Caribbean poets. *Omeros* may thus be read as an attempt at rapprochement with fellow practitioners like Brathwaite, which Walcott hopes will outlive present rivalries, by bringing to bear on the formal experiments and linguistic effects they pioneered his own poetic "energy, discipline and drive".

II

Irascibility, querulousness, suspicion, exasperation, uncertainty, shame – these qualities suffuse the exchanges between the St Lucian fishermen

Hector and Achille, whose rivalry over the local beauty, Helen, provides one main narrative strand in *Omeros*:

> *"Touchez-i, encore: N'ai fendre choux-ous-ou, salope!"*
> "Touch it again, and I'll split your arse, you bitch!"
> *"Moi j'a dire – 'ous pas prêter un rien. 'Ous ni shallope,*
>
> *'ous ni seine, 'ous croire 'ous ni choeur campêche?"*
> "I told you, borrow nothing of mine. You have a canoe,
> and a net. Who you think you are? Logwood Heart?"
>
> *"'Ous croire 'ous c'est roi Gros Îlet? Voleur bomme!"*
> "You think you're king of Gros Îlet, you tin stealer?"
> Then in English: "I go show you who is king! Come!"[13]

In this, their first (and last) direct encounter in the poem, Hector and Achille sink below the level of Ajax, the "debased, bored" carthorse in *Another Life* who doubles as "a thoroughbred on race days, once a year".[14] Their epic battle is over a rusted can that even they know is not worth the trouble. Achille says as much a few lines later, when he acknowledges: "The rage that he felt against Hector // was shame. To go crazy for an old bailing tin / crusted with rust!"[15]

And yet the language of that eternal rivalry of men over their manhood cuts, crisp and startlingly beautiful, across the page, despite (or perhaps on account of) the reining in of its pace, necessitated by the alternating lines of French Creole and English translation. Walcott stitches together rhymes across the two languages: for example, between *bitch* and *campêche* in the first two stanzas quoted, and between *bomme* and *come* in the next tercet. Patterns in one language also find their echo in the rhythms of the other. Thus, even though "You think you is king of Gros Îlet" repeats a different vowel sound (think/king) in English Creole than the French Creole *"'Ous croire 'ous c'est roi Gros Îlet"* (croire/roi), the patterns of rhythm and assonance progress in tandem with each other. Walcott deploys similar techniques to splendid effect in another bilingual passage involving Ma Kilman and Philoctete:

> *"Mais qui ça qui rivait-'ous, Philoctete?"*
>   *"Moin blessé."*
> "But what is wrong wif you, Philoctete?"

>   "I am blest
> wif this wound, Ma Kilman, *qui pas ka guérir pièce*.[16]

Here the poet connects the French *blessé* ("wounded"), through an aural pun on the English *blest*, with the French word *pièce*. *Pièce* is also a sight rhyme with *piece* (as in "pieced together") for the English reader, and, by extension, *peace*, whose meaning also ties back to the Standard English *blest*.

Walcott first used Creole in his published poetry in the early sonnet sequence "Tales of the Islands", in which anglophone Creole cadences stretch the sonnets' metrical patterns beyond their conventional limits before redirecting their energy to invigorate the underlying iambic of Standard English diction. In the sixth sonnet, for instance, which starts "Poopa, da' was a fête!", the quatrains describing the speaker's carousing use Creole but the more introspective final sestet about "two practitioners of native arts" returns to Standard English.[17] At the end of the second quatrain, where the sonnet turns, the poet clearly signals a philosophical and philological tension between the disparate language registers in the grammatical lapse of the drunk, who also muddles the rhyme scheme when he claims to quote Shelley: "with 'Each / Generation has its angst, but we has none' ".[18] Although the term "native arts" seems culturally remote from "Poopa, da' was a fête!", the modulation does not seem forced, since all the language registers that Walcott introduces have their place in Caribbean speech. Indeed, most Creole speakers would agree that in Caribbean literary contexts, Standard English sounds inauthentic where it would not be used in "real life", just as the drunk in the poem sounds ridiculous when he attempts "textbook" English in a Caribbean oral context. But when the drunk lapses into Creole, he misses the ironies of his own angst, leaving us with the impression that the Creole-speaker is less self-reflexive than either the English poet he claims to be quoting or the Standard English–speaking reader. Here, as elsewhere, Walcott seems to imply that it is impossible to think in Creole – that is, to represent complex philosophical ideas in a language register other than the Standard English in which most educated West Indians, like Walcott, first encountered them.

One needs to be very careful when imputing such views to Walcott, whatever he himself may have said in an irascible moment. In fact, his position on language is a lot more complicated than a simple bracketing of Creole speech beyond rationality. In an interview with Anthony Milne, for example, he explains, "I don't think you can say that a thought is more subtle in an imperial language than it is in a colonial dialect. I know a feeling cannot be."[19] At one level Walcott is defending Creole's range here, but his claims for it as a language of reflection seem tentative in comparison to the categorical tone of his corresponding claim for Creole as a vehicle for conveying emotion. Later in the same interview, Walcott comments appreciatively on the ways in which enduring classics by such writers as Chaucer, Dante, Joyce and Synge achieve their greatness through their use of the "vulgar tongue", before lambasting the politically fashionable denigration of Standard English by some Caribbean educators for "crippling and limiting the width of a child's mind".[20] Then he again criticizes Caribbean writers who use Creole merely for humour or satire "which pretends to be nationalistic, but which [is] really poking fun at itself" because it implicitly diminishes the complex possibilities of the language.[21] His qualifications challenge fellow writers to extend or refine the ways they use Creoles. Nevertheless, that equivocation reprises the theme and limiting condition of Walcott's early sonnet sequence.

In his review of Brathwaite's *Rights of Passage*, Walcott comes close to engaging the possibilities of a different approach to Creole forms, when he singles out the poem "The Dust" for its technical mastery. Pearlie's account of how the "May dust" blocked out the sun over Barbados, after the Saint-Pierre volcano exploded in Martinique in 1902, becomes a metaphor for the imponderables of suffering in the women's experience and the region's catastrophic history.[22] Unlike the Creole monologues framed by Standard English commentary that both Walcott and Brathwaite favoured in their early poems, "The Dust" is made up almost entirely of Creole dialogue. Yet it delivers all the registers of narrative suspense, comic relief and self-reflexivity that the poet needs to convey. The dialogue first establishes the ambience of the social space in which the women interact, as well as the measure of their speech; its mostly anapaestic feet are interrupted by frequent line breaks approximating the lurching gait of the women's Bajan speech patterns, without unduly constraining the narrative flow:

> . . . How
> you, Eveie, chile?
> You tek dat Miraculous Bush
> fuh de trouble you tell me about?

Hush!
Doan keep so much noise
in de white people shop!²³

As the poem's tripartite folktale structure unfolds, the poet lingers over the minutiae of the women's everyday lives, which are bounded by the vicissitudes of their bodies, animals and crops, and the contours of the beaches and cane fields of the Barbadian landscape. This is what Walcott, writing decades later about Patrick Chamoiseau, describes as the *histoire* "of a very small territory not seen in proportion to 'the great mutations of the world' ".²⁴ Gradually the onomatopoeia – "*brugg-a-lung-go*"²⁵ – and the pithy folk aphorisms – "the body int dead"; "Mundee Dee Vee"²⁶ – with which the women pepper their exchanges take on a choric function, drawing the reader into the world view of the women, so that we begin to interpret events within the framework of their cultural assumptions.

By the time we get to the poem's final movement, which opens by reprising the women's activities – "you does eat an' sleep / an' try to fuhget"²⁷ – we are completely caught up in the rhythms of their lives. The May Dust breaks that rhythm. Although the metre is still mostly anapaestic, end-stopped rhymes now replace the comfortably meandering enjambments. The abrupt stops take the ear by surprise, occasioning an auditory confusion that echoes the cosmic uncertainty the speaker describes:

> An' then suddenly so
> widdout rhyme
> widdout reason
>
> you crops start to die
> you can't even see the sun in the sky;
> an' suddenly so, without rhyme,
>
> without reason, all you hope gone
> ev'rything look like it comin' out wrong.
> Why is that? What it mean?²⁸

These closed-off lines, shaped explicitly by repetition and rhyme, mark the point where the women confront the arbitrariness of their suffering. Their insight into the contingent nature of an existence "widdout rhyme / widdout reason" comes to us, paradoxically, via the poem's most conventionally stylized ordering of language. Thus, even though the women may be helpless to stave off suffering or to rationalize injustice, their human capacity for reflection and awe provides them with the cultural resources needed to impose symbolic order on the chaos of their lives.

Our only hint that the poet may have arrived at his own philosophical insight by a different route than the women have is the subtle modulation in the final lines from the Creole *widdout* to the Standard spelling *without* in the second iteration of the phrase, "without rhyme, // without reason". The modulation distinguishes between the folk context within which the women operate and the poet's formal education. However, unlike the ironic tension in Walcott's "Tales of the Islands" between Shelley's purported axiom ("Each generation has its *angst*") and the drunk's grammatically distorted emendation ("but we has none"), the tight rhymes connecting the Creole and Standard versions of the poem's insight suggest that the women's world view and that of the poet have indeed converged upon the same existential dilemma. The women work things out through a form of representation that they control: an oral narrative passed down from Gran to Pearlie. That process preserves the memory of a relatively remote historical event as myth, enabling Pearlie and her audience – as well as the reader and the formally educated poet – to achieve a shared response to life's exigencies.

In his review, Walcott also calls attention to Brathwaite's poem "Wings of a Dove", without commenting on its use of multiple linguistic registers. Like Walcott's sonnet sequence "Tales of the Islands", "Wings of a Dove" moves in and out of Creole – in this case, Jamaican Patwah – with Standard English carrying the narrative authority and the Creole, for the most part, confined to the equivalent of direct utterances:

> Them doan mean it, yuh know,
> them cahn help it
> but them clean-face browns in
> Babylon town is who I most fear
>
> an' who fears most I.[29]

But Brathwaite's Creole delivery diverges significantly from Walcott's. Many

of his short lines abandon conventional English metrical feet in favour of the
pure accentual verse associated with nursery rhymes and oral poetry – a set
number of beats organizing a variable number of syllables into a predictable
aural pattern which, in Brathwaite's usage, approximates the rhythm of a
drum:

> So beat dem drums
> dem, spread
>
> dem wings dem,
> watch dem fly
>
> dem, soar dem
> high dem,
>
> clear in the glory of the Lord.[30]

The pure accentual metre is most pronounced in refrains like the one cited
above. However, its persistent drumbeat achieves an incantatory effect that
infects the poem's Standard English authorial commentary. Thus the three
lines of free verse – "Brother Man the Rasta / man, beard full of lichens /
brain full of lice" – scan aurally as four lines of accentual verse, each containing two heavy drumbeat stresses:

> Bróther Mán
> the Rásta mán
> béard full of líchens
> bráin full of líce[31]

The poem retrofits its thematic allusions as well. Psalm 55:6 – "Oh that I had
wings like a dove!" – had been transformed in the 1960s by Rastafarians into
a kind of cultural anthem that spilled over into Jamaican popular culture, via
catchy ska and reggae songs by the Blues Busters and Bob Marley, respectively. Brathwaite's title, "Wings of a Dove", invokes all three indigenized
forms – the Rastafarian chant, the reggae song and the King James Bible –
allowing him to tie the biblical images of exile and longing to Rastafarian ideology and Jamaican popular culture. In this way, the poem taps into the wide
range of cultural resources available to Jamaican Creole speakers, including

(but not limited to) the ideological and aesthetic properties of Rastafarian speech. At the same time the poem resists idealizing the Rastafarian lifestyle. Infested with lice, half-crazed by "the moon / and the peace of this chalice", "Brother Man" is elevated to the status of "prophet and singer, scourge / of the gutter, guardian [of] / Trench Town" by the rhythm of his language rather than by the heroism of his life.[32] His pain, his passion and his irascibility are the authentic accoutrements of a man, not a god.

In his review of *Rights of Passage*, Walcott says of such poems as "The Dust" and "Wings of a Dove" only that they demonstrate "how masterful a technician Mr. Brathwaite has become".[33] If this first estimate seems to damn with faint praise, it may be because Walcott in 1967 still saw Brathwaite's achievement in conventional literary terms. He seems uninterested at this stage in identifying the myriad Caribbean and African-American oral forms on which Brathwaite draws to create the mosaic of responses to displacement that *Rights of Passage* attributes to the "New World Negro". Instead Walcott focuses on Brathwaite's general indebtedness to the "poetic documentary" form pioneered by T.S. Eliot, Ezra Pound and Archibald MacLeish, and on his specific borrowings (in "Wings of a Dove" and "The Dust") from Roger Mais's Jamaican novel *Brother Man* and George Lamming's Barbadian novel *In the Castle of My Skin*.[34] He commends Brathwaite's "wry, self mocking, melancholic" tone, which he associates with Hart Crane, but finds *Rights of Passage* limited by the absence of a compelling personal narrative that could provide an internal rationale for the long poem's emotional and rhetorical range.[35] Ever the consummate dramatist, he distrusts the overdetermined correspondences in Brathwaite's allegorical approach and teleological world view, looking instead for ways to motivate characters within the stories we tell about them. When one of Brathwaite's angry New World Negroes explodes into expletives in the poem "All God's Chillun", Walcott compares the poem's tone to that of Césaire's *Cahier d'un retour au pays natal* and quips, "We are pulled and nearly drowned by Césaire's tidal wave of exasperation at the stupidity of all men, including the 'good nigger', whereas Mr. Brathwaite often sounds like someone at a dance who is being ignored."[36]

It is important to remember that at this point Walcott was reading *Rights* on its own, without the benefit of seeing it in the context of the two other volumes in Brathwaite's trilogy. Because he reads the poems as a series of lyric moments rather than a collection of interlocking dramatic monologues, he seems to miss the possibility that the speaker of "All God's Chillun" is one of several versions of the New World Negro rather than the poet himself. To say that a particular character is whiny and self-indulgent merely confirms an observation the poet expects the reader to make. In fact, from the perspective of *Islands*, the third instalment in Brathwaite's trilogy, all the speakers in *Rights of Passage* are necessarily maimed. Their coping mechanisms, however brilliant, are just that, since they change nothing about their material conditions. Even when the women in "The Dust" teeter on the verge of transcendence, the poet places limits on what their language can accomplish in the face of powers beyond their control. This stands in marked contrast to the protagonist's quiet achievement in "Francina", a poem in the later volume, *Islands*. Francina saves an ancient turtle when a parking lot destroys its habitat. Rather than ordering suffering through language when confronted with loss, she takes action to preserve the material aspects of her past that give meaning to her present existence – a political solution that, on the face of it at least, seems to undermine poetic claims for language as intrinsically redemptive.

Read in this fashion, Brathwaite's trilogy derives meaning from its allegorical relationship to history and culture. It assembles an exhaustive taxonomy of New World types, each of whose varying postures represents one aspect of the complex emotions of bitterness, anger, resignation and hope that the New World Negro carries within him. After accompanying such figures on their journeys through historical and mythological time in *Masks*, the reader gains a new appreciation of the limits placed on the speakers in *Rights of Passage*. That new understanding becomes the basis of our re-engagement with the New World in *Islands*. Brathwaite is not so naïve as to try to tack a superficially happy ending onto the trilogy. Consequently, the painful stutter in the opening lines of "Negus" –

> It
> it
> it
> it is not
>
> . . . it is not enough

– which Walcott parodied so devastatingly in the BBC programme cited earlier, can be read as both an exhortation and an admission of failure. Few of Brathwaite's individual speakers in the trilogy are redeemed. However, by the end of the cycle we can place in perspective the whiny impotence behind the blustering rhetoric in "All God's Chillun", as well as the exquisite pathos that the dancer in "The Twist" wrings out of hunger.

Within four years of Walcott's initial review of *Rights of Passage*, the enthusiastic regional reception of Brathwaite's completed trilogy had begun to cross-fertilize a variety of linguistic experiments in drama, poetry and popular music, and Walcott was ready to extend the focus of his original estimate of Brathwaite's achievement. In 1973 his Trinidad Theatre Workshop mounted a stage production of some of the poems, including "The Dust" and "Wings of a Dove". In a newspaper article published just before the production opened, Walcott returned to the poems in *Rights*, this time from the perspective of a dramatist, alert to the language and music around him. Commenting on the "superb rigidity" and "precise economy" with which Brathwaite adapts the cadences of the spoken word in his poetry, Walcott now insists:

> Every exchange in "The Dust" needs to be spoken with the musical inevitability of a song, in fact can only be performed that way, by scoring it to the syllable.
> The half rhymes, pauses, and stresses may be lost on the audience, but the actors can achieve its transparency only by the singer's discipline.
> Mr Brathwaite in "The Dust" was not writing a play, but was the poet overhearing, as he is in another sequence ["Wings"] which owes as much to the feel of Roger Mais [his novel *Brother Man*] as "The Dust", in the fairest sense "owes" to Lamming [his novel *In the Castle of My Skin*].[37]

As a dramatist, Walcott now admires the way in which Brathwaite's rhetoric remains true to its folk models: in "The Dust" the old Barbadian women "quietly reminisce and as quietly hope", while the Rasta man's fulminations in "Wings of a Dove" are "no more stagey than the sidewalk passion of the wayside preacher or the destitute 'visionary' ".[38] As a poet, however, Walcott remains sceptical about the capacity of folk-forms to function as a basis for modernist poetry. In a 1964 discussion of "Negritude" he had already declared, "The mnemonic use of words, of naming things and blessing them by naming, is something which has gone out of English, since it is possible that the more complicated in syntax a language becomes the more its original impulses, worship and communication weaken."[39] In the 1970 essay "Meanings", he revises that statement to express a more personal limitation, when he consigns the mimetic elements of song, dance and storytelling to the side of his creative imagination dedicated to drama rather than poetry: "I am a kind of split writer: I have one tradition inside me going in one way, and another tradition going another. The mimetic, the Narrative, and dance element is strong on one side, and the literary, the classical tradition is strong on the other."[40] At this point Walcott was already innovating with Creole language on the stage, and he continued to see praising and naming as the primal function of poetry. Yet he seems genuinely unable to articulate how Creole forms affect Brathwaite's poetry, even when he picks up on Brathwaite's thematic and technical borrowings from other Caribbean literary sources.

Walcott's attachment to established literary forms cannot be dismissed as simply mimicry. After all, as he remonstrates in response to Naipaul in "The Caribbean: Culture or Mimicry?", all art is mimicry. For the true artist, the visible world is always already mediated by its representations. When, in *Another Life*, Walcott envisions the Vigie promontory across Castries Harbour, he sees the home of his first love, Andreuille, and the abandoned morgue that his mentor, Harry Simmons, used as a studio after the Castries fire. But he also sees Cezanne's ambers, oranges, browns and blues, and Dante's Beatrice, and he insists that these imported associations can enhance his representation of the world he inhabits. When Walcott relates Brathwaite's technical mastery in "The Dust" to the poem's debt to Lamming's prose and Eliot's poetry, he offers to his fellow-poet recognition as an artist – a person who, by approaching language and experience through art, succeeds in creating new aesthetic effects. For him, Brathwaite's incorporation into his poem of techniques borrowed from English and American poets, as well as from West Indian novelists, "is not imitation but a serious attempt at cohesion".[41]

From Walcott's perspective, one other aspect of this cohesion may have been the extent to which, in "The Dust", Brathwaite blurs the boundaries between verse and prose. Early readers of *Rights of Passage* championed "The Dust" on account of its proletarian themes and its use of Barbadian Creole. However, most interpreted its lack of a conventionally recognizable poetic form as an ideological attack on prosody, which – depending on their own ideological position – they either applauded or deplored. By contrast, Walcott's comments on the "superb rigidity" and "precise economy" of the poem's cadences make it clear that he appreciated the full implications of the poem's prosodic innovation.[42] As far back as the 1953 publication in *Bim* of the first version of the sonnet sequence "Tales of the Islands", he had expressed a long-term interest in "do[ing] away with the prerogative of modern prose in narration" and striving in his poetry for a new standard of "factual, biographical plainness" and "dispassionate observation", which he associated with the novel.[43] That aspiration had become a goal and source of anxiety. By the time *Rights of Passage* appeared, Walcott was struggling in his own work with the writing of first a prose and then a poetic version of what ultimately became his first attempt at an epic poem, *Another Life*. In a 1968 interview with Dennis Scott, he had confessed:

> I think – this is not being glib or fancy: My poetry is getting worse in a sense that it is becoming terrifyingly plain to me and I am afraid that I am writing – well you know that I have a nostalgia for obscurity in a way – I find myself at 38 writing almost so directly that I wish I were younger in terms of – well I wish I were more "important" or complicated.[44]

The appearance of Brathwaite's "The Dust" during this period, with its focus on unimportant lives – on *histoire* rather than *History* – and on language registers that, on the surface at least, appeared prosaic, may have strengthened Walcott's resolve to push on past his "nostalgia for obscurity". Brathwaite's stripped-down language set the bar for what plainness could make possible in poetry. As the first modern anglophone poem to integrate lyric, dramatic and narrative forms, *The Arrivants* set the standard for what, after Césaire's *Cahier*, could be attempted in the Caribbean epic – a form Walcott had always imagined he would establish. After the publication of *Rights of Passage*, the epic race is on. Even as Walcott is commenting drily in his 1967 review on the "astounding ambition" that allows Brathwaite to claim the collection as the first instalment of an epic trilogy, he is confiding to his publisher, Robert Giroux, that in the writing of his own first epic poem, *Another Life*, he is "attempting something never achieved before.... It has my own tone, and I can only hope that it would turn out unaffected and honest".[45]

III

There remains one other crucial distinction between the ways in which Brathwaite and Walcott approach language and form. Walcott shared a French-based rather than English-based Creole with his St Lucian community. More so, then, than for exclusively anglophone writers, his every move in representing St Lucia involved, at the most literal level, an act of translation. Describing how he stumbled over the poetic possibilities of French Creole while navigating the rigours of Latin scansion in the poem "A Latin Primer", he claims to have had "nothing against which / to notch the growth of my work / but the horizon".[46] Yet his path would have been equally indirect had he taken Brathwaite's route through Jamaican Dread Talk or the African-American blues idiom. Those languages share lexical components with Standard English, which the *bois canot* and *bois campêche* trees of Walcott's "Cul de Sac Valley" already have rejected when they hiss:

> ... What you wish
> from us will never be,
> your words is English,
> is a different tree.[47]

Walcott acknowledges his dilemma when he points out: "Today, still in many islands, the West Indian poet is faced with a language which he hears but cannot write because there are no symbols for such a language and because the closer he brings hand and word to the precise inflections of the inner language and to the subtlest accuracies of his ear, the more chaotic his symbols will appear on the page".[48] His first response to this predicament was to imagine the poet's function as "the old one of being filter and purifier, never losing the tone and strength of the common speech as he uses the hieroglyphs, symbols, or alphabet of the official one".[49] That challenge to the ear is more easily named than met for a poet steeped in the cadences of Elizabethan English and starved for textual representations of indigenous forms. Unlike the blind character Seven Seas in *Omeros*, who "saw with his ears", Walcott in his early work seems to be able to hear only with his eyes.[50] And he remains in turn both inspired by and envious of the ease with which other anglophone Caribbean writers can mine their islands' folk-forms for Creole effects that are more closely related to the English language of their poetry.

IV

In the wake of Walcott's adaptation of Brathwaite's poems for the stage in 1973, a new appreciation for the range of uses to which he could put Creole forms in his poems began to take root. Most critics associate this shift with Walcott's dramatic monologues "The Spoiler's Return" (1981) and "The Schooner *Flight*" (1979), both of which draw heavily on anglophone Creole forms associated with Trinidad calypso. But the real linguistic breakthrough comes earlier, in the 1976 *Sea Grapes* collection, where the poet experiments with the French Creole folk-forms of his St Lucian childhood. In this collection, Walcott engages Brathwaite's cultural project directly, arguing explicitly with the ideology behind Brathwaite's aesthetic choices even as he attempts to approximate their effects. In retrospect, we can read this volume as a way of preparing for the task of writing *Omeros*.

The poem "Sainte Lucie", in *Sea Grapes*, introduces several characters and thematic elements that resurface in *Omeros*, simultaneously grappling with formal and linguistic problems that the later work resolves. At the core of the poem, in sections III and IV, Walcott retails two versions, one in French Creole and the other in English and English Creole, of a St Lucian *conte* that he explains he once heard "on the back of an open truck travelling to Vieuxfort, some years ago".[51] The poem incorporates fragments of songs about a character named Corbeau (after the region's scavenging black vulture), which often features as a kind of Everyman in Caribbean literature. One storyline is about a shopkeeper called Ma Kilman who steals Corbeau's money. Another is about Corbeau's "horning" at the hands of Iona – "while you were in Curaçao, / I made two little children, come and see if they're yours".[52] A third describes how Corbeau comes to grief when he tries to make a living playing music. These themes of ambiguous paternity and the struggle to make a living, as well as Ma Kilman's name and trade, all resurface in *Omeros*, but the poem's true function as epic prolegomenon resides in its experiments with language and form, which are similar in many respects to those essayed by Brathwaite. For a start, Walcott relies – as Brathwaite does in "Wings of a Dove" – on a folksong to provide the core of the poem with its St Lucian rhythms – "Ma Kilman, Bon Dieu kai punir 'ous".[53] He does not reproduce the St Lucian *conte* verbatim but remains faithful to its tone and form. He also utilizes rhyming sentences that change subtly each time they return, in ways that intensify the narrative's ironies. When Corbeau checks to see whether Iona's children are indeed his, he says "pour moi garder ces mamailles-la!", but when he realizes they are not and decides to mind them all the same, his line is "moi kai soigner ces mamailles-la!"[54]

The poet's decision to segregate the French Creole and English Creole versions of the *conte* throws the challenges of such bilingual composition into relief. For example, the identical *double entendre* of the French Creole *corne* and the English Creole *horn* – used both as a noun to name a musical instrument and as a verb ("to cuckold") – allows him to translate "Corne-la qui cornait-a, / c'est Iona ka cornait moin" in section III as "That horn you heard / was Iona horning me" in section IV, preserving the pun in both languages.[55] But the English Creole version sacrifices the snappy tongue-twister effect the pun had in the original, a cost Brathwaite does not have to accommodate when he integrates Dread Talk puns or Bajan onomatopoeia into his poems without translation. The whole process of lining up the two versions of the *conte* serially feels laboured after a while, even though each section, taken separately, has its distinctive feel and rhythm. Nevertheless, for the first time outside his plays, Walcott commits St Lucian Creole forms to the page and experiments with techniques adapted from other Caribbean writers to manipulate them.

In section II of "Sainte Lucie", Walcott utilizes another of Brathwaite's signature forms – the short line, of which Walcott had observed earlier in his review of *Rights of Passage*: "The initial rhythm is faint, light, and studied. The poem, read aloud, subdues and arrests the onrush of its subject by closely packed rhymes, by the tautness of its short stresses."[56] Like Brathwaite, he arranges a variable number of syllables around two beats rather than using metrical feet of equal length, thereby forcing the reader to focus exclusively on the rhythms inherent in the Creole words themselves:

> Pomme arac,
> otaheite apple,
> pomme cythère,
> pomme granate,
> moubain,
> z'anananas[57]

What begins here almost as a technical exercise – listening to the Creole names of Caribbean fruits – eventually flowers into verse. As the list ends, the poet's anguished outburst "Come back to me, / my language" represents that flowering, paradoxically, as a failure of memory, as if, in the move from pure sound to signification, the language inevitably loses some of its mnemonic power. But the outburst enables new forms of hybridity as the list of names begins to blur the distinction between language registers, switching back and forth between French Creole and Standard English. Although the lines remain fairly short and arranged around two stresses, their frequent enjambment produces phrases of two or three lines that accumulate the familiar ten syllables of the pentameter, even though they do not yet quite revert to the iambic (my slashes mark the ten-syllable phrases):

> Evening opens at
> a text of fireflies, /
> in the mountain huts
> ti cailles betassion /
> candles,
> candleflies
> the black night bending /
> cups in its hard palms
> cool thin water[58]

The contrapuntal relationship between the short lines and the longer phrases preserves a residual tension between the sound patterns of the earlier Creole list of fruits and the more expansive reflective passages later in the poem, between the tautness that Walcott attributes to Brathwaite's stresses and his own, more lush style. The poet heightens that tension when he intersperses Creole phrases like "ti cailles betassion" between the lines in Standard English. Walcott thus varies pace and emotional intensity by combining the formal elements that the different language registers bring with them.

Beyond the anglophone Creole elements in the stanzas encircling the French Creole version of the *conte*, "Sainte Lucie" still begins and ends with passages fully controlled by conventional English diction. Here the language of the educated observer, tortured by an incommunicable passion for his island, remains unambiguously front and centre. In fact, his litany of Creole fruits erupts after he admits in the poem's haunting opening sequence, "I am growing no nearer / to what secret eluded the children / under the house-shade".⁵⁹ For a brief moment in the lead-up to the *conte*, the poet achieves the full emotional intensity of passionate belonging by successfully blending Standard English, French Creole and English Creole:

> I'm a wild golden apple
> that will burst with love
> of you and your men,
> those I never told enough
> . . .
> moi c'est gens Ste. Lucie.
> C'est la moi sorti;
> is there that I born.⁶⁰

But, despite the poet's triumphant tone, his is still a secret allegiance. By the end of the poem we are back at Dunstan St Omer's altarpiece in the Roseau Valley church, indulging a vision of St Lucia as the Garden of Eden, a vision that can exist only in the absence of viewers, "from time to time, on Sundays // between adorations . . . / if one were there, and not there" – like Walcott's poetry, which seems to serve his island best when it can no longer be heard or (mis)understood by the community it celebrates.⁶¹

The poems in *Sea Grapes* present Walcott's most direct concessions and challenges to Brathwaite's aesthetic project. Although they greedily incorporate many of the techniques that *The Arrivants* trilogy pioneers, they also push back against what Walcott sees as Brathwaite's privileging of African aspects of the Caribbean aesthetic landscape. In the poem "Names", which he dedicates explicitly "for Edward Brathwaite", Walcott remonstrates:

> Listen, my children, say:
> *moubain*: the hogplum,
> *cerise*: the wild cherry,
> *baie-la*: the bay,
> with the fresh green voices
> they were once themselves
> in the way the wind bends
> our natural inflections.⁶²

Like Brathwaite, Walcott employs the cadences of the Creole names for New

World objects to good effect. But he insists on respecting the European origins of many of these words, resisting Brathwaite's ideological preference for connecting the Caribbean to, on the one hand, its African past and, on the other, a posture of resistance to all forms of European cultural hegemony. In Walcott's vision, the region's inhabitants appropriate and transform all their languages of origin, asserting the creativity as well as the humanity that enslaved Africans and European masters ultimately share:

> Being men, they could not live
> except they first presumed
> the right of everything to be a noun.
> The African acquiesced,
> repeated, and changed them.[63]

"Names" echoes Walcott's sentiments in "The Muse of History", in which he derides the extravagant claims made for regional authenticity at the controversy-riven 1971 Commonwealth Literature Conference. Although Walcott does not name them directly, he clearly has in mind the self-consciously oral effects that Brathwaite's poetry had made fashionable by then, when he criticizes the cultural nationalist obsession with "the innovation of forms".[64] He seems especially wary of how such effects divert attention from the more understated Caribbean idiom he first praised in Brathwaite's *Rights of Passage*: "The normal voice of the poet, his own speaking voice is lost."[65] Under these conditions, "Certain performances are called for, including the fashionable incoherence of revolutionary anger, and everyone is again appeased, the masochist critic by the required attack on his 'values', the masochist poet by the approval of his victim."[66] Walcott's quarrel here is not with the use of non-standard language per se. Rather, he takes issue with what he sees as the posturing of middle-class poets and the "critic-tourists" who move "manically between the easy applause of dialect, the argot of the tribe and ceremonial speech" as if these were the natural registers of their everyday language.[67] That judgement, however, also prompts Walcott to attempt a poetic version of his own speaking voice in *Sea Grapes*, unencumbered by the exaggerated folksiness he so deplores, or by the elevated rhetoric that often colours his own poems in Standard English.

We can gauge how well Walcott rises to his own challenge in the wry swipe he takes at Brathwaite's trilogy in a poem from *Sea Grapes* that, with a nod to

Brathwaite's "New World Trilogy", he calls simply "New World". The contraction resists the nationalist vogue of blaming all the region's shortcomings on race, focusing instead on how the New World reinvents the human capacity for greed that motivates both white and black oppressors. An uncanny feature of this mildly parodic poem is the way in which it captures a uniquely West Indian conversational idiom. Though it is not a dramatic monologue, its tone evokes a certain kind of educated middle-class West Indian speaker, recognizably male, chasing rum with coconut water on a Friday evening. I imagine him affectionately heckling the solemn pieties of a Black Power poetry reading, à la Brathwaite, by volunteering an irreverent second take on its portentous New World imagery, its biblical allusions and its earnest moralizing:

> So when Adam was exiled
> to our New Eden, in the ark's gut,
> the coined snake coiled there for good
> fellowship also; that was willed.
>
> Adam had an idea.
> He and the snake would share
> the loss of Eden for a profit.
> So both made the New World. And it looked good.[68]

The parody encompasses the biblical serpent's diminishment to the status of intestinal hookworm, as well as the way in which the biblical "God saw ... and it was good" gets overlaid by the shallow insouciance of the regional obsession with "looking good". Moreover, the sly enjambment that splits the phrase "for good / fellowship" allows readers to hear it as *for good . . . or evil* or just *for good* – the preferred West Indian form of *forever*. Thus the poem reduces the serpent, that harbinger of mankind's fall, to an importunate hanger-on, like the new nationalist politicians waiting for handouts from their former colonial masters – or the masters themselves, whose departure *for good* seems always delayed by the prospect of another round of profiteering at someone else's expense. As a matter of fact, the poem's relationship to Brathwaite's trilogy is rather similar: Walcott, the laid-back "Trini" by adoption, throwing *picong* at the more earnest Bajan poet's industry, even if, like the snake in his poem, he privately "admire[s] labour".[69]

Like its pesky intestinal parasite, Walcott's poem feeds off of Brathwaite's. Indeed, it takes this dialogic context – one poet's response to the other's ideological position – to move Walcott away from his obsession with conventional literary forms. Stung into riposte by the need to demonstrate that there is an authentic language register between "the easy applause of dialect" and "ceremonial speech", the poet taps into a linguistic register closer to his everyday West Indian middle-class idiom than that of Shabine in "The Schooner *Flight*" or the calypsonian in "The Spoiler's Return".[70] As with Achille's quarrel with Hector in *Omeros* over a rusted tin, however, the passion just under the surface in "New World" places the reader on alert. Something is at stake here that belies the poem's artfully offhand tone. That something is nothing less than the poet's defence of his craft, his conviction that a more understated, colloquial voice can convey the unique combination of casual violence, benign exploitation and banal ennui that characterizes everyday evil in the Caribbean. From this poem's perspective, a histrionically self-righteous Creole rhetoric merely lets the New World Negro off the hook for his contribution to the ubiquity of evil.

Despite these reservations, Brathwaite is the only anglophone Caribbean poet whose formal experiments elicit a sustained literary response from Walcott. Such direct engagement is a rare luxury for a poet who sees few of his peers as offering him a calibre of writing against which it is even worth pushing back. Walcott's attempts to manipulate the spoken word thus have a complicated relationship with Brathwaite's experiments with regional folk-forms. He distrusts Brathwaite's politics and his claims for the organic verisimilitude of "nation language". Nevertheless, until poets and novelists like Brathwaite and Lovelace – or singers like Bob Marley and the calypsonian Spoiler, for that matter – made the aesthetic possibilities of regional folk-forms visible on the page, Walcott rarely attempted anything similar in his poetry. As soon as he saw their formal experiments, he could think of a myriad ways in which to improve upon them or to translate them into a St Lucian context or a middle-class West Indian idiom. Their experiments spurred him on to augment, embellish and invigorate his own poetic production and to purify "the language of the tribe" in much the same way that he continued to refine his classical models.[71]

V

Brathwaite's formal influence on Walcott culminates in the successive revisions of *Omeros*'s opening sequence. The final published version of Walcott's epic poem gives its opening lines to Philoctete, who delivers them in a stylized version of St Lucian English Creole. However, earlier drafts of the manuscript (preserved at the library of the University of the West Indies in Trinidad) reveal that he originally intended to open each book of the poem with a set piece about the landscape or action, written in Standard English diction and arranged in irregularly rhymed lines of iambic pentameter.[72] Manuscript 0564:3:1, for instance, gives us this version of the opening sequence:

> This was how, in green sunrise, they chose the canoes.
> On a cold ridge, as the hazed sea was waking,
> they stood in dewy ferns. Now their gaze follows
> the masts of mossy trunks, the top leaves shaking
> in windy light like the noise of emerald shallows,
> with that identical noise. Also, the slow, creaking
> branches creaked like the screech of pulleys,
> so that the running hills, the fog-thinned valleys
> were to these fishermen, extensions of the sea's
> early sound, and they saw the wind agreeing
> with their rooted judgment, the axes in their eyes,
> that had already hacked and trimmed the cedars.
> Columns are brought down, and towering cultures
> from the root, from the speckled blight at the base
> of Troy, the way those cedars slowly leaned towards
> the ferns, with a long, sideways groan, leaving a space
> for the new sky, where no sky was before.
> The fishermen leapt back, then, like barbarians
> storming a breach, or a beach where a breaker
> surges between black rocks, the fallen giants
> of the cedars were hacked in the joyous war
> of pygmies, leaving them bare.[73]

In this version, the narrator's elevated diction seems so remote from the characters it describes that the poet has difficulty attributing some of his more refined flights of fancy to the fishermen. When their "gaze follows / the masts of mossy trunks", we know at once that the conceit is the narrator's, not the fishermen's, since all along the narrator has been working the land/sea substitutions in his own descriptions. A few lines later, the connection becomes so attenuated that the poet has to signal explicitly "that the running hill, the fog-thinned valleys / were *to these fishermen* extensions of the sea's / early sound" (my emphasis).

The poet brushes aside such token nods towards the fishermen's imagination as he hurries on to Troy to connect the island scene to its epic model. His passive construction describing how "Columns are brought down, and towering cultures / from the root" effectively cuts the fisherman out of all significant action, while his ornate epic similes reduce them further, to "barbarians / storming a breach", stripping the trees in the "joyous war / of pygmies". Both pygmies and barbarians have their literary precedents; however, the poem provides no organic link between the St Lucian fishermen and these images, apart from their uncomfortable popular associations with derogatory ways of describing black men. In a subsequent revision, Walcott crosses out *barbarians* and replaces it with *gommiers*, the French Creole name for gum trees, as well as for the canoes made from their trunks.[74] The revision conflates the fishermen's strength with that of the trees, making the men equals in a heroic struggle with nature rather than uncivilized barbarians with no respect for the dignity of their foe. However, the move feels out of step in a train of images that stresses the unequal proportions of the men and the trees. Nor do the three equal stresses in *gommiers* succeed in breaking the stride of the iambic with the syncopated grace of the phrase "ti cailles betassion" inserted between lines of Standard English in the poem "Sainte Lucie". The isolated substitution of *gommiers* for barbarians feels like too little, too late, and the poet abandoned that line of development.

The next major reworking of the opening sequence is preserved three versions later. By this point Walcott has shifted the verse form to tercets and the line length to hexameter, borrowed from Dante but capable in the Caribbean poet's hands of suggesting the incessant, irregular heaving of the sea, "from whose groundswell the great hexameters come / to the conclusions of the exhausted surf".[75] He also has given the narration, in the form of a dramatic monologue, to Philoctete, into whose Creole speech, however, the original narrator's metaphorical flights fit awkwardly:

'This is how, foreday morning, we make choose them canoes. –
We stand in wet roots, while the ground mist was making
just like a snake, thigh deep in fern. We watch the noise

at the top of the tall trunks, their young leaves shaking
in the (cold) emerald light, with the same noise that the shallows
make in the sunrise. The smooth ones would be oars.

The heights was cold, boy. The forest shaft its shadows,
but our breath was smoke. We jam hands in our jacket
and pass the white rum around. We heard the valleys

of bananas below, and, when wind came back, it
was like standing in the very sea that feed us
all our life[76]

The Trojan War, thankfully, is gone, but Walcott has not yet won the battle with his literary antecedents. His Creole speech in particular remains in their thrall: "foreday morning", for example, is Walcott's translation for the French Creole *au bout de petit matin*, but in English Creole this is a Barbadian expression for dawn that feels inappropriate in a St Lucian context. *Boy*, as a tag at the end of a sentence ("The heights was cold, boy"), has pretty widespread usage in the anglophone Caribbean. However, because Creole raconteurs often use it for comic effect, the term has become a clichéd marker of the burlesque, making its presence in this context confusingly jocular. Such random imports of anglophone Creole literary conventions sound as jarring as the earlier draft's references to Troy. Walcott's most felicitous gesture towards St Lucian language registers is his use of the verb *make* in the Creole manner, as an intransitive verb – as in "the ground mist was making / just like a snake, thigh deep in fern". However, the land/sea simile he now transfers to Philoctete – "it was like standing in the very sea that feed us / all our life" – still seems laboured. The sound that the Standard English *very* makes, as it jangles up against the uninflected Creole forms of *feed* and *life*, is about as discordant to the West Indian ear as the Creole *we has* sounds to a Standard English speaker listening to the drunk in "Tales of the Islands".

Walcott still seems to be struggling with the problems of translation he encountered in "Sainte Lucie" as he moves in his mind's ear between French and English Creoles, as well as between both Creoles and Standard English, or between the classical precedents he hopes to embellish and conventions for representing Creole forms on the page that he has picked up from other writers. But just as Brathwaite channels the conversational voices of the women in "The Dust" – both by reading Eliot and Lamming and by listening to the women in the corner shops of his childhood – Walcott finally gets his opening sequence right by channelling Brathwaite's techniques and attending more closely to the formal properties of the language around him.

Walcott's most significant final change allows Philoctete to address a specific audience rather than leaving his words to hover without context until the poet folds them into his larger rhetorical project. This is the same dialogic move that made Pearlie's voice in Brathwaite's "The Dust" come alive. The tourists listening to Philoctete are already there in at least one of the earlier drafts written in hexameter, but they are relegated to the end of his monologue, where their presence reinforces the distancing effect of the Standard English narration:

> ... The trees had to dead. The ferns said 'yes'
> the moment the axe of sunlight hit the cedars
>
> and we measure them with the axes in our eyes.
> And that first stroke wound the <u>gommiers</u> into canoes'.
> So, daily, Philo gives this spiel to the tourists
> who keep taking his soul with cyclops cameras
> squinting in the sun, while he grips a hull with wrists
> as gnarled as a sea-grape branch[77]

The idiomatic incongruity between the self-consciously folksy "the trees had to dead" and the Yiddish-American colloquialism *spiel* leaves Philoctete's soul at the mercy of the tourists' cameras as well as the poet's intrusive omniscient narration, so that the familiarity of calling him Philo sounds patronizing; who in his audience could possibly be on such intimate terms with the fisherman? Presenting Philo's "spiel" as spectacle also harkens back to Walcott's words of scorn for those who celebrate anything and everything folksy: "The critic-tourist [who] can only gasp at such naturalness ... [but] wouldn't care to try it himself, really".[78] Moreover, the distance between the fisherman's language at one extreme and that of the narrator at the other, even after the tourists have gone, makes it difficult to discern who is agent and what is object in this tableau.

Once Walcott blocks in an interactive relationship on his poem's stage – among Philoctete, the narrator and the listening tourists – the poem can finally move freely between the abstract and the mimetic, between the part of his imagination that Walcott claims to reserve for poetry and the part devoted to drama. The new synergies thus created allow him to place his entire repertoire of oral forms and dramatic techniques at his Creole-speaker's disposal, without compromising the self-reflexivity of his opening sequence: "'This is how, one sunrise, we cut down them canoes.' / Philoctete smiles for the tourists, who try taking / his soul with their cameras."[79] In this the final published version, *sunrise* has replaced the anachronistic *foreday morning* and *cut* replaces *choose, make* and the earlier passive *are brought down*. Thus the violent action of cutting down "them canoes" now belongs fully to the fishermen, as opposed to the narrator or the Greek warriors of Walcott's literary imagination. Philoctete's language also draws perceptibly closer to that of the narrator. Thus, a few stanzas later, the Yiddish-American *spiel* is gone but the Creole phrase "the trees had to dead" has also been replaced – by the more standard "the trees have to die", leaving it to the line's rhythm to preserve its Creole inflection. That convergence of Creole and Standard English mirrors the narrative convergence of speaker and omniscient narrator through the mediation of free indirect discourse. Conversely, Philoctete's relationship to the tourists becomes less one-sided. Whereas in the previous version they *keep* taking his soul, now they can only *try* to do so, suggesting that the speaker too is an actor in this arena, rather than an exotic icon. Moreover, the cross-cultural engagement's final outcome is no longer a foregone conclusion.

The fishermen's relationship to their classical counterparts has also shifted. Like Pearlie and the other women in "The Dust", who understand cosmic uncertainty because they have encountered it in their lives, the fishermen grasp the metaphysical implications of their battle with nature. This is not because they have read Homer but because the task at hand is actually difficult and dangerous on its own terms – either the trees or the men are literally going to die. It is this mortal extremity, not the mere existence of a classical parallel, which gives an epic dimension to their struggle. The white rum, the shivering of the men and the leaves, the axes in the sun's rays reflected in the men's eyes can now function as both vehicle and tenor for Walcott's complex metaphors.

When the images of pygmies and barbarians return several pages later, they do so in the context of the immense relief the fishermen experience after having conquered those towering, dangerous trees:

> Like barbarians striding columns they have brought down,
> the fishermen shouted. The gods were down at last.
>
> Like pygmies they hacked the trunks of wrinkled giants
> for paddles and oars. They were working with the same
> concentration as an army of fire-ants.[80]

By allowing his barbarians to sit astride the tree-trunk columns, Walcott refines his initially vague epic simile to home in on a direct parallel between the historical barbarians' sacking of Rome's columned temples and the actual work the fisherman do to turn the logs into canoes. The rest of the opening sequence has already represented the forest grove as a temple of the fallen Aruac civilization. It is thus no longer a stretch to see the exuberance of the fishermen/barbarians who take down its columns as a sign of their ignorance about the civilization they are destroying, as well as a celebration of the vigour of a new race that in turn will leave its own unique mark on this landscape. Rather than mourning the ruins, therefore – one of Walcott's pet peeves about epic poetry – the classical allusion points to fresh beginnings. Similarly, the reference to pygmies, rather than invoking some recondite connection to a "joyous war", now focuses solely on the contrast between the stature of the men and the massive size of the *gommiers* before miniaturizing them even further into swarming fire-ants. This final image connects the effort still required to turn the logs into canoes with the ants' industry in breaking down fallen logs to create vast half-buried catacombs.

As he does in the second section of "Sainte Lucie", Walcott slips the French Creole *laurier-cannelles* into *Omeros*'s opening sequence to anchor his hexameter's rhythms in the cadences of French Creole speech. But this time, instead of offering a separate translation, he only inserts the English alternative, *cedars*, into the next line, where it helps maintain the metre. Translation in this context, therefore, is active rather than passive, pushing forward both the story and the rhythms of the poem. By the time chapter III assaults us with the violent Creole exchange between Hector and Achille – *"Touchez-i, encore: N'ai fendre choux-ous-ou, salope!"* – we are fully versed in the multilingual properties of the St Lucian discursive landscape.[81] Rather than hissing "*your words is English, / is a different tree*", the trees here utter "as one nation, // ... [teaching] their saplings: from the towering babble / of the cedar to green vowels of *bois-campêche*".[82] Like Brathwaite, Walcott now moves effortlessly between language registers within a single line. Not only does Achille express his anger in both French and English Creoles, the language through which we are given access to his reflections – "To go crazy for an old bailing tin / crusted with rust!" – also retains an unmistakable Creole cadence.[83] Walcott (or at the very least his narrator) is thinking in Creole!

Perhaps the most moving image of this perfected opening sequence is Philoctete's phrase "Dew was filling my eyes".[84] Walcott refines it from a French Creole expression that describes dew or mist, like tears, as actively "falling" or "breaking". In Philoctete's phrase, the dew's action simultaneously reveals and obscures the emotions that well up in him as he approaches his grim task through the early morning mist. The fact that Walcott derives that image from an actual Creole expression excises any coyness in its usage here. We hear it first as a statement of fact, even as, on account of the terse beauty of the image, dew breaks in the eyes with which we contemplate the page.

VI

Readers unfamiliar with Brathwaite's long association with such formal techniques are wont to credit Walcott with inventing them, and indeed, Walcott probably appropriated them unconsciously. However, without appreciating how *Omeros* echoes and refines Brathwaite's original experiment, we risk losing much of the nuance and richness of Walcott's achievement. In a move of consummate cathexis, Walcott instructs his readers on how to measure his achievement in *Omeros* by drawing attention to how Patrick Chamoiseau uses similar techniques in *Texaco*. Commenting on how classic folktale structures inform Chamoiseau's opening, as well as the poetry of Aimé Césaire and the Guadeloupian St John Perse, Walcott avers:

> Césaire's incantation in his poem invokes an island dawn, "*Au bout du petit matin*," just as Chamoiseau's "*Nous tait ka*" does. Join the three beginnings "In those days" (Perse in Guadeloupe), "At foreday morning" (Césaire in Martinique), and "We used to" (Chamoiseau), and you have the elegiac Caribbean memory, as calm as smoke rising from blue hills: "In those days, just before sunrise, we used to ..." [...] That "*Noutéka*," that "We used to," of *Texaco* is the real history, the *histoire* seen for itself of a very small territory not seen in proportion to "the great mutations of the world" but one bounded by small, thickly forested hills, or *mornes*, rusted roofs, bright bays, and bleached villages, and far from wars and changing empires.[85]

Extend the list of beginnings and Walcott might as well be writing his ideal reviewer's appreciation of the opening lines of *Omeros*: "This is how, one sunrise, we cut down them canoes." But the technique he commends in Chamoiseau is almost identical with the bounded "*histoire* ... of a very small territory not seen in proportion to 'the great mutations of the world'" in Brathwaite's poem "The Dust", in which a description of the everyday also unfolds from the mist of an island dawn.

In his 1967 review of *Rights of Passage*, Walcott had rated Brathwaite just outside that charmed circle of Caribbean writers into which he now inducts Chamoiseau: "There is nothing in 'Rights of Passage' that equals the fan-poem 'Cahier d'un Retour Au Pays Natal', or the sustained ram's horn splendours of Perse's 'Eloges' and 'Pour Feter Un Enfance'. Wry, self mocking, melancholic. Brathwaite is at his best."[86] The review adequately appreciates the challenge Brathwaite has mounted to Naipaul, pointing out: "Where Naipaul fumes with exasperation at the deracinated wreckage that makes every island a compost heap, Mr. Brathwaite picks his way through the wreckage, selecting broken artifacts, unshaped memories."[87] It commends the "refined, anguished sensibility" of Brathwaite's tone, "bent on achieving not power, but grace, not grandeur but sharp, piercing truths".[88] It even urges aspiring West Indian poets to learn from *Rights of Passage*'s stylistic achievement. Nevertheless, that estimate of Brathwaite's accomplishment seems tepid when compared to Walcott's fervent praise for Chamoiseau:

> I would press your book into the hands of every West Indian as if it were a lost heirloom, even on those who cannot read. After that formality, I would run through the markets with vendors in the shade of huge umbrellas, past aban-

doned fountains, stopping traffic with an uplifted hand, entering dark retail stores selling fading ledgers and disintegrating chalks, preaching, "You have to read this book, it is yours! It has come to reclaim you!"[89]

The language in this expansive tribute is deliberately hyperbolic, aiming, in homage to Chamoiseau, at a declamatory style that allows Walcott, like his francophone counterpart, to be "impulsive, elliptical, to indulge in that simultaneity which you call 'opacity' ".[90] Its almost sophomoric veneration has a lot to do with Walcott's anxiety that, to a Martinican ear, the less developed St Lucian French Creole probably sounds "cautious and awkward, enthusiastic, ungrammatical".[91] But until this time, Walcott, alone among the major anglophone Caribbean writers, had been forced to negotiate this unique linguistic tangle of English, French, English Creole and French Creole on his own. As he unravels it here, the poet also experiences a tremendous sense of vindication upon discovering how many of the technical and linguistic choices he made in *Omeros* work as well as or better than those in *Texaco* or its English translation. Even as he fusses about Chamoiseau's decision to go with the phonetic spelling *noutéka* for *nous tait ka*, and the translator's decision to replace the French Creole names for the trees with Standard English equivalents, we can sense his excitement at finally having a chance to wrangle with a fellow writer over this quadruple linguistic challenge:

> The word *gommier*, for example, translated into "gum tree," is not only the tree itself but also the dugout canoe manufactured by the indigenous Caribs; and as the tree, its sound contains the activity of a light breeze in the gum tree's boughs or branches; "boughs," however, is archaic, containing a mild assonance – "*gommier,*" "boughs" – but it is so right a sound for the Carib canoe in its buoyancy and elegant length, its riding and shearing of water, the carved trunk of the floating tree and the blue echo around the word.[92]

Walcott's elation in such passages arises from more than having encountered in Chamoiseau a writer worthy of emulation. It is also a measure of his linguistic isolation, which keeps a very vital part of his literary identity separate from that of an anglophone writer like Brathwaite. After all, fresh and expansive as he makes it sound, not even Walcott could sustain the hothouse francophone rhetorical style he reproduces here, in emulation of Chamoiseau, for the length of an entire English novel or epic poem without exasperating an anglophone reader. That rhetorical affectation lies at the other extreme from the unadorned English style of the "poetic documentary", replete with "biblical conjunctions" and "liturgical responses", that Walcott identifies in Brathwaite's borrowings from Lamming, Mais, MacLeish, Eliot and Crane.[93] Chamoiseau indulges the "nostalgia for obscurity" by which Walcott confesses he has often been seduced even as he disciplines his poetry to eschew its worst excesses.[94] Yet facets of the St Lucian French Creole heritage partake to a significant degree in this hyperbolic Gallic tradition. If Walcott discerns in the work of Chamoiseau, Césaire and Perse elements that he misses in his reading of Brathwaite, it may be because the linguistic culture that links St Lucia to its francophone neighbours is not wholly contiguous with the political history that binds it to the former British West Indies. The burden of negotiating those competing traditions subtends many of the virtuoso effects that Walcott achieves in *Omeros*.

It is tempting to see in Walcott's expansive tribute to Chamoiseau, rather than in his tempered praise for Brathwaite, a more fitting correspondence to Achille's eulogy for Hector:

> You never know my admiration, when you stood
> crossing the sun at the bow of the long canoe
>
> with the plates of your chest like a shield; I would say
> any enemy so was a compliment.[95]

There is, however, one important caveat: when Walcott celebrates Chamoiseau, he expresses reverence at a distance for a newly discovered hero, but the unspoken tribute that Achille never quite offers to Hector (it is, after all, the prayer he "could not utter"[96]) acknowledges a long, intimate history of personal rivalry and mutual irritation that resembles much more closely Walcott's relationship to Brathwaite. Then too there is Achille's discomfiting awareness that he may have stolen his rival's "craft" – a word that Walcott puns on throughout *Omeros* to connect the fisherman's boat, the poet's art and the Creole term for a sexually attractive woman. Achille considers himself a better man than Hector; after all, he has won the "craft" and survived to eulogize his *compère*. But he will never know if the child that Helen is carrying is his or Hector's. And if Hector had not died, the two men would probably still be quarrelling over rusted tin cans in the bellies of leaking crafts.

Walcott may consider his writing to have "a stronger energy, a stronger discipline, and a stronger drive" than that of his Caribbean contemporary, but he cannot know whether posterity will deem legitimate or stolen his appropriation of the formal effects that Brathwaite pioneered in *Rights of Passage*, or whether, for that matter, anyone will care.[97] Already these two writers' mutual anxieties about regional authenticity are being eclipsed by the preoccupations of a new generation of Caribbean writers. This new generation can take its linguistic and cultural hybridity for granted, in ways that nationalist writers of Walcott and Brathwaite's generation – with their colonial educations and their insecurities about their relationship to the common folk – cannot. When Walcott offers his allegiance to Chamoiseau, he represses an old debt to Brathwaite, even as he sublimates a nagging anxiety that both he and Brathwaite may be battling over what is merely "an old bailing tin / crusted with rust".[98]

Beyond their rivalry over Helen, Achille claims solidarity with his rival on account of Hector's mastery of the craft they both ply, "'Cause no / African ever hurled his wide seine at the bay // by which he was born with such beauty".[99] Despite his review's parsimonious praise for *Rights of Passage* and his poetic refusal in *Sea Grapes* of the ideology behind *The Arrivants*, one senses in Walcott too a grudging admiration for his rival: for Brathwaite's technical prowess, his willingness to risk mockery and isolation in pursuit of his craft, and his loyalty to a regional literary fraternity, whatever its shortcomings. Although, like Achille, Walcott refuses the easy pieties of class and racial solidarity, he acknowledges those things that he shares unequivocally with his West Indian *compère*: their passionate allegiance to their island homes – figured as Helen for Walcott, mother for Brathwaite – and their devotion to their craft. His unspoken accolades for his rival sustain a fervent hope for the possibility of a regional literary fraternity that can transcend insular boundaries and the ravages of time.

10

FOR WALCOTT

> ... This is why you have ended, to pass,
> praising the feathery swaying of the casuarinas
> and those shudderings of thanks that so often descended,
> the evening light in the shafts of feathery grass,
> the lances fading, then the lights of the marinas,
> the yachts studying their reflections in black glass.[1]

> peel your own image from the mirror.
> Sit. Feast on your life.[2]

I

"Love after Love" may be the most widely circulated poem in Walcott's oeuvre. It has been set to music in countless YouTube videos and expatiated upon (with varying degrees of calumny) by generations of students who have had to write standardized exams in Britain and its former colonies. It even graced the pages of Oprah Winfrey's *O* magazine in March 2004, complete with floral border and the magazine's recurrent heading "Live Your Best Life". Certainly its feel-good message – "you will love again the stranger who was your self" – fits well with the kind of therapeutic self-affirmations for middle-aged women for which *O* is best known.[3] So it may be outing myself to admit that, when I unexpectedly encountered the poem in the magazine, midflight between Trinidad and Boston, I was moved to tears before I registered that it was Walcott's work. I was overcome by "shudderings of thanks", like those Walcott says descend on you when the evening light filters through shafts of feathery grass as the sun sets over the Caribbean Sea.

But who exactly is this *you* we so often encounter with fresh emotion when we read a Walcott poem? Poem 14 from *The Bounty*, cited in my first epigraph, opens with an imperative – "Never get used to this" – that seems to call the unfocused reader to attention.[4] But it continues: "since that is all you need to do now at your age / and its coming serene extinction like the light on the shale / at sunset, and your gift fading out of this page".[5] Here the speaker seems to warn himself not to take for granted either the landscape's beauty or his God-given poetic gift. Alternatively, *you* grammatically signals the indeterminate third person, here standing in for all mortals who sense their oneness with the earth to which they eventually will return. Neither reading eliminates the original assumption that the poem is addressing its readers directly when it urges "you" not to take for granted the landscape's beauty or the poetic gift that recreates that vista through language.

The popular appeal of "Love after Love", the second poem cited in my epigraph, demonstrates the dizzying effects that such pronominal ambiguity can produce when taken to extremes. The images through which the poem establishes its self-reflexivity – the act of writing, the act of looking into a mirror, the miracle of transubstantiation – are embedded in a conceit about hospitality extended to a stranger or a loved one:

> The time will come
> when, with elation,
> you will greet yourself arriving
> at your own door, in your own mirror,
> and each will smile at the other's welcome,
>
> and say, sit here. Eat.
> You will love again the stranger who was your self.
> Give wine. Give bread. Give back your heart
> to itself . . .[6]

Like several of the shorter poems discussed in previous chapters, "Love after Love" first appeared in the 1976 *Sea Grapes* collection, completed just before Walcott relocated to America, and it can be read as his response to a series of personal crises. Walcott's second marriage was disintegrating at the time, and his working relationship with the Trinidad Theatre Company had fallen apart. The culture wars that pitted his work against Brathwaite's were still raging and Walcott was seriously strapped for cash.[7] The entire debacle was as much a consequence of Walcott's actions as those of his collaborators and detractors. Such tough times may have called for a poem that affirmed the possibility of future reconciliation with this ethical subject's best self.

Readings that see the rhetorical *you* in "Love after Love" as standing in for Walcott inform many of the online comments posted by students. They go back and forth about whether the poet is writing about loving himself or loving someone else, with the debate becoming heated enough at times to bring participants to virtual blows ("LEARN TO SPELL, DUMBY"[8]). A perspicacious teenager on YouTube enumerates with alarming composure the details of each of Walcott's failed marriages before pronouncing that the poem is about Walcott forgiving himself for betraying women.[9] Responding to another video that superimposes the poem on images of swans, kittens and sunsets,[10] "glasgowsteamboat" enthuses about "us[ing] the poem for my uni exam tomorrow" to demonstrate Walcott's feelings of isolation as a Methodist growing up in a Roman Catholic community. A post on a different site insists that Walcott is writing about reclaiming the white side of his identity:

> "Love After Love" is an extended metaphor for the reuniting between the two sides "give wine, give bread, give back your heart to itself to the stranger who has loved you". This quote is a beautiful representation of the overriding theme of the poem. Calling the 'white' side a stranger, demonstrates the neglect Walcott feels his fellow contemporaries [sic] have been showing. Saying that they should "give back your heart" illustrates Walcott's desire for reconciliation.[11]

Non-student commentators tend to bypass the autobiographical, poaching lines from the poem for greeting cards and T-shirts dealing with their personal crises. Although I have yet to come across a reading that positions Walcott as a breast cancer survivor, web searches reliably turn up posts claiming this poem as inspiration for moving on after a mastectomy or the loss of a loved one to cancer. Like a blot in a Rorschach test, the poem seems endlessly appropriable, capable of meaning all things to all men – and women!

The poem produces its radical indeterminacy by allowing its multiply refracted pronoun *you* to collapse the triangulation of speaker, subject and reader that characterizes many lyric poems. Its imperatives (*take, give back, peel, sit, feast*) suggest a speaker with transcendent authority – perhaps the embodied divinity of the New Testament who also commands his disciples, "Give wine. Give bread", or the father who recognizes "the stranger at your door" as his prodigal son. Whether these commands are directed inward at the speaker or outward to the reader, the syntax creates a hermetically sealed circle of reciprocity. "You" is urged to offer sustenance to "the stranger who was yourself", as well as to accept reconciliation with "the stranger who has loved you // all your life".[12] The poem even constructs the mirror in which the addressee encounters this estranged self, out of words and images that self has created: "the love letters from the bookshelf, // the photographs, the desperate notes".[13] At the same time, *you*'s focus on "yourself" also affirms the second-person pronoun's communal interpellation. *You*'s selfhood is given meaning by the loved ones who send or receive the desperate letters, the family or spiritual community with whom bread is broken, or the gaze exchanged between photographer and photographed subject.

The poem's final exhortations – "peel your own image from the mirror. / Sit. Feast on your life" – take the addressee back to the time before the infant divines that the mother's body, its source of sustenance, is not an extension of its own. In Lacanian psychoanalytical theory, the individuated self originates when the infant moves past this realization into the mirror stage and constructs a stable self-image through which to differentiate *I* from *you*. But the poem urges its addressee to peel this reified image from the mirror, to "feast on yourself" without being denied or consumed. We know from Lacan that entry into the symbolic order forecloses such reunification of the split subject. Yet the poem's proliferating pronoun *you*, echoing back to *yourself* across enjambed lines and refracted from multiple subject positions, represents that aspiration towards reunification so forcefully that readers, like devotees at a religious shrine, experience its message as a miraculous transubstantiation. *You* can indeed consume *yourself*.

II

Walcott's rhetorical *you*, like the other mirroring techniques he employs across his oeuvre, informs *Omeros*'s reckonings with posterity. It complicates my introduction's claim that, in order to constitute themselves as speaking subjects, the three writers I consider construct subaltern interlocutors in relation to whom they define their subjectivity. Unlike Naipaul's elusive *I* or Brathwaite's multiple personae, Walcott's *you* replaces the solipsism of *I and I* and the alienation of *I* from *me* with a pronoun that embraces the other, while stopping short of the total erasure of distinction inherent in *we*. Walcott's *you* also pushes back against a wider tendency in modernist poetry to limit the lyric's address to *I* – an inward-looking speaker who, according to T.S. Eliot, talks "to himself – or to nobody".[14] As W.R. Johnson explains, Eliot designated this form "meditative verse", and he considered it superior to the lyric's outmoded and somewhat disingenuous *I–you* dialogic: "For in Eliot's view the older meditative poets, when they pretended to address their poems, their sentiments, and their thoughts to another person, were in fact disguising their interior monologues by presenting them as utterances of praise or blame, as attempts at communication with other beings, as shared speech."[15]

Walcott distances himself from such modernist introversion when he replaces *I* with *you* in all the subject positions available to the speaker or addressee in "Love after Love". The switch preserves, even heightens, the authorial self-reflexivity that the modernists endorsed, but it also reaches out to embrace both reader and poetic subject as fellow travellers on this journey of self-discovery. Paradoxically, that embrace foregrounds the gap between *I* and *you* that readers elide when they identify effortlessly with the lyric *I*. In addressing both himself and his readers as "you", the poet forces us to register the transference that occurs every time we take for granted our identification with the lyric *I*.

Walcott's strategy depends on the multiple syntactical functions that *you* facilitates in modern English usage, as well as the way in which such functions interface with pronominal conventions in many Caribbean Creoles. Unlike the third-person pronoun – which becomes *he* in the singular and *they* in the plural when replacing a subject, and *him* and *them* when standing in for objects – *you* indicates both singular and plural forms of the second-person subject and object. Moreover, in informal usage, English-speakers often replace the third-person pronoun *one* with *you*. Caribbean English-speakers in particular invariably use *you* rather than *one* to indicate an indeterminate third person or to draw an interlocutor into the complicity of *we*, as happens in the passage from Naipaul's *Mimic Men* discussed in chapter 8, where the French Creole patriarch Deschampneufs expounds to Ralph Singh, "where you are born is a funny thing".[16] Walcott relies heavily on all these uses of *you* when speaking with interviewers about his poetry and his life.[17]

Walcott's signature use of the second-person pronoun thus exploits the ways in which the Standard English pronoun *you* resembles the uninflected first-person pronouns *mi* and *moi* in English and French Creoles respectively.[18] Like these Creole first-person pronouns, *you* blurs the distinction between subject and object. In my introduction I discussed how the tension between the uninflected Creole pronoun *mi* and its inflected Standard English counterparts *I* and *me* recapitulates the power dynamic between master and slave. The Creole-speaker re-inscribes his status as the object *me* in relation to the dominant *I* of Standard English whenever he uses *mi* to refer to himself as subject. Rastafarian Dread Talk's tautological doubling "I and I", to indicate both subject and object, challenges this hierarchy. But its impact depends on the listener's subliminally registering the power differential between the Standard *I* and the Creole *mi* that *I and I* subverts. By contrast, Walcott's recourse to the uninflected *you* in both Creole and Standard English contexts, especially his reliance on its syntactical function as indefinite third-person pronoun or self-reflexive first person, opens up fresh options for representing the subject. It destabilizes the boundaries between self and other, creating infinitely proliferating degrees of intimacy among Walcott's poetic subject, his readers and his authorial self.

It is worth noting that Walcott's poems rarely use the second-person pronoun in the manner of the traditional sonnet to express the speaker's aspiration to become one with the object of his desire. His published lyric poems addressed to loved ones tend to take on an elegiac tone rather than expressing a desire for greater intimacy. The direct addresses to Maman and Anna in *Another Life* fall into this category, as well as the "you" addressed in the poem "Islands", Walcott's beautiful tribute to his second wife, Margaret. Despite – or perhaps because of – the poem's unambiguous tenderness, such lines as "So, like a diarist in sand, / I mark the peace with which you graced / Particular islands" consign the relationship with the loved one to the past tense rather than desiring, in Petrarchan terms, a future consummation.[19]

Two decades later that elegiac tone recurs in "Early Pompeian", dedicated to the poet's third wife. He describes the young wife's suffering as she delivers their stillborn child:

> In their black sockets, the pebbles of your eyes
> rattled like dice in the tin cup of the blind Fates.
> On the black wings of your screams I watched vultures rise,
> the laser-lances of pain splinter on the gods' breastplates.[20]

The heroic imagery in this section of the poem focuses our attention on the life-and-death struggle of a woman for whom the speaker cares deeply. Later, however, the speaker redirects the poem's second-person address to the unborn child, leaving readers who are unfamiliar with the details of the poet's biography to wonder if the young wife survived her ordeal. The poet acknowledges the violence this pronominal shift implies, at the end of the poem begging the reader's pardon for "the pride I have taken / in a woman's agony".[21] Nevertheless, the pronouns in the poem's later stanzas struggle to meld *I* and *her* into *we*, dramatizing the poem's insight that suffering is, ultimately, a solitary experience. Since we cannot feel another's pain, we can only hope to transcend it through love:

> And what can I write for her
> but that when we are stoned with pain,
> and we shake our heads wildly from side to side,
> saying "no more," "no more again," to certain things,
> no more to faith, no more hope, only charity,
> charity gives faith and hope much stronger wings.[22]

These beautifully elegiac poems addressed to mothers, wives and unborn children use the second-person pronoun to mark distance. They also anticipate some of the roles that writing and nature will play in establishing the mirror in which the poet will encounter himself, his subjects and his readers. However, their use of the second-person pronoun is still a far cry from the intimate and indeterminate rhetorical *you* that Walcott goes on to make a hallmark of later poems that address his aesthetic lineage and legacy.

The poem "Exile" marks one of Walcott's earliest attempts to use the rhetorical *you* for purposes other than elegiac address. Unlike the poems dedicated explicitly to wives, children or deceased friends, "Exile" does not name its addressee, although many of its details suggest that its subject is V.S. Naipaul. The *you* the poem addresses is an exile whose writing reconstructs the Indo-Caribbean peasant culture he has left behind, until

> invisibly your ink nourishes
> leaf after leaf the furrowed villages
> where the smoke flutes
> and the brittle pages
> of the Ramayana stroke the mulch fires[23]

Walcott himself had no first-hand knowledge of the kind of emigrant experience he ascribes to this exile. Although in the 1950s there had been talk of his going to England to complete a graduate degree or to seek his fortune as a writer, he first visited the country in the summer of 1964, on his way home from an international writers' conference in Berlin, and he did not make the journey by boat.[24] As a regular reviewer of early West Indian literature, however, he would have encountered descriptions of emigrants arriving in England that were similar to the one he reconstructs here:

> Wind-haired, mufflered
> against dawn, you watched the herd
> of migrants ring the deck
> from steerage. Only the funnel
> bellowing, the gulls who peck
> waste from the ploughed channel
> knew that you had not come
> to England; you were home.[25]

These opening lines recall the first movement of Brathwaite's poem "The Emigrants", whose title and leading images in turn echo George Lamming's 1954 novel of the same name.[26] Brathwaite writes:

> So you have seen them
> with their cardboard grips,
> felt hats, rain-
> cloaks, the women
> with their plain
> or purple-tinted

coats hiding their fattened hips.

These are The Emigrants.[27]

The two poets approach their migrant subjects through similar images but from different angles. Brathwaite's poem emphasizes the flimsiness of the emigrants' material possessions, their inchoate aspirations – "Where to? / They do not know. . . . // Why do they go? / They do not know" – and the way their vulnerability reduces them to the level of animals being fattened for slaughter.[28] In Walcott's version, the image of the migrant herd ringing the deck, while still dehumanizing, draws the emigrants closer to other pastoral images through the bellowing funnel, the gulls pecking at the waste in the ploughed water.

More significantly for the purposes of this discussion, the pronouns function differently in the two poems. Brathwaite's "So you have seen them" positions the reader outside the scene in conversation with the speaker, as enfranchised observers taking in the spectacle of vulnerable travellers waiting like cattle in "patient queues" for their travel papers to be processed.[29] As it progresses, the poem redeems the emigrants' abjection by linking their ignorance and unpreparedness for what lies ahead to the excitement and openness to possibility with which "Columbus from his after- / deck" approaches the New World, "watch[ing] stars, absorbed in water, / melt in liquid amber drifting // through my summer air".[30] The personal pronoun *my* now situates the speaker (but not the reader) among the Caribbean natives watching Columbus approach. The poem comes to a momentary halt when the poet isolates the line "I watched him pause", near the end of the Columbus sequence, from the stanzas that precede and follow it. That hesitation invites the reader to fantasize about alliances among all the poem's subjects: among different kinds of observers, between observer and observed, and between the two sets of emigrants – one group from the Caribbean to Europe in the 1950s, and the other from Europe to the Caribbean in the fifteenth century.

Columbus chooses conquest over solidarity, "splashing silence" as "he walk[s] towards our shore", crabs scattering before him.[31] Meanwhile, the speaker, having abandoned the privileged perspective that the indeterminate observing "you" enjoys in the poem's opening stanza, now aligns himself with the 1950s emigrants. The "I" who watches Columbus pause morphs into a succession of first-person subjects assaulted by the stifling summer heat of the metropole, the impersonality of its technology and the artificiality of its inhabitants. Eventually these first-person subjects are subsumed into a communal "we" that links educated blacks in Europe to working-class Caribbean emigrants in Britain, on account of their shared experience of racism. With the reassertion of the self-reflexive "you" in its final stanzas, the poem comes full circle. This time, though, the speaker ventriloquizes the frustrations of a range of victimized subjects from the embodied distance of dramatic monologue:

> So what to do, man?
> . . .
> Put a ban on all
> marriages? Call
> You'self X
>
> wear a beard
> and a turban
> washing your tur-
> bulent sex
>
> about six
> times a day:
> going Muslim?[32]

The dramatic monologue's built-in ironies allow readers to gauge the limits of the poet's solidarity with that collective *you* "washing your tur- / bulent sex // about six / times a day". By triangulating the speaker's address among "I", "you" and "them" and shifting poetic genres from lyric to narrative to dramatic monologue, Brathwaite continuously recalibrates the distance between reader, subject and speaker.

In "Exile", Walcott's *you* occupies all the subject positions that Brathwaite's shifting personal pronouns in *The Arrivants* negotiate. Rather than watching the emigrants from afar, as Brathwaite's *you* does initially, Walcott's *you* encompasses his observing subject in the poem, as well as the reader observing this subject beyond the text. The first *you* travels on the same ship as the emigrant herd he observes, although at a slight remove, in steerage. Shifting the vehicle of the cattle metaphor to the "scarred leather" of a suitcase, the speaker divines that this educated *you* brings fantasies as naïve as those of the working-class immigrants to the moment of disembarkation, and remains as susceptible as his shipmates to dehumanization:

> Even her wretched weather
> was poetry. Your scarred leather
> suitcase held that first
> indenture, to her Word,
> but, among cattle docking, that rehearsed
> calm meant to mark you from the herd
> shook, calf-like, in her cold.[33]

The "you" here does not simply stand in for Naipaul, the objectified other. It also gives substance to the speaker's private anxieties and to a more generalized colonial angst. Fantasies about England as home motivated many ambitious West Indian emigrants in the 1950s, as the accounts of exile and migration in such works as George Lamming's *Pleasures of Exile* and Samuel Selvon's *Lonely Londoners* testify. And Walcott would probably have been the first to concede that he had shared such fantasies. Many of his poems embrace his "indenture" to the English language – a wound, as he says after his narrator's encounter with Plunkett in *Omeros*, which he had "no wish to remove".[34] Walcott's rhetorical *you* here thus locates itself somewhere between the *one* in "everyone knows" and the *we* implicit in "I, like you, have felt", even as it registers Naipaul's ethnic specificity through such terms as "wind-haired" and "indenture".

Like Brathwaite's "The Emigrants", Walcott's "Exile" shifts its focus to the Caribbean in its second movement. After the wistful ironies of the line "Never to go home again, / for this was home", the poem's rhetorical *you* does return home – imaginatively, by writing about a remembered Caribbean. Later stanzas recuperate the opening images of ploughing seagulls and bellowing smokestacks to reconnect the poem's addressee, as well as the emigrants in the previously dehumanized herd, to their pastoral roots, through the act of writing:

> And earth began to look
> as you remembered her,
> herons, like seagulls, flock-
> ed to the salted furrow,
> the bellowing, smoky bullock
> churned its cane sea,
> a world began to pass
> through your pen's eye[35]

Walcott reaches here for all the techniques of mirroring, empathy and imagination mediated through art that define his mature work. On the biographical level, he conflates the creative process of this Naipaulesque *you* with his own, drawing on his early experiences of homesickness, which spurred him to produce the entire script of his play *Ti-Jean and His Brothers* in a mere three days, during his first extended stay in New York in 1957.[36] Walcott channelled this nostalgia in *Ti-Jean* to represent his first significant move away from home as a rehearsal for the ultimate separation that death brings. Like *Ti-Jean*, the book that this poem's *you* is writing incorporates early memories and communal myth as well as reflections on the limits of mortality. But even as it does so, the ambiguous syntax in the lines "the earth began to look / as you remembered her" calls the reliability of these memories into question. Is the earth that the writer re-presents the world he left behind, or has memory revised that landscape to accommodate the gendered imaginary of his nostalgia? Like the islands fixed in the diarist's memory because they have become conflated with images of his wife, the act of writing inevitably reifies the lost homeland.

Beyond superimposing his memories of homesickness and isolation in New York onto what he imagines Naipaul's situation in England must have been like, Walcott integrates into his poem the still-fresh images of his encounter with a richly diverse Indo-Trinidadian culture. He had moved to Trinidad in 1958. By the mid-1960s, when he wrote "Exile", Walcott's explorations had taken him to the island's interior, where he would have encountered the cultural artefacts that his poem references: Bollywood movies, "in language half the country cannot read", purveyed by travelling cinema vans; flags hoisted on bamboo poles announcing the presence of Hindu family shrines; and the Ramlila pageant, a local re-enactment of the Ramayana's central myth. The experience affected Walcott's imagination profoundly, culminating almost three decades later in his Nobel Prize lecture's famous characterization of the Ramlila pageant: "Break a vase, and the love that reassembles the fragments is stronger than that love which took its symmetry for granted when it was whole."[37] But Walcott's rural Trinidad, like everything else in his writing life, would also have passed through the pen's eye, this time through his reading of Naipaul's epochal novel *A House for Mr Biswas*, which Walcott had reviewed at some length when it appeared in 1961.[38] Thus, although the poem's themes draw on Walcott's personal experiences and perennial preoccupations, its images are refracted through Naipaul's novels and its form through Brathwaite's poems. It is as if Walcott were addressing himself in a mirror constructed in part by Brathwaite, but seeing Naipaul reflected there; as if his rhetorical *you* represented both them and *I*.

The poem's structure also re-enacts this mirroring process. The way it repeats and transposes images of ploughing birds and bellowing bullocks and funnels has been noted already. Similarly, the "rheum-eyed windows" of winter become the "rheum-eyed" pauses of "the old men, threshing rice".[39] More subtly, "the bullock's strenuous ease is mirrored / in a clear page of prose", while the mirroring wordplay when the exile registers loss – "Never to go home again, / for this was home!" – finds its poignant afterimage in the Indo-Trinidadian labourers' fading dreams of a Mother India to which they too will never return.[40] Rather than securing his place in the bosom of an originary community, the exile's attempts to recuperate his lost homeland through writing connect him to a previous cycle of yearning and displacement. The poem's *you* allows us to insert ourselves as well as the not-yet-exiled poet into this cycle, imagining with him the yearnings and possibilities of a future outside the region, already apprehended through its expatriated writers' representations of loss.

"Exile" filters all these images of home – anticipated, transposed and remembered, but never fully inhabited – through the vapours wreathing from bellowing funnels, steaming cattle and temple offerings, as well as through the smokescreens thrown up by Bollywood movies. By the time we arrive at the poem's closing lines – "Your memory walks by its soft-spoken / path, as flickering, broken, / Saturday jerks past like a cheap film"[41] – Walcott's rhetorical *you* has extended to encompass everyone and everything through which the poem filters loss or possibility, without effacing each potential addressee's unique experience of that process.

Walcott deliberately plants many specific references in "Exile" that allow us to link the poem's rhetorical *you* to Naipaul and Brathwaite, and thus to other exiled or alienated Caribbean writers, including himself. The poem "Oddjob, a Bull Terrier", by contrast, works with more generalized representations of loss, so that its rhetorical "you" addresses the reader as well as an ethical subject internal to the poem: "You prepare for one sorrow, / but another comes."[42] And indeed, less than halfway through the poem, the indeterminate second-person address folds seamlessly into the first-person plural, when the speaker acknowledges:

> Your companion, the woman,
> the friend next to you,
> the child at your side,
> and the dog,
> we tremble for them[43]

As with the shifts in "Early Pompeian", however, the restlessly alternating subjects in "Oddjob" ration the comforts of shared grief. Although the speaker's rhetorical *you* seems more dialogic than the lyric *I*, something about it remains unremittingly singular, as each of the mourners must confront alone a "silence / ... stronger than thunder".[44] Over and over in poems addressed to "you", Walcott worries the boundaries between separate subjects, especially those that isolate us in the presence of loss. Thematically he suggests in such poems as "Islands", "Exile" and even "Early Pompeian" that the act of writing creates mirrored surfaces within which reader and speaker can re-encounter shared experiences. Syntactically, however, the second-person pronoun both distances and embraces the reader. Every time *you* affirms the privacy of loss, it risks pulling *I* back into an objectifying distance from *them*. Each time this *you* reaches out to close the gaps occasioned by loss, it risks effacing essential distinctions in a communal, amnesiac *we*.

III

In *Lyric Poetry*, Mutlu K. Blasing points out that the lyric *I* is a metaleptic figure; that is, that the sound *I* stands in for the "illusion of an 'individual' projected upon, to use Nietzsche's words, 'a piece of fate'".[45] She argues that this *I* does not derive its authority from the specific ethical subject it represents – Walcott, Brathwaite or Naipaul, in this study, for instance – but draws on the authority that a community attaches to the sound associated with the first-person pronoun in its linguistic code. We impute the existence of an authenticating subject with a particular relationship to the reader and to the poem's world when a lyric poem invokes that *I*. This happens even though the lyric *I* of modernist poetry so often "talks to itself or to nobody in particular and is not primarily concerned with narrating a story or dramatizing an action".[46] The linguistic conventions authorizing the meaning that we agree to give to particular sounds in a specific language ground the speaking subject's authority in the national, since "Native readers recognize both the necessities of the code as facts and their constitutive emotional history in that code."[47] Thus, Blasing infers, "they are predisposed to an acute personal recognition of the real-life givens they might otherwise feel as only vaguely concerning themselves".[48]

Blasing assumes that the speaking subject has a relatively stable relationship with a socially constructed, historically individuated first-person pronoun, when she propounds:

> The truth spoken in the language in which one undergoes the transition into words is "one's own truth"; it is who one *is*. The lyric "I," which has no reality other than its audibility as an "I," re-sounds the originary mediation of the mother tongue that makes the socializing/individuating history of a subject. The cultural institution of the lyric safeguards the site for the re-cognition of that lived history. The poet's personal memories and associations in the mother tongue are formalized and thus socialized as a generic discourse of a virtual "I," so that other speakers with other, different, memories and associations can recognize their "own truths" as socialized/individuated subjects in language.[49]

Such assumptions do not always hold true in a Caribbean Creole context, where the speaking subject enters a socio-symbolic order that already defines her subjectivity in terms of the object *mi*. Indeed, that internally focused *I* – which addresses no one in particular yet takes its authority for granted because it draws on a shared linguistic code – has frequently eluded the writers in this study. When Naipaul's first-person narrator in *The Enigma of Arrival* resists the historical identifications that would relegate him to the role of representative of his marginalized ethnic or regional community, or define him purely in terms of his autobiography, and when Brathwaite has to insist that the *I* he invokes in *Barabajan Poems* represents Kamau, not Edward, we can see this slippage at work. Conversely, enfranchised readers are happy to empathize when Brathwaite frames his emigrant's abjection by reference to Columbus's mitigating agency. Yet they are unlikely to "recognize their 'own truths' as socialized/individuated subjects in language" when the poet trades his observing, indeterminate subject position at the beginning of the poem for the embodied objectification of the *I* who watches Columbus pause, or the sex-obsessed *you* of the closing dramatic monologue.

Walcott too, like the rhetorical *you* his poem "Exile" addresses, has often been self-conscious about his ambiguous dialogic positioning: on the one hand, as observer and interpreter of a Caribbean creole community to which he does not always fully belong, and on the other, as a colonial whose subject position is one that readers beyond the region assume they can inhabit effortlessly. Moreover, as we have seen in previous chapters, when Walcott moves between language registers, between literary precedents and between perceived audiences, he often worries that his creative process is diminished to the level of mere translation. From Blasing's perspective, translation undermines poetry's affective charge, since only the shared linguistic code of the mother tongue – as opposed to the mere object that the language names – guarantees poetry's emotional authenticity. Her insistence that "Certainly, the sound shape of a poem, formally spelling the necessities of a specific language, cannot be translated"[50] is a lot like the warning the *bois campêche* and *bois canot* trees issue in Walcott's "Cul de Sac Valley", when they hiss:

> ... What you wish
> from us will never be,
> your words is English,
> is a different tree.[51]

Walcott's reservations about appropriating the Caribbean subjects he addresses – like Beauty in the poem "The Light of the World" or Helen in *Omeros* – thus may mask deeper anxieties about the appropriation of his own literary legacy by the colonizing *I/eye* of his Standard English–speaking reader. From that perspective, I read his recourse to the second-person pronoun as an attempt to pull both his provincial textual subjects and his local and international readers into the indeterminate subject position that he occupies. The strategy does not completely efface the lyric *I*. After all, the reader must presuppose the existence of an *I* who addresses the poem's *you*. Nevertheless, the pronominal shift exposes how the gap between *you* the reader and *I* the speaker never quite closes in a Creole context, forcing us to register the transference taking place every time we identify with a first-person speaking subject.

IV

Because *Omeros* contains both narrative and dramatic elements, it uses the second-person pronoun for multiple purposes, several of which have already been discussed. *You* turns up in conventional dialogue that advances the epic plot. It also signals the poem's subliminal address to other writers, especially Naipaul and Brathwaite, through its elegiac apostrophes to various fictional characters. But there are other moments in *Omeros*, like those in Walcott's lyric poems, that stand outside narrative time, where the poem, in Blasing's terms, "talks to itself or to nobody in particular and is not primarily concerned with narrating a story or dramatizing an action".[52] Such moments rarely announce themselves by invoking an authenticating first-person subject. The poet seems to share Blasing's notion that *I* is a metaleptic figure – a pronominal stand-in that is never quite identical with Walcott himself. And he has a little fun with this critical claim when he digresses during his description of Plunkett's war wound to make such distinctions clearer – or murkier:

> This wound I have stitched into Plunkett's character.
> He has to be wounded, affliction is one theme
> of this work, this fiction, since every 'I' is a
>
> fiction finally. Phantom narrator, resume:[53]

The poet also draws attention to the "phantom narrator's" sleight of hand when he points out how the authenticating *I* negotiates the distance between the poet's imagination and the words on the page:

> he plays tricks with time because there are two journeys
> in every odyssey, one on worried water,
>
> the other crouched and motionless, without noise.
> For both, the 'I' is a mast; a desk is a raft
> for one, foaming with paper, and dipping the beak
>
> of a pen in its foam, while an actual craft
> carries the other to cities where people speak
> a different language, or look at him differently[54]

In both these instances, Walcott's "I" is consummately self-aware of its provisional status. Moreover, even when the poem contemplates the community, it rarely restricts the lyric *I*'s consciousness to that of the narrator. In lines that channel Whitman's *Song of Myself*, "I" organizes the consciousness of an entire community:[55]

> ... I heard the sizzle
> of fried jackfish in oil with their coppery skin;
> I smelt ham studded with cloves, the crusted accra,
>
> the wax in the varnished parlour: Come in. Come in,
> the arm of the Morris chair sticky with lacquer;
> I saw a sail going out and a sail coming in,
>
> and a breeze so fresh it lifted the lace curtains
> like a petticoat, like a sail towards Ithaca;
> I smelt a dead rivulet in the clogged drains.[56]

An isolated observer, like Walcott's speaker in the early lyric poem "Laventille", might have dwelt on the foetid stench of the "clogged drains" rather than the rivulets they have choked, to signal a level of poverty in the face of which he feels pity, revulsion or guilt. Walcott's sensory interlude here, however, asks us simply to smell the way life abuts death, the way the stench from the open sewers that are still ubiquitous in some parts of the Caribbean become inextricable from the vibrant life we associate with the community's culture – the smells of fried fish, Christmas hams and furniture polish – and the iodine-laden scent of the sea breeze that lifts the curtains.[57] The poet's choral "I" here, like the chorus in a Greek tragedy, takes the first-person pronoun's function in an altogether different direction from its previously enumerated uses. It speaks less to the sensations and aspirations of a specific ethical subject and more to the way an imagined community celebrates itself.

You on the other hand, the poem insists, is real, both in the sense that the poem addresses its readers directly and in the Lacanian sense that it mirrors back to its speaking subject a reified version of the self. It also marks the reader's distance from and solidarity with the poem's addressees. Thus, even at its most self-reflexive, *Omeros* chooses the dialogic possibilities of argument, apostrophe, accusation, solidarity, communion and didacticism over introversion. Its speaking subjects address the reader or the poet directly, even when they are speaking to each other.

Walcott most explicitly defends the second-person pronoun against the modernist charge of disingenuousness when his poem intones "O Thou, my Zero, is an impossible prayer, / utter extinction is still a doubtful conceit. / Though we pray to nothing, nothing cannot be there."[58] Ironically, he gives these lines – which reject the idea of a non-existent interlocutor – to his father's ghost, which, along with the ghost of Homer, addresses the poem's rhetorical *you* to the reader as well as to the poet's fictional alter ego. As fictions within a fiction, both apparitions already stand at several removes from the reader. Like the unspecified speaker who prophesies *you*'s reconciliation with "your self" in "Love after Love", they occupy a transcendent space – none of the other characters interact with them and their presence does not advance the plot. Walcott is therefore under no constraint to fit either ghost into a specific role, beyond that of mirror or prism through which to refract his preoccupation with his legacy and craft.

Cut off in his prime at a younger age than the poet-narrator, and without access to the international opportunities from which his adult son benefited, Walcott's paternal ghost represents the poet's younger self, as well as his inevitable end. An amateur watercolourist like his son, and a dabbler in poetry, Walcott Senior functions as a mirror in which the poet can reflect upon what it means to be a provincial artist. He also lays down the standards by which the poet hopes posterity will judge his legacy. The poem thus establishes a self-referential circle, similar to the one in "Love after Love", that reconnects "you" to "the stranger who was your self" when it stakes out a dual role for the paternal apparition: as mirror and foil for his painter/writer son.[59]

When the father addresses his son's artistic duty and legacy directly after dismissing the claim that the poet's "thou" addresses nothing or no one, we can assume that his didactic *you*, though addressed to the phantom narrator, conveys a message to the reader as well:

> Kneel to your load, then balance your staggering feet
> and walk up that coal ladder as they do in time,
> one bare foot after the next in ancestral rhyme.
>
> Because Rhyme remains the parentheses of palms
> shielding a candle's tongue, it is the language's
> desire to enclose the loved world in its arms;[60]

These often-quoted stanzas use sound almost to elide metaphor. The dual denotations of *kneel, balance* and *feet* precede the connotations with which the poet's simile freights them. The pun on *feet* denotes metrical feet, as well as the bare feet of the women carrying baskets of coal on their heads. The wordplay in the command to kneel, which the women must do to hoist their immense loads onto their heads, also directs the poet to treat his weighty God-given talent with reverence. Both kinds of feet strive to maintain a rhythm in order to balance their respective loads. All these readings coexist in the first line cited, before the formal brokering of simile in the next line explicitly compares the women's gait to the poem's rhythms. The next stanza moves into a more explicitly metonymic realm, to subsume rhyme into parentheses, parentheses into palms, and palms into arms, through the repetition of sounds and serial displacements of a shape. Yet the language retains some of its unmediated naming power in the way that synecdoche allows the single word *tongue* to simultaneously denote both language and the candle's flame.

After the many readings in this study that have concentrated on how the anglophone Caribbean's three major writers negotiate their relationship to specific socio-historical legacies, it is worth noting here that Walcott stakes his most direct claim on posterity by challenging us to consider how he controls language itself, rather than evaluating the faithfulness of his representations. Puns, rhythm, metre and rhyme are all features of language that reside in the sounds words make, and, as Blasing points out, language's affective charge is inextricable from that sensory appeal. In invoking the coal-carriers' pacing and poise, the poet does not seek to advocate on these women's behalf or to augment their historical significance. The women's disciplined, balanced feet have already elevated their labour. Rather, he focuses our attention on the craft and grace to which he aspires when manipulating such semiotic properties. The poet's accomplishment rests on whether he can achieve with language what they have achieved with their bodies, whether he can live up to the demand that he "give those feet a voice":[61]

> . . . only by its stages
> like those groaning women will you achieve that height
> whose wooden planks in couplets lift your pages
>
> higher than those hills of infernal anthracite.
> There, like ants or angels, they see their native town,
> unknown, raw, insignificant. They walk, you write;[62]

Walcott makes here a simple yet radical argument for poetry: that the poetics of the poem constitute its highest reason for being. Just as we measure the women's achievement by the rhythm and poise with which they perform their menial task (the "grace of effort", as Walcott terms it in his Nobel lecture), the poet demands that we judge his achievement by how well his craft moves language itself – its tones, sound, rhythms, metre and rhymes.[63] And just as the repeated sound of *you* in "Love after Love" allows both speaker and addressee to embrace "your self", these innate features of speech in *Omeros* enable "the language's / desire to enclose the loved world in its arms".[64]

    The mutually encompassing relationship between language and the world in *Omeros* collapses time and space. I have already noted how the poem's use of single sounds – *feet, kneel, tongue* – creates the momentary illusion that it has eliminated the difference that subtends metaphor. Similarly, the poet's craft collapses the conceptual space between text and reader. Unlike painting or performance, the images that poetry helps us to see exist only in the mind's eye; its rhythms beat only in our hearts. Everything else is black marks on a white page. When the paternal ghost tells us that the poet's task is to "give those feet a voice", it names that magical moment of poetic transubstantiation when the word becomes flesh, when the sounds and images that the poem conjures on the page pulse in time with our living breath. And it asks us to judge the poet's achievement by this measure.[65]

When Homer's ghost in its turn addresses Walcott's fictional narrator, the poet expands the scope of his rhetorical *you* to encompass his future readers, as well as to place his work in retrospective dialogue with its classical precedents. Walcott invokes Homer in terms of sound – the sounds his name makes when spoken in Greek and the meanings those sounds convey to the Caribbean poet's ear:

> and *O* was the conch-shell's invocation, *mer* was
> both mother and sea in our Antillean patois,
> *os*, a grey bone, and the white surf as it crashes
>
> and spreads its sibilant collar on a lace shore.
> Omeros was the crunch of dry leaves, and the washes
> that echoed from a cave-mouth when the tide has ebbed.[66]

While echoes of the Latin *os* and the Creole *mer* speak to the poet's hybrid linguistic heritage, other sounds that the word conjures are drawn directly from nature. Its alliterative sibilance suggests the hissing noise the waves make as they are sucked back from the shore, while the repeated O sound mimics the way the hollows between the rocks distort the booming noise of the surf. If we think of this strategy in terms of Blasing's certainty that "the sound shape of a poem, formally spelling the necessities of a specific language, cannot be translated",[67] it becomes clear that Walcott is not interested in mere translation. When he chooses to address Homer by his Greek name rather than its English translation, he does not lay claim to what Blasing calls the name's "constitutive emotional history"[68] in the native language of the Greek girl who first says the word. Instead, the Caribbean poet domesticates the sound of the word *Omeros*, filtering it through his specific cultural experiences: his colonial education in classical languages, his Creole mother tongue, the legacy of slavery, the ever-present sound of the sea, even the race and gender politics of his casual sexual liaison with a white woman. Each of these experiences contributes to how this particular ethical subject experiences the word *Omeros*. Transliteration here intensifies language's affective charge. It vindicates the

Creole-speaking subject's appropriation of the colonizer's languages, which in other contexts has been represented as mere mimicry or abjection.[69]

But neither nature exclusively nor language accounts for the properties of the sound with which the word *Omeros* begins. Produced in nature by human agency, the amplified breathing sound that the blown conch shell makes to announce dawn or to call the community together in times of crisis seems to transcend speech and subjectivity. In Walcott's usage, it becomes the originary breath of his epic poem, the apostrophe that inaugurates language's attempt to enclose the world in its arms:

> O open this day with the conch's moan, Omeros,
> as you did in my boyhood, when I was a noun
> gently exhaled from the palate of the sunrise.
> . . .
> . . . Only in you, across centuries
> of the sea's parchment atlas, can I catch the noise
> of the surf lines wandering like the shambling fleece
>
> of the lighthouse's flock[70]

The randomly alternating open and closed O sounds in the progression "O – open – conch – moan – Omeros – boy – hood – noun" in the first tercet quoted above find their distorted echo in the fluctuating A sounds in the last line of the tercet, as well as in the tercet that follows in my citation, until the O sounds resurface at the opening of the final tercet cited. That pattern repeats itself for much of the rest of this canto, so that, if we listen carefully to those alternating Os and As, we can almost hear the poem, like the blower of the conch shell, breathing.

The echoing sounds within chapter II, in which the conch summons Omeros, and the echoes between chapter II and chapter LVI, in which the bard finally responds, inscribe on an epic scale the kinds of mirroring techniques that Walcott employs more generally in his lyric poems. The two scenes take place at the same location on the St Lucian shore, and aurally, the O and A sounds in each chapter expand and contract in similar ways. However, by the time Homer's ghost resurfaces (literally!) in chapter LVI, the poet has had time to develop all the sensory associations that accrue to the St Lucian landscape in the course of his poem. His rhythms in chapter

LVI, therefore, come freighted with associations that echo far beyond the images and scenes from chapter II, and even beyond the poem itself. Like the sound of incoming surf, these rhythms convey a sense of portentous anticipation:

> ... I heard a moan from the village
> of a blowing conch, and I saw the first canoe
> on the horizon's glittering scales. The old age
>
> of the wrinkled sea was in that moan, and I knew
> that the floating head had drifted here. The mirrors
> of the sky were clouded ...[71]

As in the Revelation of Saint John the Divine, whose cadences inform the poem's syntax here – "And I heard a voice from heaven say, Write!" (Revelations 14:13) – the urgency builds from the repeated verbs of witness in the passage cited – "I heard", "And I saw", "and I knew".[72] However, the narrator in this case does not hear the transcendent voice of God or receive his prophecy from heaven:

> ... and I heard my own voice
> correcting his name, as the surf hissed: "Omeros."
> The moment I named it, the marble head arose,
> fringed with its surf curls and beard, the hollow shoulders
>
> of a man waist-high in water with an old leather
> goatskin or a plastic bag, pricking the dog's ears,
> making it whine with joy.[73]

Having substituted his voice for the voice of God, the phantom narrator moves readers between images of Homer's bust, "marble with a dripping chiton"; of Seven Seas, the "foam-headed fisherman"; and the blind St Omere "in his white, torn / undershirt", making it clear that he fully controls all the magical transformations, translations and transubstantiations to which we have borne witness.[74] Thus, even as Walcott pays his dues to Homer, his direct appeal to the master becomes a challenge. It throws down the gauntlet to the epic tradition, demanding that we take note of how his poetic intervention echoes and distorts that tradition in much the same way that the hollows in the rocks along the Caribbean coast distort the sound of the sea.

As Walcott's phantom narrator wrangles with Homer's ghost over the meanings of their respective literary legacies, both poetic apparitions direct their second-person address to the reader, as well as to each other. Walcott first uses their dialogue to address the problem of obscurity in his poetry. When the narrator admits shamefacedly to never having read the Homeric epics in their entirety, because he found their mythical underpinnings impenetrable – " 'The gods and the demi-gods aren't much use to us' " – Omeros sets him and the reader straight: " 'Forget the gods,' Omeros growled, 'and read the rest.' "[75] The message to Walcott's readers here is hard to miss. Whether we are intimidated by the length of *Omeros*, its many literary allusions or its provincial specificities, the poem demands that we read "the rest". The poet defines that *rest* in several ways. First, his narrator describes to Omeros what, as a child, he took away from his early encounter with a massive epic work that eluded full comprehension:

> . . . when I was a boy
>
> your name was as wide as a bay, as I walked along
> the curled brow of the surf; the word 'Homer' meant joy,
> joy in battle, in work, in death, then the numbered peace
>
> of the surf's benedictions, it rose in the cedars,
> in the *laurier-cannelles*, pages of rustling trees.
> Master, I was the freshest of all your readers.[76]

In these lines, Walcott once again directs readers' attention to the aesthetic properties of sheer sound: the ways that rhythms in language – even in languages we do not fully understand – can transport the listener. The patterns these sounds create facilitate the relationship in poetry between action and emotion, producing a counterintuitive elation even when its themes are dire: "joy in battle, in work, in death".[77] But the Greek bard insists in response that a "girl smells better than a book" and "Her image rises out of every battle's noise".[78] Rather than reading such lines as conveying only a crassly objectified notion of femininity, I see them as also asserting the ways in which, for Walcott, lived relationships trump abstract aestheticism. At the very least, these lines acknowledge that art can attain its full value only in the service of such relationships. Finally, Homer's ghost extends this claim even further, by pointing out how the highest bond a poem can aspire to represent is a communal one, rather than merely the romantic bond between two individuals, the Petrarchan desire to become one with the beloved: "Love is good, but the love of your own people is // greater".[79] Through these exchanges between Omeros and the narrator, Walcott arranges poetry's virtues in ascending order: joy in battle, work and death; love for the beloved; and a greater love for your own people. He asks us to gauge the intimacy and expansiveness of his literary legacy according to how well it embodies these virtues.

Omeros's astounding ambition to enclose the loved world in its arms excludes no rival, master or lover. The poet acknowledges his debt to Homer when he declares, "That's why I walk behind you".[80] But in doing so he positions himself as Homer's successor, rather than his imitator or translator. In a final act of emulation and appropriation, the phantom narrator joins Omeros in reciting lines that could have opened a chapter in *The Odyssey* – "'In the mist of the sea there is a horned island / with deep green harbours where the Greek ships anchor'"[81] – only to have the bard's voice merge with his in praise of the Antilles:

> "It was a place of light with luminous valleys
>
> under thunderous clouds. A Genoan wanderer
> saying the beads of the Antilles named the place
> for a blinded saint. Later, others would name her
>
> for a wild wife. Her mountains tinkle with springs
> among moss-bearded forests, and the screeching of birds
> stitches its tapestry.[82]

As the poets' joint recitation progresses, images that we have followed all through Walcott's epic poem begin to dominate. We still hear echoes of Homer in the way the recitation reminds us that the island named St Lucia, "for a blinded saint", has also been nicknamed Helen, "for a wild wife" over whom armies came to blows. At the same time, however, we begin to pick up echoes of Walcott's own words earlier in *Omeros*. Maud's tapestry of birds screeches to life; the tinkling spring water and the moss-bearded trees hearken back to Philoctete's opening description of the forest in which the fishermen cut down trees for their canoes. Having already established the associations we bring to these words, the poem is free to cite itself, to repurpose the images it has brought to life even as it refurbishes those it borrows from Homer.

V

A poem on the scale of *Omeros* can defeat even the most sustained attention. Yet even if we despair of charting the appearance of every swift that darts through its pages, or every time its manipulation of assonance and alliteration makes the sounds in the word *Omeros* hiss and echo, we cannot fail to respond to the cumulative power of that repetition. Helen's beauty and the rivalry over her, for instance, are never far away when the poet invokes Castries Harbour through the image of a horned bay. Moreover, almost any passage from *Omeros* can be parsed for the moments when it refracts another of Walcott's works. My earlier discussion of how the long poem "Sainte Lucie" in *Sea Grapes* anticipates the shifting linguistic codes in *Omeros* provides one such example. The Whitmanesque passage about the smells of Christmas ham and furniture polish and foetid drains, cited earlier to distinguish among the uses to which Walcott puts the pronoun *I* in *Omeros*, is another case in point. Its sensory impressions distil the emotions conveyed in "The Three Musicians", a ballad from *The Arkansas Testament* that describes the annual Christmas preparations a childless couple makes. Conversely, this couple's private grief over their barrenness is amplified in the passages in *Omeros* surrounding Plunkett's inability to conceive an heir. Indeed, any close reading of *Omeros* must come to terms with the sheer plethora of recycled lines, images and phrases that Walcott weaves into his epic poem. Eventually, like the speaker in "Islands", we come to trust the poem's rendering of its Caribbean landscapes, because we, like the poem's characters, "have loved in them".[83] With fully realized characters in a story to connect us to specific places, we can develop a richly textured sense of Caribbean topography that a casual reader of a single lyric poem might miss. *Omeros* thus gives Walcott the grand canvas he needs to develop many of the images, sounds and rhythms that his shorter lyric poems, perforce, have to circumscribe.

Repetition has its pitfalls, however, and Walcott has always been aware of these. Looking back at the work of his middle period in an interview with Edward Hirsch (during which he repeatedly invokes the rhetorical *you*), the poet reflects:

> There's a vague period in any poet's life between thirty and forty that is crucial because you can either keep working in one direction, or you can look back on your earlier work as juvenilia, a nice thing to look at from a distance. . . . Yet you also have the fear that your work really has been basically mediocre, a failure, predictable. You find yourself at a point at which you say, ah, so you have become exactly what you were afraid of becoming: this person, this writer, with a certain name and a certain thing expected of you, and you are fulfilling that mold.[84]

Walcott is here discussing the 1970s, when he began to transition away from the Caribbean to America – the period whose concerns he captures so well in the *Sea Grapes* volume, with all its regrets and hopes for the future, summed up in the prophetic lines with which "Love after Love" opens: "The time will come / when, with elation, / you will greet yourself".[85] With the completion of *Omeros*, Walcott may have felt that this time had come, and that his stated ambition to fulfil "Adam's task of giving things their names" had been achieved.[86] The poems in *The Bounty*, the collection Walcott published after *Omeros*, challenge us to take that achievement for granted. Having attained his rhyme's ambition to enclose the world in its arms, Walcott seems to feel entitled to follow his earlier poem's command to "peel your own image from the mirror. / Sit. Feast on your life."[87]

Yet when Walcott followed *Omeros*'s epic accomplishment – and the Nobel Prize it netted him – with a collection of elegies mourning his mother and the loss of friends, "dying / as if from some medieval plague",[88] some prominent reviewers found the new work anticlimactic. Its repetition of well-worn images did not sit well next to its obscure references to people nobody who read the *New York Times* had ever heard of. Moreover, its tone of constant lament seemed the work of an old man who had spent himself in one final brilliant burst of creativity and had little left to give.[89] We know now that Walcott would go on to write some of his finest verse after *Omeros*, but *The Bounty* was no false start. Its unrelievedly elegiac tone masked a deeper elation. To read the poems in this short collection after having read *Omeros* is to re-encounter every previous image in Walcott's poetry. Like colonials who, on seeing England for the first time, recognize its buildings, its vegetation and even the quality of its light from years of immersion in English literature, we readers of *Omeros* recognize locations in *The Bounty* that we have never visited and vistas we have never seen. Not only does Walcott's art in this collection seem almost to eclipse the world it represents, at a deeper level, the world we re-encounter through the poems cannot be said to have existed before Walcott created it in language.

Walcott had postulated just before *Omeros*'s publication that landscapes exist only after they have been represented in art. In a 1986 BBC interview he explains why, as a colonial reared on British literature, for him the names for English trees were imbued with a poetic resonance that the words for tropical vegetation lacked:

> I think the difference lay not in a longing to see elms and oaks, really. The point was the alleged embarrassment . . . the presumed inferiority of mangoes next to elms or palm trees next to eucalyptus or pines . . . those things are named by the literature. Somebody in Warwickshire who says elm says elm, but if Shakespeare says elm then that's a noble tree. The difference simply is that there was no articulating of that vegetation. It was not sanctified by literature. . . . But the people of my generation . . . who hesitated on the fringe of writing down the word breadfruit, on the fringe of writing down the word mango, didn't mean that the mango was not a beautiful tree. . . . the penalty of colonialism was the mango couldn't possibly have the dignity of an oak, in the same way that a black West Indian could not possibly have the dignity of an Englishman in Warwickshire.[90]

The sounds of *elm* and *oak*, in Walcott's example, are not without resonance in the Caribbean context. If anything, they suffer from an excess of signification; they are freighted not only with the virtues and passions that English literature associates with them but also with the feelings of inadequacy that overwhelm colonized readers when they encounter them in literature. Such readers recognize the values and emotions those sounds convey but locate them beyond the expressive capacities of their world. Conversely, the breadfruit, from the colonial's perspective, is no blank slate either. Unnamed in poetry, the contours of its leaves are invisible. On the page they become risible at best, and at worst, a source of deep humiliation.

Walcott's observations thus add a fresh caveat to Blasing's claims for the affective limits of poetry in languages other than the native tongue. The Creole-speaking subject's double consciousness ensures that the separate languages of art and everyday life signify doubly and differently, facilitating no straightforward contiguity between sign and signifier. Walcott addresses this dilemma in the epigraph to "The Divided Child" in *Another Life*, when he recycles an observation from Malraux's *Psychology of Art* about the artist Cimabue admiring the shepherd boy Giotto sketching sheep: "But, according to the true biographies, it is never the sheep that inspire a Giotto with the love of painting: but, rather, his first sight of the paintings of such a man as Cimabue. What makes the artist is the circumstance that in his youth he was more deeply moved by the sight of works of art than by that of the things which they portray."[91] The poet whose development Walcott portrays in *Another Life*, however, does not have the luxury of merely copying other artists' representations of nature. The works of art by which he was first moved represented sheep to him in a world where only goats existed, and elms in a vista populated with breadfruit trees. *Another Life* demonstrates how, in order to move through art to the representation of his own reality, the young poet either made Negro heads "woolly", as other Caribbean writers had done, or transposed the techniques used to represent sheep onto the representation of goats. After *Omeros*, the mature poet could experiment with a third alternative; having established a rich repertoire of images to represent his world, he could attempt to copy those. He could play Cimabue to his own Giotto. Thematically and formally, the poems in *The Bounty* engage that method.

VI

The Bounty shares its name with Captain Bligh's ill-fated ship, which first attempted to transport breadfruit-tree cuttings from Tahiti to the Caribbean to feed enslaved Africans. Together with other such foreign imports as the mango, the coconut and the banana, these trees are now so ubiquitous in the Caribbean that they define the landscape Walcott describes.[92] Parallelling this originary moment of repetition, Walcott also uses the idea of bounty to represent, in Wordsworth's famous phrase, "the spontaneous overflow of powerful feelings" that his mother's death released in him. And he draws on the bounty of his own poetic repertoire to do so. One mourning poem for his mother repurposes the images associated with the chorus of forest creatures that frame the action in *Ti-Jean and His Brothers*, in which Walcott uses the death of Ti-Jean's mother to contemplate the limits of mortality:

> Bounty!
>   In the bells of tree-frogs with their steady clamour
> in the indigo dark before dawn, the fading morse
> of fireflies and crickets, then light on the beetle's armour,
>
> and the toad's too-late presages, nettles of remorse
> that shall spring from her grave from the spade's heartbreak.
> And yet not to have loved her enough is to love more,
>
> if I confess it, and I confess it.[93]

The poems mourning Alix Walcott are raw with grief, but despite their many intertextual allusions they share an unfettered ease of tone. There is none of the self-conscious deference and lining up of parallels between the Caribbean and Europe that marked the appearance of "Thomas Alva Lawrence's dead child" in *Another Life* as a symbol of untimely death.[94] They invoke the English poet John Clare as savagely and hyperbolically as they ventriloquize Walcott's *Ti-Jean*. Another poem draws unabashedly on a reference in Yeats's work to "the bounty of Sweden". The reference connects the financial stability that both Yeats and Walcott secured by winning Nobel Prizes to the good fortune of their being able to live surrounded by the bounteous landscapes that inspired their poetry:

>   ... No bounty is greater
> than walking to the edge of the rocks where the headland's
> detonations exult in their natural metre,
> like white wings at Coole, the beat of his clapping swans.[95]

Walcott does not invoke the Irish poet as a model. Instead he represents the details of the two poets' lives as equivalent: both are islanders, both Protestants inspired by the beauty and struggle of the poorer Catholic communities in which they were raised, both are boosters of national theatre companies who champion the poetic properties of local languages, in poems that take the English language to new heights. Walcott no longer stops to spell out these connections. After *Omeros* he seems to assume that his literary legacy and the critical apparatus surrounding it delivers the same kinds of historical and biographical details we take for granted when we read Yeats's life into his work. He can connect, without embarrassment, the natural metre of the waves detonating against the headlands of a St Lucian bay with the clapping beat of the swans' white wings at Coole.

The uses to which Walcott puts the second-person pronoun address in *The Bounty* also begin to shift. As the interpretive flights of student readers and magazine browsers demonstrate, "Love after Love" invited the reader's identification precisely because it did not name a specific interlocutor or refer explicitly to details about Walcott's private life. Many of the intensely dialogic poems in *The Bounty*, by contrast, are stubbornly personal. They force readers to engage the "you" the poems address as if we were eavesdropping on Derek Walcott's actual conversations, leaving it to the allusions culled from the poet's larger *oeuvre* to flesh out the context for those exchanges. In *The Bounty*'s series of linked "Italian Eclogues", for example, the poet jokes with his deceased friend and fellow poet Joseph Brodsky, as familiarly as Plunkett in *Omeros*, scrubbing his back in his bathtub, converses with his dead wife:

> Say you haven't vanished, you're still in Italy.
> Yeah. Very still. God. Still as the turning fields
> of Lombardy, still as the white wastes of that prison
> like pages erased by a regime. Though his landscape heals
> the exile you shared with Naso, poetry is still treason
> because it is truth.[96]

Brodsky's international stature identifies him easily. The Italian landscape in which Walcott converses with his departed friend epitomizes the pastoral setting that produced the eclogue form associated with the classical poet Virgil. In addition, Naso is one of Ovid's names. Thus the reference to Ovid's exile to the Black Sea and Brodsky's exile from Russia converge in a relatively unforced manner, tying all these poets, including Walcott, to a shared poetic form and familiar literary landscape hallowed by history and repetition. The poet says as much to his dead friend in the fourth eclogue, which ends:

> I am going down to the shallow edge to begin again,
> Joseph, with a first line, with an old net, the same expedition.

> I will study the opening horizon, the scansion's strokes of the rain,
> to dissolve in a fiction greater than our lives, the sea, the sun.⁹⁷

The rhetorical second-person address in these eclogues, although directed to a famous ghost in a celebrated landscape, is deliberately conversational. The speaker does not declaim or apostrophize. He simply chuckles: "Yeah. Very still." Brodsky would have enjoyed the pun.

Walcott reaches for a similarly conversational style in "A Santa Cruz Quartet" to commune with his deceased Trinidad Theatre Workshop friend Charles Applewhite. The poet feels entitled to rifle through his own literary repertoire to attempt a similar convergence. The quartet's four movements are set mostly in Santa Cruz, the Trinidad home of Walcott's adult children. Its scenic views are familiar from many of his poems, as well as his paintings, such as the one that graces the cover of *The Bounty*. Moreover, the fertile Santa Cruz Valley, in the foothills of the Northern Range, is a site of racial convergence, having been home to successive waves of Spanish Creole ("Coco-pagnol"), French mulatto, black and Indo-Trinidadian farmers of cocoa, citrus and market vegetables since Walter Raleigh's time. In one of those uncanny biographical twists so common in small island communities, the French mulatto Maillard family of Walcott's second wife, Margaret, sold its cocoa estate to Naipaul's family in the 1940s.⁹⁸ This is the estate that Naipaul memorializes as "The Chase" in *A House for Mr Biswas*, where the protagonist has his nervous breakdown. It is also the landscape of blighted cocoa trees that Naipaul tells us he shares with Blair in *A Way in the World*, and into which he claims the history of successive generations of its inhabitants has sunk without leaving a trace.⁹⁹ Its repeated representation in both Naipaul's and Walcott's work thus makes these valleys in Trinidad's Northern Range one of the more recognizable literary landscapes in the Caribbean. Like Shakespeare's elms and oaks, its vegetation has been "sanctified by literature".

The first movement of "A Santa Cruz Quartet" describes oranges as "yellow globes in the leaves glow[ing] like Marvell's lanterns" – a reference to Andrew Marvell's poem "Bermudas", which reads, "He hangs in shades the orange bright, / Like golden lamps in a green night".¹⁰⁰ However, Walcott is also citing himself. He used an ironic allusion to the same poem for the title and title poem of his first internationally published poetry collection, *In a Green Night*, as a way of pushing back against utopian European visions of the tropics.[101] Fifty years later he draws on all the colonial emulation and anticolonial zeal of his earlier poem to inform a much more nuanced response. In "A Santa Cruz Quartet" Walcott overlays both Marvell's images and his earlier response to them with his memories of family and friends associated with Santa Cruz, while incorporating resonances from the region's representation in the works of other writers and painters. As the poet reflects near the end of the quartet's second movement,

> Perhaps it is the fog that erases the sins
> of history, that no longer looks or sounds foreign
> in the mouth of the valley, despite the visible echo
> of Spanish and French in roads in bright gusts of rain,
> and, when the rain passes, a shining language.[102]

The second movement in "A Santa Cruz Quartet" refers to the "squat chapel" of a locally venerated icon, La Divina Pastora – the "Holy Shepherdess" – to whom Octavio, one of the cuckolded lovers in Walcott's play *The Joker of Seville*, appeals before facing down Don Juan.[103] Octavio's aria invokes the serenity of another mountain valley, this one in Trinidad's Southern Range, where La Divina Pastora's shrine is located:[104]

> *O Divina Pastora,*
> *Holy Shepherdess,*
> *I see that valley still*
> *in times of stress,*
> *seas of bright grass*
> *where, like a pearl, my soul*
> *sleeps in its shell of grace.*[105]

The allusion to *The Joker*'s "holy shepherdess" in "Santa Cruz Quartet" allows Walcott to reference the eclogue's pastoral conventions as he does in the poems addressed to Brodsky, without shifting his focus away from the Trinidadian landscape that his speaker contemplates. When the speaker finally addresses Charles Applewhite in the quartet's third movement, all the repetitions accreted from Walcott's earlier work have created a context for the poet's conversation with this fallen "pillar of the Theatre Workshop", who played the role of Don Gonzalo in the original production of *The Joker of Seville*. Here Walcott effortlessly associates his absence with holy shepherdesses, Marvell's brilliant fruit, the Santa Cruz Valley and Trinidad's French, Coco-pagnol, black and Indio-Trinidadian communities, as well as other quotidian details of his island bucolic:

> The junction. Divina Pastora. Napkin clouds over Jean's
> Hot Roti Shop: a grill with an iron table, a round
> of rain from the bamboos like idling engines,
> the shadows on Saturday gaining more and more ground
> as the week loosens its grip. Sabbath. Now silence
> takes root on the roadside like weeds and runs
> through Santa Cruz . . .
> . . .
>   . . . Into the blue disappears
> every Indian vendor with her open-mouthed baskets: tangerines,
> eggplant, bodi, and the echo of the name Aranguez,
> and the role, Don Gonzalo, in the play's final scenes
> in that stone-dusted chapel where you stride up the aisle
> with your gravedigger's cough, like a crested palm, to grip
> the Joker's wrist and drag him to Hell with a smile
> like a crack in concrete.[106]

Fifty years earlier, such scenes would not have supported the depth of resonance that Walcott hopes he can now take for granted when referring to the Caribbean landscape. Just as he appropriated Western literary tradition to invoke Brodsky's memory in an Italian landscape hallowed by Ovid and Virgil, Walcott now stakes his legacy's claim on his right to delineate his island pastoral through his own imagery, without embarrassment or fear of opacity. It matters to him that the breadfruit and the coconut, through his art, have become "noble trees"; in the late afternoon light their "lower leaves" take on a "waxen viridian" hue as the poet registers the way in which "faces that I love harder every year turn / towards the dusk and deepen also under the coconuts".[107] When, in another poem, the rhetorical "you" doubts "yourself" – asking (rhetorically) "Can you genuinely claim these, and do they reclaim you / from your possible margin of disdain, of occasional escape" –

the speaker does not have to wait another half-century to peel a response from the mirror.[108] The answer returns quickly a dozen lines later, with assurance and humility:

> Yes, they reclaim you in a way you need not understand:
> candles that never gutter and go out in the breeze,
> or tears that glint on night's face for every island.[109]

VII

So who exactly is this "you" whom we so often encounter with fresh emotion when we read a Walcott poem? In the context of his lifetime of poetic achievement, Poem 14 of *The Bounty*, from which the first epigraph for this chapter is taken, invites another question: What exactly is the *this* you so often encounter with fresh emotion when you read a Walcott poem? Positioned dead centre in the short collection, surrounded on both sides by poems that memorialize fallen friends and family members, loved landscapes and communities, Poem 14 contemplates at its own dead centre "infinity behind it, infinity ahead of it".[110] Like the addressee in "Exile", through whose transforming pen "the earth began to look / as you remembered her", the soul now travelling towards "its coming serene extinction" knows of death "Only what you had read of it, / that it was like a flame blown out in a lowered lantern, / a night, but without these stars".[111] But the book from which that knowledge comes is one of the poet's own making, as the lines about the night "without these stars" repurpose yet another series of images from *The Joker of Seville*, when Don Juan chooses to embrace death:

> *Don Juan Tenorio knows when to retire:*
> *a night like this with its fine sweat of stars,*
> *a laughing tropic night, as this one was,*
> *not marbled into fable like your heroes,*
> *but flesh, with all its blemishes and scars!*[112]

Similarly, the "this" of Poem 14's opening line and the syntax of its closing sentence – "This is why you have ended, to pass, / praising the feathery swaying of the casuarinas" – recall the lines from *Omeros* in which the poet, following in Homer's wake, exults: "If this was where it ended, the end was easy – / to give back the borrowed breath the joy that it gave, / with the sea exulting, the wind so wild with love."[113] Poem 14 not only recycles familiar tropes from earlier poems, but its opening and closing sections mirror each other in sound and image so that its structure repeats and reverses the dimensions of the scene it describes. A marina at sunrise surrounded by headlands in the poem's opening movement returns, as the poem closes, in the boats at rest, "studying their reflections in black glass".[114] The white lances of the yachts' sails in the opening lines become fading lances in the poem's penultimate line. The "growling *Aves*" of the morning surf reverberate in "those shudderings of thanks that so often descended" at sunset.[115] Even the opening end rhymes that connect *casuarinas*, *grass*, *marinas* and *grace* return in the final five lines of the poem, which rhyme *casuarinas* and *marinas* around and against the repeated sounds in *pass*, *grass* and *glass*, heightening both assonance and alliteration as the poem draws to a close: "all that it knew was this craft, all that it wanted".[116]

Here, then, is the *this* that Walcott urges "you" not to take for granted. Not merely the natural beauty his poetry celebrates, the destitution behind the picturesque poverty of his islands' inhabitants, or the vexed questions of language and power that entangle their history, but the craft itself, with which he has transformed this vista into art. The "you" the poem addresses may be the poet himself, but it is also Walcott's reader, whom he hopes will continue to respond to the poet's craft with astonishment and delight. The borrowed breath of language flows from the poets who preceded "you" into those to whom "the wind so wild with love" will give it next.[117] It is *you*'s duty, as the poet, to transform that breath into art. After all, "This is why you have ended, to pass, / praising the feathery swaying of the casuarinas / and those shudderings of thanks that so often descended".[118] But it is also *you*'s duty, as the reader, "Never [to] get used to this" communal celebration of life.[119] Although the "poet's personal memories and associations in the mother tongue", in Blasing's terms, cannot always be "formalized and thus socialized as a generic discourse of a virtual 'I' ", *you* can engage the world. [120] Having followed the progression of new words and their associated images across Walcott's oeuvre, we find ourselves suffused with elation as now-familiar sounds and techniques repeat in endlessly proliferating combinations. The poet's craft allows us to contemplate with fresh eyes our "coming serene extinction", just as earlier variants of the same sounds allowed us to reflect on the nostalgia of exile, the devastation of loss, the hope for love reclaimed, the vigour of a language that no longer embarrasses. The self-love that such a poem as "Love after Love" urges may be great, but, as Omeros reminds us, "love of your own people is // greater".[121] And it is language's duty, above all, "to enclose the loved world in its arms".[122] This, ultimately, is Walcott's literary legacy, his wager with the word, his appeal to you and his challenge to himself.

ACCIDENTS
An Afterword

> What shall I do to be forever known,
> And make the age to come my own?[1]

Will these writers' legacies last? And who will be their future readers? One of the most intense aspects of being a Caribbean reader of Caribbean literature is that, as I make my way through the worlds these writers have imagined, I am constantly, unpredictably turning corners and crashing into myself. I think of these intersections as happy accidents, in the complex sense that I imagine Phyllis Wheatley, the early African-American poet, thought of her enslavement when she described it as felicitous – arbitrary, enabling, but always somehow painful.

 The first words I read of *A Way in the World* were the passages about the coo-coo and the gefilte fish. An English department colleague, who writes reviews for highbrow literary magazines, had placed his review of the new Naipaul novel in my departmental mailbox, with one of his characteristically clipped, erratically typed notes attached, asking me to take a look at it for possible factual inaccuracies. Skimming the article quickly, mail in hand, in the corridor of our red-brick office building, with its trademark white pillars and clock tower overlooking a typical New England college quad, I am jolted into another landscape and moment so unexpectedly that my stomach turns over. I am six years old and my Barbadian grandmother is visiting us in Trinidad. She has brought with her a navy-blue grip packed full of small-island delicacies: coconut pone wrapped in brown paper, the oil oozing through the wrapping, creating shiny dark patches that seem to expand stealthily every time I take my eyes off them; flying-fish fillets, breaded and fried, arranged in neat rows and pressed together inside a heavy rectangular biscuit tin tied shut with fuzzy white string. And then this indefinable monstrosity, this shuddering yellow mass of cornmeal, okra and other, nameless things, glistening ominously in its embarrassingly common aluminium pan. It is the kind of pan that road labourers stack one on top of the other to carry their ground-provision lunches, so that the various flavours don't run together until it is time to eat. I am incensed by this shuddering mass, revolted by its implacable yellowness, outraged that I am expected to eat it – to *like* it! I am embarrassed that my almost white grandmother could be associated with such black small-island food.

For years I remain revolted by the idea of eating coo-coo, widening my prejudice to take in crab and callaloo, black pudding and souse – anything slimy that makes your hands feel disgusting. Much later, in West Africa, I learn to eat such foods with equanimity. In international settings I come to celebrate them proudly as authentically Caribbean. But that original revulsion, nurtured by decades of class and racial prejudice, passed along over generations within my middle-class brown family, is also authentically Caribbean. Underneath, it never quite goes away. My stomach is churning before I even realize that I am reading Naipaul's descriptions of not being able to eat coo-coo or gefilte fish, alongside my colleague's bemused comments about how unnecessary it seems for Naipaul to go on and on about such an insignificant detail.

Landlocked, insomniac, recovering from minor surgery in a German hospital, I am surfing my way for the first time through Brathwaite's hypertext *Barabajan Poems*, flipping to the notes sometimes, sometimes not; skipping over passages where the whimsical typeface becomes too rococo; jumping ahead to look for my favourite poems from *The Arrivants* that I just know he has to include:

> We who are born of the ocean can never
> seek solace
> in rivers: their flowing runs on like our
> longing,
> reproves us our lack of endeavour &

> purpose,
> proves that our striving will founder on that[2]

Or that other favourite of mine, from *Mother Poem*:

> praaaaze be to
> praaaaze be to
> praaaaze be to
> gg[3]

Without warning, a sharp pain shoots through the inner corner of my right eye and my hurt head is throbbing. I move to ring for a nurse. Maybe the drugs in my drip are wearing off. Maybe Brathwaite's extravagant typeface and my poorly positioned reading lamp have finally done me in.

But instead I am back in the wooded space behind Mary Seacole Hall, on the Mona campus of the University of the West Indies, an undergraduate in the 1970s. They have invited a group of pocomania dancers to give a demonstration of their possession rituals for the edification of students and professors in the newly liberated post-occupation Creative Arts Centre. Something is going terribly wrong. The time allotted for the cultural demonstration has long been exceeded, but even when one of the organizers steps forward to move along the proceedings, one woman is refusing to stop. She is groping her crotch and moving her body in shuddering spurts that seem threateningly obscene, all the time never missing the beat of the drums, even after they have stopped playing. The other dancers hold her, push her, whip her, spin her – nothing helps. Finally the drummers start up again, moving her with them out of the auditorium into the wooded space behind Mary Seacole Hall. The dancers form a tight circle around the woman, blocking her body from the view of the students who have trailed out behind them, half curious, half frightened, like voyeurs at the site of a fatal crash.

Inside the auditorium, the organizer is introducing the next feature, a Rastafarian drumming ensemble, and droning on about possession rituals and African retentions. But I have fled both venues, head throbbing, heart thumping in dangerous synchrony with the beat of the pocomania drums. I am overwhelmed by cultural overload and terrified by my connection to what I have just witnessed – just as the poet-professor in *Barabajan Poems* is experiencing those same emotions on the page I am reading now, as he shuts down his tape recorder, turns off the video cameras and switches off the Niagara lights at the possession ritual he thought he could merely observe. His tiny, frightened font is squashed up against the margin, clinging to the edges of the page in a way that makes me squint and hurts my head, leaving an echoing hollowness in the body of the text. Like Lamming's Fola, like McKay's Bita, like Brodber's Nellie. So much repression. So many denials.

Pursued by impossible deadlines, I sit hunched in my winter coat, waiting for the visiting writer I am driving to Connecticut for a reading at another college. It is cold outside and overheated in the car, but I do not want to go into the house and get caught up in conversation, because I am reading to the finish line of Walcott's *Omeros*, which I have to present to my department colleagues at next week's staff course meeting. I have read most of the poem in one breathless marathon on the long flights to and from London the previous week, where I was attending a conference on black women writers and giving a series of talks as part of the South Bank Cultural Festival. Still, it has been hard keeping track of all the turns in this gargantuan poem, and I have practically given up at this point on being able to say anything useful about the "Catherine of the Plains" sections in next week's meeting.

Mentally I am cursing staff courses and poets who, as Walcott says elsewhere, write poems to give their children homework. Coming on top of the tightly packed London itinerary, the growing stack of unmarked papers, my courtesy chauffeur detail for the visiting writer, and the fact that I am up for tenure next month, the notes I am expected to produce for my colleagues seem like the proverbial last straw. The tears overwhelm silently, like the unannounced tide creeping up the Caribbean beach I am lying on, making the towel under my body damp, then straining salt through my hair. Walcott's text has crept into my consciousness without my registering what I have been reading:

> ... strong as self-healing coral, a quiet culture
> is branching from the white ribs of each ancestor,
>
> deeper than it seems on the surface; slowly but sure,
> it will change us with the fluent sculpture of Time,
> it will grip like the polyp, soldered by the slime[4]

The sobs, when they come, suck the air out of me like an undertow of anguish, drawing me out to the rocks before hurtling me back up the beach. Then the cadences of the poem wash over me, calling me back from the edge of the abyss, telling me that those revulsions and denials, the slime and the hollow spaces, are things we all share – the nothing out of which our something grows.

Walcott, Brathwaite, Naipaul. These writers are the mediums who have drawn me through the *tonelle*. The humour and luminosity in their writing, their irascibility, their elation, their failures, their petty grievances and self-deceptions, their ambition and their mortality have mirrored my own and enabled my survival.

And those images! A crust of coral, a lump of coo-coo, a woman plucking her body taut as a drum. Hard to believe that someone besides me knew about all this; that these, my most intimate of memories – now hurling themselves off the page into my body, jolting my stomach, lancing my head, seeping like spilt blood into my innermost recesses – are out there now for everyone else to see. But there they are, these Caribbean images, in books I have bought in America and that I am reading in Europe. Books that take me back to the islands when I am loneliest, that I must talk about next week with my New England colleagues, and that I will read about in this weekend's highbrow literary magazines, if I ever find the time. Writers whose reputations we will squabble over noisily between kaiso and reggae at the next Labour Day fête in Flatbush, or between rounds of drinks, overlooking the Savannah, next time I am home. The accidents that join their images to my life have become part of the cultural currency of all the worlds I inhabit. In spite of the pain, I steady myself by clutching their words to my body.

NOTES

Introduction

1. Derek Walcott, *Omeros*, 2nd ed. (New York: Farrar, Straus and Giroux, 1992), 321.
2. Ibid., 320–21.
3. V.S. Naipaul, *The Enigma of Arrival* (1987; New York: Vintage, 2012), 158.
4. Edward Kamau Brathwaite, *The Zea Mexican Diary* (Madison: University of Wisconsin Press, 1993), 199.
5. V.S. Naipaul, "Jasmine", in *The Overcrowded Barracoon and Other Articles* (Harmondsworth, UK: Penguin, 1976), 26.
6. Simmons's death is the centrepiece of "The Estranging Sea", the final section of Walcott's autobiographical poem *Another Life*, in which Walcott's father also figures prominently.
7. Derek Walcott, *The Bounty* (New York: Farrar, Straus and Giroux, 1997), 57.
8. Naipaul describes his response to his sister's death in an epilogue to *Enigma of Arrival*, which he also dedicates to the memory of his brother; the effect of his father's death while he was away at university is rendered fictionally at the end of *A House for Mr Biswas*. Naipaul returns obsessively to this paternal loss in his introduction to the collection of his father's short stories, *Gurudeva and Other Tales*, in "Prologue to an Autobiography", and in *Enigma of Arrival*.
9. The Ghanaian poet Kofi Awoonor and the Kenyan novelist Ngũgĩ wa Thiong'o have often spoken about Brathwaite's influence on their ideas about language and orature. Brathwaite's sister, Mary Morgan, quotes their comments in "The Silver Feather", an essay describing the events surrounding Brathwaite's 1994 receiving of the Neustadt International Prize for Literature, for which Awoonor nominated him. Apart from Awoonor, the prize committee also included the African writers Nuruddin Farah, J.M. Coetzee and Nawal El Saadawi. Ngũgĩ delivered the encomium at the award ceremony. For a discussion of some of the cultural developments in the Caribbean to which Brathwaite contributed

during this period, see Brathwaite, "The Love Axe/I: Developing a Caribbean Aesthetic", *Bim* 61 (June 1977): 53–65, and also his anthologies, particularly the issue of *Savacou* (14–15 [1979]) devoted to new writers from Jamaica.

10. Brathwaite has written about his wife's death in *Zea Mexican Diary* and about the other personal disasters that precipitated his moves in *DreamStories* (Harlow, UK: Longman Caribbean, 1994).

11. Jean-Luc Nancy, introduction, in *Who Comes after the Subject?*, ed. Eduardo Cadava, Peter Connor and Jean-Luc Nancy (New York: Routledge, 1991), 5.

12. Fanon lays out this argument most succinctly in his chapter "The Negro and Language", in *Black Skin, White Masks* (New York: Grove Press, 1967), 17–40. But here I am relying verbatim on Diana Fuss's restatement of his positions in her essay "Interior Colonies", in *Identification Papers: Readings on Psychoanalysis, Sexuality, and Culture* (New York: Routledge, 1995), 144.

13. Fanon, *Black Skin*, 215.

14. Fuss, *Identification Papers*, 144.

15. Fanon, *Black Skin*, 211.

16. Fuss, *Identification Papers*, 9.

17. Ibid., 144.

18. Rhonda Cobham-Sander, "Colin Ferguson, Me and I: An Anatomy of Creole Psychosis", *Transition* 67 (Fall 1995): 16–21.

19. For a discussion of some of the cultural forms such pathologies take in the Caribbean, especially neuroses related to "studiation", or "feeling white", see Lawrence E. Fisher, *Colonial Madness: Mental Health in the Barbadian Social Order* (New Brunswick, NJ: Rutgers University Press, 1985).

20. Jacques Derrida, "'Eating Well', or the Calculation of the Subject: An Interview with Jacques Derrida", in Cadava, Connor and Nancy, *Who Comes after the Subject?*, 106.

21. Walcott, *Bounty*, 39.

22. V.S. Naipaul, *A Way in the World: A Novel* (New York: Vintage, 1995), 89.

23. Edward Kamau Brathwaite, *Barabajan Poems* (New York: Savacou North, 1994), 300.

24. Derek Walcott, *Collected Poems* (New York: Farrar, Straus and Giroux, 1986), 149. (Hereafter identified in the notes as *CP*.)

25. For a discussion of *Caribbean Voices* and Naipaul's contribution to it, see Rhonda Cobham-Sander, "The *Caribbean Voices* Programme and the Development of West Indian Short Fiction: 1945–1958", in *The Story Must Be Told: Short Narrative Prose in the New English Literatures*, ed. Peter O. Stummer (Würzburg: Königshausen und Neumann, 1985), 146–58.

26. V.S. Naipaul, review of *Of Age and Innocence* by George Lamming, *New Statesman* 56, 6 December 1958, 827.
27. Gordon Rohlehr, *The Shape of That Hurt and Other Essays* (Port of Spain: Longman Trinidad, 1992), 38. For a wonderfully detailed contextualization of the period in Caribbean literary history during which Walcott produced these essays, see Gordon Collier's introduction to his massive two-volume collection of Walcott's early prose, *Derek Walcott, the Journeyman Years: Occasional Prose, 1957–1974*, vol. 1, *Culture, Society, Literature, and Art* (New York: Editions Rodopi, 2013), xi–xlii.
28. Edward Kamau Brathwaite, "Jazz and the West Indian Novel", *Bim* 44 (January–June 1967): 275–84; 45 (July–December 1967): 39–51; 46 (January–June 1968): 115–26. Brathwaite, "The Love Axe", *Bim* 61 (June 1977): 53–65; 62 (December 1977): 100–106; 63 (June 1978): 181–92. For a full listing of Brathwaite's most influential essays, see Doris Monica Brathwaite, *A Descriptive and Chronological Bibliography (1950–1982) of the Work of Edward Kamau Brathwaite* (London: New Beacon, 1988).
29. In note 47+ of *Barabajan Poems* (321–22), Brathwaite offers a blow-by-blow account of his most celebrated face-off with Naipaul, at the 1971 Commonwealth Writers Conference in Jamaica. Naipaul attacked claims for the folk culture in Brathwaite's keynote address, then refused to appear with him on Jamaican television. Before this, however, Brathwaite had frequently written with admiration about Naipaul's novels. Brathwaite and Walcott have been contrasted implicitly and explicitly by many critics; see, for example, Patricia Ismond, "Walcott versus Brathwaite", in *Critical Perspectives on Derek Walcott*, ed. Robert D. Hamner (Washington, DC: Three Continents, 1993), 220–36. However, the writers maintained a circumspect public cordiality until Walcott's mischievous parody of Brathwaite's poem "Negus" during a BBC Channel 4 programme, *Caribbean Nights*, in September 1986. Asked to comment on the literary merits of the piece, Walcott borrowed the well-known opening movement of the poem to quip:

> It
> It
> It
> It is not
> It is not
> It is not a very good poem.

See also his poem "Names" (*CP*, 305–8), dedicated to Edward Brathwaite, from the *Sea Grapes* collection.

Walcott broke his silence on Naipaul in a review of *Enigma of Arrival*, when he accused Naipaul of finally having gone too far in his Anglophilism and denigration of the Caribbean; see Derek Walcott, "The Garden Path", *New Republic* 196, no. 15 (13 April 1987): 27. (Subsequent references in this book are to the version published as "The Garden Path: V.S. Naipaul", in *What the Twilight Says: Essays* [New York: Farrar, Straus and Giroux, 1998].) In his poetry, however, Walcott acknowledges a more nuanced if still ambivalent relationship with Naipaul. See, for example, "Laventille", from *The Castaway and Other Poems* (London: Jonathan Cape, 1965), which he dedicates to Naipaul, and the calypsonian's invocation of "V.S. Nightfall" in "The Spoiler's Return", from *The Fortunate Traveller* (New York: Farrar, Straus and Giroux, 1981).

30. Walcott, *Bounty*, 26.
31. Walcott, *Another Life*, CP, 282.
32. Ibid., 147.
33. Recorded 7 January 1981 at Walcott's home in Petit Valley, Trinidad and Tobago. The interview has since been titled "Derek Walcott Interview with Ken Ramchand" in the Banyan archive, http://www.pancaribbean.com/banyan/digitisedarchive.htm.
34. Shortened versions of three chapters from this book, one from each section, have appeared in festschrifts. An early version of "For C.L.R. James" appeared in *Anthurium* 5, no. 2 (Fall 2007), a special issue marking Naipaul's seventy-fifth birthday, as "Consuming the Self: V.S. Naipaul, C.L.R. James, and *A Way in the World*". "For Kamau" appeared as "K/Ka/Kam/Kama/Kamau: Brathwaite's Project of Self-Naming in *Barabajan Poems*", in *For the Geography of a Soul: Emerging Perspectives on Kamau Brathwaite*, ed. Timothy J. Reiss (Trenton, NJ: Africa World Press, 2001), 297–315. "For Brathwaite" appeared as "'Any Enemy So Was a Compliment': Walcott, Brathwaite and the Formal Possibilities of Creole", in *Interlocking Basins of a Globe: Essays on Derek Walcott*, ed. Jean Antoine-Dunne (Leeds: Peepal Tree, 2013), 100–122.

Chapter 1

1. Naipaul, *Way in the World*.
2. Ibid., 171–72.
3. Ibid., 163, 175.
4. Ibid., 3.
5. Ibid., 172.
6. Ibid.
7. The Hakluyt Society edition of Sir Walter Raleigh's *Discoverie of Guiana* includes

this advertisement, although, characteristically, Naipaul seems to have taken liberties with its content. Raleigh concedes that many of his sailors had brought back marcasite, which they thought was gold, but he insists that the small samples of white spar they chipped out of rocks in Guiana did indeed contain gold. His reference to North African (Barbary) gold, however, occurs in a circumlocutious sentence that seems to say he did not use it to mislead his audience, but this sentence could be read otherwise: "I am not so much in loue with these long voiages, as to deuise, thereby to cozen my selfe, to lie hard, to fare worse, to be subiected to perils, to diseases, to ill sauours, to be parched and withered, and withall to sustaine the care and labour of such an enterprize, excepte the same had more comfort, then the fetching of *Marcasite* in *Guiana*, or bying of gold oare in Barbery"; Sir W. Raleigh, *The Discovery of the Large, Rich, and Beautiful Empire of Guiana* (London: Hakluyt Society, 1848), 89.

8. Alfred Tennyson, *In Memoriam. Authoritative Text – Criticism*, ed. Erik Irving Gray (New York: W.W. Norton, 2004), 76.
9. Naipaul, *Way in the World*, 214.
10. Ibid., 215.
11. Ibid., 338.
12. Walcott, "Garden Path", 128.
13. Naipaul, *Way in the World*, 178.
14. Ibid., 180.

Chapter 2

1. Naipaul, *Way in the World*, 160–61.
2. I am indebted for this information to Patricia Haward, of Highbury, London, whose time in Uganda at Makerere University overlapped with Naipaul's. Haward was Naipaul's contemporary at Oxford and an editor at the *New Statesman* during the late 1950s when Naipaul contributed to the journal. I have used her memories of these venues throughout to help me reconstruct the social and intellectual circles within which Naipaul circulated during the 1950s and 1960s. Patrick French's biography of Naipaul also cites "Jim Allen (Kenya-born and bred, but of simplish Australian background)" as the model for De Groot; Patrick French, *The World Is What It Is: The Authorized Biography of V.S. Naipaul* (New York: Knopf, 2008), 255.
3. The original correspondence between James and Naipaul is now housed in the West Indian special collection at the University of the West Indies, St Augustine, Trinidad. Naipaul's official biographer, Patrick French, and Farrukh Dhondy, in

his more impressionistic version, offer fairly detailed accounts of the friendship between the two men; French, *World Is What It Is*, 236–39; Farrukh Dhondy, *C.L.R. James: A Life* (New York: Pantheon, 2001), 161–71. I am indebted to my colleague Biodun Jeyifo for suggesting a possible source for the name Lebrun in the historical figure of the French syndicalist Pierre Le Brun (1906–70), who would have been a contemporary of James's within the European Left. French notes that Lebrun was also the name of Learie Constantine's father; Constantine, a cricketer and politician, was the other black Trinidadian who rose to prominence in England after the Second World War. Finally, Naipaul seems to borrow minor details for Lebrun's early political career from that of the Trinidadian French creole politician Cipriani, about whom James had written in *The Case for West-Indian Self Government* (New York: University Place Book Shop, 1967). Perhaps more importantly, Naipaul is playing here with the auditory associations between the name Lebrun and the French *le brun* ("the brown one") – an appropriate sobriquet for Naipaul's character, as well as for his narrator.

4. James died in 1989. In the decade leading up to and following his death, several volumes of his selected writings were reissued and retrospective studies of his literary and political accomplishments began to appear. So James's intellectual legacy was very much in the spotlight when Naipaul was working on *Way in the World* in 1991–92.
5. Naipaul, *Way in the World*, 131.
6. In his introduction to *The Adventures of Gurudeva*, Naipaul tells us that an autobiographical piece his father had written "was read, long after it had been written, to a Port of Spain literary group which included Edgar Mittelholzer and, I believe, the young George Lamming"; V.S. Naipaul, *The Adventures of Gurudeva* (New Delhi: Buffalo, 2001), 9. This group included those members of the *Beacon* circle still in Trinidad in the 1940s.
7. Naipaul, "Jasmine", 27.
8. Naipaul, "Sporting Life", in *Overcrowded Barracoon*, 23.
9. I have not been able to locate a review of Naipaul by James that matches this description. However, Naipaul may be signifying the left-leaning sympathies of the *New Statesman* magazine, in which, according to Dhondy's biography, James published a favourable review of *The Mystic Masseur* in 1958; Dhondy, *C.L.R. James*, 162. Naipaul may also be conflating aspects of this review and the favourable reviews that both Brathwaite and Walcott wrote of *A House for Mr Biswas* in later years.
10. Naipaul, *Way in the World*, 114.
11. V.S. Naipaul, *The Middle Passage: Impressions of Five Societies – British, French and Dutch – in the West Indies and South America* (New York: Vintage, 1981), 29.

12. Naipaul, *Way in the World*, 117.
13. For examples of readings of Naipaul as betrayer that appeared before the publication of *Way in the World*, see Selwyn Cudjoe, *V.S. Naipaul: A Materialist Reading* (Amherst: University of Massachusetts Press, 1988), 33, especially his introduction, where he explicitly compares Naipaul's take on the Caribbean to that of James; and Rob Nixon, "London Calling: V.S. Naipaul and the License of Exile", *South Atlantic Quarterly* 87, no. 1 (Winter, 1988), 1–37. The two most high-profile of these attacks are Chinua Achebe's essay on *A Bend in the River* (in "Viewpoint", *Times Literary Supplement*, 1 February 1980, 113), in which he dismisses the book without having read it, and Edward Said's critical remarks in "The Post-Colonial Intellectual: A Discussion with Conor Cruise O'Brien, Edward Said and John Lukacs", *Salmagundi* 70–71 (Spring–Summer 1986): 65–81, in which O'Brien and Lukacs argued for Naipaul. Other examples of what Nixon calls "Naipaul worship" include Eugene Goodheart, "V.S. Naipaul's Mandarin Sensibility", *Partisan Review* 50, no. 2 (1983): 224–56; and Joseph Epstein, "A Cottage for Mr Naipaul", *New Criterion* 6, no. 2 (October 1987): 6–15.
14. Kent Worcester identifies the woman on whom Naipaul probably based this description of Lebrun's woman friend as James's second wife, Selma, who was Jewish; Kent Worcester, *C.L.R. James: A Political Biography* (Albany: State University of New York Press, 1995), 174.
15. Naipaul, *Way in the World*, 120.
16. Ibid., 80.
17. See Naipaul, *Middle Passage*, 72.
18. See Mighty Sparrow's calypso "Saltfish" (YouTube video, 3:08, uploaded 21 December 2008. http://youtu.be/o1aYB2nlFbo.). The relevant stanza goes:

> Very well, I like the taste
> Though the smell sometimes out of place
> It hard to take
> But make no mistake
> I want you to know
> Is because it extra sweet that it smelling so.

The popular refrain reiterates, "When you want to eat, all saltfish sweet." Espinet's essay "Indian Cuisine" provides independent corroboration of my hunch that eating coo-coo has a special set of sexual connotations associated with creole promiscuity among Indo-Trinidadians. Describing her own first attempts at making this meal, she recounts the revulsion with which most of her family greeted it, as well as her mother's consternation when her father ate the meal with the practised gusto of a long-time connoisseur: "I heard the hiss in her voice, 'Yuh know bout coo-coo? Where yuh know bout coo-coo?' I was still doing home-work on the big table outside and listened attentively. I had heard a neighbour whispering to Muddie that Da-Da had a Creole woman and that it wasn't really the gambling job that took up so much time"; Ramabai Espinet, "Indian Cuisine", *Massachusetts Review* 35, nos. 3–4 (Autumn–Winter 1994), 570.

19. Naipaul, *Way in the World*, 89.
20. *Creole* is a vexed term in Trinidad usage. Technically it means someone born in the Caribbean, but among black Trinidadians it is most often used to refer to white Trinidadians or people of indeterminate race, as in a "creole callaloo" or "French creole". Indo-Trinidadians tend to use the term to distinguish between themselves and other Trinidadians, especially black Trinidadians, perhaps because at first they did not consider themselves natives of the islands. One can also speak of a "creole Indian" to indicate a particularly "assimilated" person of Indian descent. Given the social and linguistic hybridity of Trinidad society, my informal attempts to define the term turned up as many usages as I had informants, suggesting that this is one more Caribbean word whose precise meaning varies with context. It may be significant, however, that although Naipaul uses the term *creole* when talking about cultural matters such as Lamming's influence, or about the street on which he was raised, he uses *black* or *Negro* when talking about Trinidadians of African descent where the stakes are political.
21. Edward Baugh, "Cuckoo and Culture: *In the Castle of My Skin*", *Ariel* 8, no. 3 (July 1977): 23–33.
22. Naipaul, *Way in the World*, 127.
23. Williams acknowledges that the idea for *Capitalism and Slavery* was an elaboration of the thesis about the economic motivations of the "Owners" put forward in chapter 2 of James's *The Black Jacobins: Toussaint L'Ouverture and the San Domingo Revolution* (1963; reprint: New York: Vintage, 1989) ; see Robert Hill, "In England: 1932–38", in *C.L.R. James: His Life and Work*, ed. Paul Buhle (London: Allison and Busby, 1986), 79. The break between the two men occurred during 1958–62, when James worked as editor of the *Nation*, the official organ of Williams's party, the People's National Movement. They differed on the question of the party's willingness to compromise with the US government over the matter of ownership of the Chaguaramas naval base in Trinidad. Williams offers a summary of his version of their political falling out in his autobiography but does not mention James's earlier influence on his intellectual development; Eric Williams, *Inward Hunger: The Education of a Prime Minister* (Chicago: University of Chicago Press, 1971), 267–68. For a summary of James's explanation of the split, see Worcester's comments in *C.L.R. James*, 153–54.

24. Naipaul, *Way in the World*, 120.
25. Ibid., 121.
26. Ibid., 119.
27. Ibid., 128.
28. Kenneth Ramchand suggests another intertextual dig here – at Edward Said, one of Naipaul's most vociferous critics, who had referred to Naipaul as a "scavenger" – in the naming of Leonard Side and Side/Said's association with dead bodies and unmentionable worked-over things.
29. Naipaul, *Way in the World*, 11.
30. Ibid., 128.
31. Ibid., 160–61.
32. Ibid.
33. Worcester, *C.L.R. James*, 175.
34. Caryl Phillips, "The Voyage In", review of *A Way in the World*, by V.S. Naipaul, *New Republic* 210, no. 24 (13 June 1994): 43.
35. Naipaul, *Way in the World*, 160–61.
36. Phillips, "Voyage In", 43.

Chapter 3

1. Naipaul, *Way in the World*, 27–28.
2. Ibid., 181.
3. Ibid., 77.
4. Ibid., 76.
5. In "Prologue to an Autobiography", Naipaul mentions that his early writing sacrificed much of the social nuances of his Trinidad society for the sake of speed and pace, elements without which, he suggests, the story would not ring true, however accurate he might have made their details; V.S. Naipaul, *Finding the Center: Two Narratives* (New York: Knopf, 1984), 1–72. Here he seems to carry the point a step further to suggest that distortion, rather than verisimilitude, is the essence of good writing even when, as happens in this novel, the distortion makes the work seem formless. Naipaul seems to have come full circle, to embrace the unreadability for which he critiqued Lamming in his 1958 review of *Of Age and Innocence*, cited in my introduction.
6. Naipaul, *Way in the World*, 77.
7. Ibid., 78.
8. Ibid., 163.
9. Consider, for example, the role given to the lone dark-skinned group member

in such classic adventure films as *The Bridge on the River Kwai* (1957), *The Dirty Dozen* (1967), *Jurassic Park* (1993) and *Pacific Rim* (2013). He is always the first character to fall off the bridge, to be eaten by dinosaurs, bombed out of existence or sacrificed for the good of the group. His expendability enhances our investment in the hero's charmed existence. Naipaul's fellow Trinidadian, novelist Earl Lovelace, develops this idea in *Is Just a Movie*: that novel's protagonist refuses to die quietly as prescribed by his role as an extra in an American movie being shot in Trinidad.

10. Naipaul, "The Crocodiles of Yamoussoukro", in *Finding the Center*, 73–176.
11. Naipaul, *Way in the World*, 373.
12. Ibid.
13. Ibid.
14. French, *World Is What It Is*, 394, 401. French claims that Blair was "inspired by Walter Rodney, the author of *How Europe Underdeveloped Africa* (London: Bogle-L'Ouverture, 1972), a pan-Africanist and devotee of C.L.R. James"; ibid., 456. However, this claim seems less defensible. Rodney was physically small and intellectually intense, while Naipaul makes Blair a large, affable man, similar to Wooding. Moreover, the laissez-faire views that Naipaul gives Blair are at the opposite end of the political spectrum from those Rodney espoused.
15. Naipaul, *Way in the World*, 29.
16. Ibid.
17. Ibid., 373.
18. Ibid., 378.
19. Ibid., 374.
20. Ibid., 375.
21. Ibid., 159.

Chapter 4

1. Naipaul, *Way in the World*, 379–80.
2. Naipaul, "Jasmine", 27.
3. In *The Middle Passage*, he writes, "I had never wanted to stay in Trinidad. When I was in the fourth form I wrote a vow on the endpaper of my Kennedy's *Revised Latin Primer* to leave within five years. I left after six; and for many years afterwards in England, falling asleep in bedsitters with the electric fire on, I had been awakened by the nightmare that I was back in tropical Trinidad" (41).
4. Quoted in Walcott, "Garden Path", 127.
5. Ibid.

6. Derrida, "Eating Well", 106.
7. Certainly when Trinidad fêted him royally on his seventy-fifth birthday in April 2007, all the contradictions of this relationship were still on display. Naipaul reportedly wept with emotion at a banquet organized in his honour by his former classmates at QRC. A few days later the airwaves crackled with reports that he had lashed out at a class of Trinidadian schoolchildren for asking what he thought were inane questions. For a description of Naipaul's visit, see Al Creighton, "Return of the Enigma: Naipaul Goes Home for 75th Birthday", *Stabroek News* (Georgetown, Guyana), 29 April 2007, http://www.landofsixpeoples.com/news702/ns0704299.html.

Chapter 5

1. Brathwaite, *Barabajan Poems*, 364; italics in the original.
2. The piece was finally published as *Shar: Hurricane Poem* (Kingston: Savacou, 1990).
3. For Brathwaite's personal and aesthetic responses to the destruction of the hurricane, see *Shar*, and also "Open Letter to the Vice Chancellor of the University of the West Indies" (18 November 1988) describing the threatened archive at his Irish Town home and pleading for help in preserving and cataloguing it; cited in Gordon Rohlehr, introduction to Brathwaite's *DreamStories*, iv.
4. Edward Kamau Brathwaite, *Trench Town Rock* (Providence, RI: Lost Roads, 1994), 68. The work is built around the ordeal of the robbery (see also "Open Letter"). Brathwaite mentions the detail of the wedding ring in *Zea Mexican Diary*, 183.
5. Rohlehr, introduction, vii.
6. Winnie Risden echoes a version of this sentiment in her review of *Masks*, when she complains: "The small private moments when the conscience is shattered through contact to new perceptions are excluded by the poem's very nature. Brathwaite's success is to have endowed a familiar theme with the dignity of public ceremonial. He offers no message to the heart." She wants to know who speaks from behind the masks, "which face is his among the strange and terrible"; Winnie Risden, review of *Masks*, by Kamau Brathwaite, *Caribbean Quarterly* 14, nos. 1–2 (March–June 1968): 147. I am less critical of this formal distancing of the poet because I see it as a useful strategy for addressing a pressing aesthetic dilemma in Caribbean writing – the absence of a literary tradition in which to ground the personal – that can all too easily become an excuse for endless narcissism.
7. In the preamble to the volume, Brathwaite explains that the lecture was one in a

series of memorial lectures sponsored by the Barbados Central Bank and named for Sir Winston Scott, the first native governor general of Barbados. It was held in the bank's Frank Collymore Auditorium, named after the founder and editor of *Bim*, the literary magazine that gave both Brathwaite and Walcott their start as creative writers; Brathwaite, *Barabajan Poems*, 11. Brathwaite claims that he produced *Barabajan Poems* in frustration over the bank's almost decade-long failure to produce a published version of his lecture. Sections of the talk may have existed for a much longer time in manuscript, however; Gordon Rohlehr in *Pathfinder* quotes from personal communications with Brathwaite dating to 1974 that reproduce almost verbatim some of the material now integrated into *Barabajan Poems*; ibid., 5. Ironically, the bank's version of the talk finally appeared weeks after the launch of the present volume. See also note 1, where Brathwaite describes the historical context in which his speech was delivered; ibid., 286.
8. Ibid., 377.
9. Ibid., 185.
10. Ibid., 189.
11. Ibid., 202.
12. See Rohlehr's comments in his introduction to *DreamStories* and also Brathwaite, *X/self* (New York: Oxford University Press, 1987), 80–87. See also the note to the reader at the beginning of the story "Chad", in which Brathwaite's two muses, Chad and Zea, merge through his computer to warn him of the impending destruction of his Irish Town home; Brathwaite, *DreamStories*, 47–50.
13. Edward Kamau Brathwaite, *Mother Poem* (New York: Oxford University Press, 1977), 46–47.
14. Brathwaite, *Zea Mexican Diary*, 72–73.
15. Brathwaite, *Barabajan Poems*, 316.
16. Brathwaite's poetic vision has been the object of some feminist criticism, most notably Beverly Brown's "Mansong and Matrix: A Radical Experiment", in *A Double Decolonization: Colonial and Postcolonial Women's Writing*, ed. Kirsten Peterson and Anna Rutherford (Coventry, UK: Dangaroo Press, 1986), 68–79. Brown accuses Brathwaite of manufacturing exclusively male myths and reducing women in his work to a voiceless, passive, inert landscape. She is especially critical of what she perceives to be Brathwaite's recourse to "androcentric birthing, so that even foetal blood may be credited to a male figure and the sea is the recipient of Father-ancestor rivers" (70). Rohlehr mounts a spirited defence of Brathwaite that mostly faults Brown for not having read Brathwaite closely enough; Gordon Rohlehr, "Brathwaite with a Dash of Brown: Crit, the Writer and the Written Life", in *Shape of That Hurt*, 229–43. Nevertheless, I think

Brathwaite's work is open to charges of male-centredness, not because it is not sympathetic in its presentation of women but because he does (understandably!) write from a male perspective, and there is often an implicit opposition in his work between woman – as place, land and mother – and man – as intellect, alienated subject, keeper of the word of the father. Most of the time I see this as a productive opposition. Given the poet's subject position and historical moment of insertion into Caribbean literary discourse, it seems inevitable that he would work best through such images, and predictable that eventually they would attract disapproving attention from feminist critics. What interests me here, however, is how this dialogic process is extended and refracted by re-inscription of Brathwaite's poems within the latticework of autobiographical interventions provided in *Barabajan Poems*.

17. Brathwaite, *Mother Poem*, 112.
18. Brathwaite, *Barabajan Poems*, 328.
19. Kamau Brathwaite, "The New West Indian Novelists: Part 2", *Bim* 8, no. 32 (January–June 1961), 274.
20. Brathwaite, *Zea Mexican Diary*, 153. His statement about the individual's relationship to community is made in the course of criticism of the narcissistic introspection that he divines as a flaw in both the author and the protagonist of Lamming's *Of Age and Innocence* (London: Allison and Busby, 1981). I find it significant that both Naipaul and Brathwaite identify in this particular novel – which they both read in important ways as having failed – problems that became central to the aesthetic dilemmas of their own later work.
21. Brathwaite, *Barabajan Poems*, 334.
22. Ibid., 333.
23. For a discussion of the psychological implications of this grammatical move, see my introduction to this book, as well as Cobham-Sander, "Colin Ferguson", 16–21.
24. Brathwaite, *Barabajan Poems*, 222.
25. Ibid.
26. Ibid., 239–40.
27. Ibid., 263, 264.
28. Ibid., 236.
29. Ibid., 189.
30. Ibid., 167.
31. Ibid., 268.
32. Ibid., 364.
33. Gordon Rohlehr writes perceptively about what he perceives as the central irony of Brathwaite's life as a public poet who, in order to create, needed to remain

the most private of persons but who failed to understand this need in others. When, in the aftermath of his wife's death, Brathwaite upbraided the university community at Mona, Jamaica, for their lack of support, Rohlehr contends, he was asking other, equally private people in this "community of isolatos" to step out of their own needed private space: "Brathwaite was demanding from Mona far more than it could ever have given: a support system of continuous concern and caring, that is possible only within the warmth and immediacy of a family. And Brathwaite had lost his"; Rohlehr, *Shape of that Hurt*, 211–12.

Chapter 6

1. Brathwaite, *Barabajan Poems*, 141. In Standard English, without the lisp, this passage translates into something like "And you are not going to be the one to unscrew the cap under the bonnet of this lorry; you, who think you are such a big-shot man, nor are you going to get a chance to crank up this fan with that handle of yours you think you can handle and pump [interrupts here with epic simile to describe the change in her tone]. You see, you see, you see what I told you! That is all you billy-goats want to do with us: pump gas into our tanks – without so much as a thank-you, as my mother always says. And when you're through driving us about any way you like, you go back to town and forget all about the bill when an accident happens and the lorry ends up in the dump. But listen to me, Mister Full-of-Yourself, nobody has driven this little lorry yet [showing him where it was in the tree], and nobody is going to get a chance to ride it either, unless they show me a licence before they get in."
2. Ibid., 313–15, 319–20.
3. Ibid., 141.
4. Ibid., 314.
5. Ibid., 320.
6. Ibid., 139.
7. Ibid., 316.
8. Ibid., 134.
9. Ibid., 314.
10. Ibid.
11. Ibid., 166.
12. According to a Caribbean folk adage, "Gap-tooth girl have a bag of sugar"; that is, women with widely spaced front teeth are perceived to be sexier and more licentious than others. Another possible reading of Esse's lisp that would support my reading here is that it associates her with the Anansi trickster figure

of Caribbean and West African folklore, who, at least in the New World, is represented as having a nasal drawl and a lisp – qualities that in a man suggest a certain effeminacy, an indeterminacy of signification appropriate to a figure whose place in the power hierarchy is constantly shifting.

13. M.M. Bakhtin, *The Dialogic Imagination: Four Essays*, trans. Caryl Emerson and Michael Holquist; ed. Michael Holquist (1981; Austin: University of Texas Press, 2004), 294.
14. M.M. Bakhtin, *Problems of Dostoevsky's Poetics* (1984; Minneapolis: University of Minnesota Press, 2003), 292–93.
15. Walcott, *Omeros*, 294.
16. Jamaica Kincaid offers just such a rereading of the struggle for domination in the master–slave dynamic when she refigures the black woman as playing out an aggressively sadomasochistic fantasy in which she "directs" the master's invasion of her body, ultimately saving her truest pleasure for those masturbatory moments when she dispenses altogether with his services; Jamaica Kincaid, *The Autobiography of My Mother* (New York: Farrar, Straus and Giroux, 1996).
17. Brathwaite, *Barabajan Poems*, 132–33.
18. Hilary Beckles, *Black Rebellion in Barbados: The Struggle against Slavery, 1627–1838* (Bridgetown, Barbados: Antilles, 1984), 1–8, 52–53.
19. Gordon Rohlehr has observed that the Barbadian sensibility in George Lamming's novels is both titillated and terrified by the idea of social upheaval, and that many of Lamming's images of the vortex of social transformation conceal their negative double, the void. In discussing the ending of Lamming's *Water with Berries*, Rohlehr notes: "Catastrophe in the present renders the future far less 'open' than the unresolved issues at the end of each novel may suggest"; Rohlehr, "Possession as Metaphor", in *Shape of That Hurt*, 95. Brathwaite often seems more sanguine than this, but his deep private insecurities about the absence of personal support for his artistic project undermine his public optimism about the possibility of a restructured community. In Brathwaite's later confessional texts, the poet grows increasingly pessimistic about the level of unchannelled violence and chaos within the black underclass. One thinks, for example, of his description of the plumber in the story "Grease", whose rape of his wife is not ameliorated by any of the more sympathetic images Brathwaite associates with similarly dehumanized men in the earlier *Mother Poem*; Brathwaite, *DreamStories*, 112–33.
20. Most poor white Barbadians are the descendants of indentured Irish servants brought to Barbados before and during the first importations of African slaves in the sixteenth century. For a history of their presence, see Jill Sheppard, *The "Redlegs" of Barbados: Their Origins and History* (Millwood, NY: KTO Press,

1977). Hilary Beckles reports that at various moments in Barbadian history, poor whites made common cause with enslaved Africans against the planter class; Beckles, *Black Rebellion*. Many "redlegs" rose in the island's social and economic hierarchy once race came to define social status during the colonial period. However, it is altogether conceivable that the fortunes of other white Barbadians declined.

Chapter 7

1. Edward Kamau Brathwaite, *Sun Poem* (New York: Oxford University Press, 1982), 61.
2. They are James Edward, born 1844; Henry Lawson, 1874; Edward Hilton, 1908; Lawson Edward [Kamau], 1930; and Michael Kwesi, 1958.
3. Brathwaite, *Barabajan Poems*, 152.
4. Ibid., 132–33.
5. (that was our space)
   (my 3 sisters slept in our mother's room till Aunt Lucille died)
   I am grateful to Gordon Rohlehr for drawing my attention to the single direct reference Brathwaite makes to his father in *Barabajan Poems*: "My first memories are there - when I first or even before I first saw th/(e) sea - coming from Hart's Gap when I was about 7 years old - retur/ning to a Round House I before this don't remember and falling aslee/(p) - emotionally, I χpect - on arrival and then waking up in the Simmonds bed I was to share (that was our space) with my father for the 20 years I lived in Barbados (my 3 sisters slept in our mother's room till Aunt Lucille died) and watching the light from the sea on the wall of the room and not knowing/understanding what it was"; Brathwaite, *Barabajan Poems*, 109. Brathwaite's unconventional line breaks and his use of an undersized typeface for the shockingly intimate information in the allusion – itself a digression within a digression – only deepens the mystery surrounding his absent father. His association of this first memory with falling asleep emotionally, as well as with primordial beginnings and death, would give a Freudian psychoanalyst a field day!
6. Brathwaite, *Sun Poem*, 62.
7. Ibid.
8. Edward Kamau Brathwaite, *Ancestors* (New York: New Direction, 2001), 283.
9. Edward Kamau Brathwaite, *The Arrivants: A New World Trilogy* (London: Oxford University Press, 1973), 239, 242.
10. Brathwaite, *Barabajan Poems*, 156–61.

11. Ibid., 131.
12. Brathwaite, *Arrivants*, 239.
13. Brathwaite, *Barabajan Poems*, 162.
14. Brathwaite, *Sun Poem*, 87.
15. Ibid.
16. Ibid., 87, 88.
17. Ibid., 103.
18. Ibid., 90.
19. Ibid., 88.
20. See also my comments in note 5 on a similar moment of strategic forgetting in Brathwaite's parenthetical remarks about sharing a bed with his father.
21. Brathwaite, *Sun Poem*, 89.
22. Ibid., 90.
23. From the third-century Greek spelling of Jesus Christ, which was sometimes shortened, particularly in Christian inscriptions, to IC and XC or IHS and XPS, for *Iesous Christos*. These Greek monograms continued to be used in Latin during the Middle Ages. Eventually the right meaning was lost; erroneous interpretation of IHS led to the faulty orthography *Jhesus*. Saint Ignatius of Loyola adopted the monogram IHS for his seal as general of the Society of Jesus (1541), and thus it became the emblem of the Jesuits. IHS was sometimes wrongly understood as "Jesus Hominum (or Hierosolymae) Salvator", i.e., Jesus, the saviour of men; "IHS", in *Catholic Encyclopedia*, vol. 7 (New York: Robert Appleton, 1910), http://www.newadvent.org/cathen/07649a.htm. The monogram often appears inscribed on prayer books or in stained glass windows in Roman and English Catholic churches.
24. Brathwaite, *Sun Poem*, 88.
25. I use the modality *should* deliberately. Although the die for sixpences bearing the head of Edward VIII was struck in 1937, the coins were never minted because the monarch abdicated the throne. The use of his name to identify the missing sixpences, therefore, is my conceit, not that of the poet. I am assuming that the story about the missing sixpences is set in 1937–38, when the child in the poem would have been seven or eight years old, and both sets of sixpences are now "missing". The iterations of the given name Edward in the Brathwaite family map onto its recurrence in the British royal family, as it was not uncommon in the British Caribbean for children to be named after the most recent addition to the royal family or in honour of the most recently crowned monarch. Brathwaite's great-grandfather (b. 1844) was christened James Edward, three years after the birth of Edward VII (b. 1841), and the poet's father, Edward Hilton, was born seven years after Edward VII's coronation in 1901. Edward VIII's 1937 abdication

for love of the American divorcée Mrs Simpson made him a wildly popular figure in the Caribbean, which he had toured in the early 1930s while he was Prince of Wales. The refrain of a calypso commemorating the scandal – "It was love, love, love alone that forced King Edward to leave the throne" – provided Naipaul with the title of one of his sketches in *Miguel Street* and has now passed into the popular musical repertoire of the region. It may be stretching the conceit a bit too far, however, to attach significance to the fact that the last Edwards in both the British and Bajan patrilineages ended up choosing to expunge their name from their respective family trees.

26. Brathwaite, *Sun Poem*, 88.
27. Ibid., 88–89.
28. Ibid., 89.
29. Ibid. It is worth noting the parallels here between Brathwaite's use of the motif of the disappearing coin and a similar series of images in Lamming's *In the Castle of My Skin* (New York: McGraw-Hill, 1953) involving the pennies the boys scrutinize and hide and the penny the drunken schoolmaster loses. The two authors use lost British coins to indicate colonial impotence on the part of adults and the desire for agency on the part of the boys, in such similar ways that it is tempting to read Brathwaite's image as derivative of Lamming's – like Naipaul's appropriation of Lamming's description of the meal of coo-coo. It is important to keep in mind, however, that Brathwaite claims to have written several sections of *Sun Poem* very early in his career, as part of a fictionalized memoir that he abandoned when Lamming's novel appeared, because he feared the two works would be considered too similar; Brathwaite, *Barabajan Poems*, 300.
30. Brathwaite, *Sun Poem*, 61.
31. Strictly speaking, Frank Collymore (1885–1980) was not white. In the first chapter of his biography of Collymore, Edward Baugh traces the genealogy of the family from the Scots-descended Robert Collymore (born ca. 1750), an attorney for large estate owners and a land speculator, who purchased and manumitted the mulatto slave Amaryllis Rebecca Phillips, with whom he had eleven children. Although he never married her, Robert left Amaryllis a small estate in his will. She ran the estate successfully, increasing the number of slaves she owned from forty-four to sixty-five and diversifying her assets by purchasing a number of medium-sized town properties. Amaryllis's descendants intermarried with other landed mulatto families and they ranged across the colour spectrum. One of her grandchildren, Joseph Richard Collymore (1796–1891), was Frank Collymore's great-grandfather. His son, James Pharor Collymore (1828–87), married an Englishwoman, and their son, Joseph Appleton Collymore (1857–1932), who was Frank's father, married into a white Barbadian family. Thus, by Frank

Collymore's generation, his branch of the family could easily pass for white. Moreover, as would have been common for his time and class, Frank did not consider himself a "Negro"; however, he never claimed that he was white and occasionally corrected those who assumed he was. Such racial indeterminacy is typical of the Caribbean mixed-race upper middle class. For our purposes, however, it is clear that, socially and ideologically (except perhaps for that very tiny portion of the Barbadian population that claimed pure white descent), Frank Collymore signified as white. Like "Tom Redcam" (Thomas MacDermott) in Jamaica a generation earlier, it was precisely this presumption of whiteness that made his dedication to the advancement of "black" Caribbean writers so noteworthy, although both men are rightly remembered as personally generous, ideologically free of prejudice and culturally dedicated to their communities. See Edward Baugh, *Frank Collymore: A Biography* (Kingston: Ian Randle, 2009).

32. Brathwaite, *Barabajan Poems*, 19.
33. Walcott, *Another Life*, CP, 257. Dunstan St Omer, Walcott's teenage running-mate, becomes the inspired intuitive fellow artist Gregorias in Book Two of *Another Life*. Andreuille, his first love, she of the golden hair, becomes Anna, the first in a long line of female muses in Walcott's oeuvre who fuel his erotic fantasies and his poetic imagination. Harry Simmons's relationship to Walcott was similar to Brathwaite's relationship with Collymore; he taught Walcott to paint and introduced him to Caribbean poetry. His suicide, committed while Walcott was working on *Another Life*, provides the closing "cut" for the poem: "When I began this work, you were alive, / and with one stroke, you have completed it!"; ibid., 282. For a full discussion of the autobiographical aspects of *Another Life*, see Edward Baugh, *Derek Walcott: Memory as Vision: Another Life* (London: Longman, 1978).
34. Brathwaite, *Barabajan Poems*, 19.
35. Brathwaite, *Sun Poem*, 90.
36. Brathwaite, *Barabajan Poems*, 41.
37. Ibid., 41–42.
38. Ibid., 40.
39. Brathwaite and other Caribbean intellectuals borrow the phrase "New World Negro" from the anthropologist Melville Herskovits, whose controversial classic, *The Myth of the Negro Past* (1941; repr., Boston: Beacon Press, 1990) rejected the notion that African Americans lost all traces of their past when they were taken from Africa and enslaved in America. See, for example, Edward Kamau Brathwaite, introduction, in Melville Herskovits, *Life in a Haitian Valley* (1937; New York: Doubleday, 1971), and Brathwaite, "The Contribution of M.J. Herskovits to Afro-American Studies", *ASAWI Bulletin* 5 (December 1972): 85–94. Both are

cited by David Scott in his discussion of Brathwaite's relationship to Herskovits and to anthropology more generally, in *Refashioning Futures: Criticism after Postcoloniality* (Princeton, NJ: Princeton University Press, 1999), 109–10.

40. Brathwaite is explicit about this inclusivity in *Barabajan Poems*. See, for example, his description of Julian Hunte in footnote 14: "a white ITAL Baje for those who glad to note that some at least white Bajans continue - increasingly so, I think, since the 80s - to contrib to Bajan life & letters"; *Barabajan Poems*, 289. He cites *Contradictory Omens: Cultural Diversity and Integration in the Caribbean* (Kingston: Savacou Mona, 1974) as the piece in which he makes this argument most explicitly, although that essay has often been (mis)read as insisting upon the exclusively African origins of Caribbean culture. Brathwaite returns to this issue in footnote 19+, where he voices his exasperation at Caribbean writers and critics who interpret any explicit expression of the African origins of Caribbean culture as dangerously exclusive, or an indication of atavistic excess: "on the one hand the 'negro' is a brute and has nothing to contribute. Next - suddenly - he/she is being accuse/(d) of being bute & FADDIST, producing all or too much/ though no one in the Caribb has ever seriously argued (see **Contradictory Omens**) for an xclusively 'Negro' interview"; ibid., 299.
41. Ibid., 40.
42. Ibid.
43. Walcott, "Che", *CP*, 123.
44. *The Entombment of Christ* (1602–3) is generally considered the most monumental of Caravaggio's paintings. The symmetrical composition of its human subjects is built up from the stone slab onto which the body of Christ is being lowered, which juts diagonally out of the background. The painting is from the altar of the Chiesa Nuova in Rome, which is dedicated to the Pietà. The embalming of the corpse and the entombment are actually secondary to the mourning of Mary, which is the focal point of the lamentation.
45. In the estimate of most art historians, nothing distinguished Caravaggio's paintings more strongly from the art of the Renaissance than his refusal to portray the human individual as sublime, beautiful and heroic. "His figures are bowed, bent, cowering, reclining or stooped. The self-confident and the statuesque have been replaced by humility and subjection"; Hermann Bauer and Andreas Prater, *Baroque*, ed. Ingo F. Walther (London: Taschen, 2006), 30.
46. Derek Walcott, "The Muse of History", in *What the Twilight Says*, 36.
47. Brathwaite, *Mother Poem*, 112.
48. Brathwaite's most controversial statement of this position is delivered in *Contradictory Omens*, but he returns to this claim in all the major essays now

collected in the volume *Roots*. For a perceptive discussion of the face-off between Brathwaite and the Trinidadian poet Eric Roach on this point, see Gordon Rohlehr, "West Indian Poetry: Some Problems of Assessment", in *My Strangled City and Other Essays* (Port of Spain: Longman Trinidad, 1992), 107–32.
49. Edward Kamau Brathwaite, *Roots* (Ann Arbor: University of Michigan Press, 1993), 45–46.
50. Ibid., 48.
51. Brathwaite, *Barabajan Poems*, 134–37.
52. Brathwaite, *Mother Poem*, 20.
53. Brathwaite, *Arrivants*, 162.
54. Brathwaite, *Barabajan Poems*, 130.
55. Brathwaite, *Sun Poem*, 67.
56. Edward Kamau Brathwaite, *Other Exiles* (New York: Oxford University Press, 1975), 7.
57. Brathwaite, *Barabajan Poems*, 58.
58. Ibid.
59. Ibid., 58–59.
60. Brathwaite, *Other Exiles*, 7.
61. Brathwaite, *Barabajan Poems*, 62.
62. Ibid., 65.
63. Catherine Hall, *Civilising Subjects: Colony and Metropole in the English Imagination, 1830–1967* (Chicago: University of Chicago Press, 2002), 19.
64. Ibid.
65. Homi Bhabha, "Of Mimicry and Men: The Ambivalence of Colonial Discourse" (1984), in *The Location of Culture* (New York: Routledge Classics, 2004), 130.
66. Homi Bhabha, "Signs Taken for Wonders: Questions of Ambivalence and Authority under a Tree Outside Delhi, May 1817" (1985), in *Location of Culture*, 172.
67. Brathwaite, *Arrivants*, 239.
68. Brathwaite, *Sun Poem*, 61.

Chapter 8

1. Walcott, *Omeros*, 266.
2. Ibid.
3. Ibid.
4. Ibid., 28.
5. *Enigma*'s narrator describes spending two years working on a book whose themes

touch upon "discovery, the New World, the dispeopling of the discovered islands; slavery, the creation of the plantation colony, the coming of the idea of revolution; the chaos after revolutions in societies so created"; Naipaul, *Enigma of Arrival*, 101. He reports having such great faith in "the grandeur of [his] story" that he packed up and moved back to Trinidad after completing the manuscript, in the expectation that this book would "find the readers that my books of the previous twelve years had not found" (ibid.). He was devastated when it failed to attract favourable critical attention. The details of this account map closely onto the description in French's biography of Naipaul's unsuccessful attempt to relocate to Trinidad after having completed *The Loss of El Dorado*. Naipaul's attempts in *El Dorado* to define his relationship to Trinidad by writing himself into its history suggest interesting parallels between this work and Walcott's *Another Life*, especially their mutual concern with the original native inhabitants of the Caribbean.

6. Walcott, "Garden Path", 125.
7. Caryl Phillips, in his review of *The Arkansas Testament*, describes Walcott as one of the "poetic gang of four (Josef Brodsky, Czeslaw Milosz and Seamus Heaney being the other three), the internationally displaced poets who teach in America"; Caryl Phillips, "No Man Ever Dies in His Own Country", *Los Angeles Times Book Review*, 6 September 1987, 1–9.
8. Wayne Brown, "Caribbean Booktalk: Derek Walcott – His Poetry and His People", *Caribbean Affairs* 1, no. 3 (1988): 176.
9. Ibid., 184.
10. Derek Walcott, *The Arkansas Testament* (New York: Farrar, Straus and Giroux, 1987), 73.
11. Brown, "Caribbean Booktalk", 181.
12. Rohlehr, "The Problem of the Problem of Form: The Idea of an Aesthetic Continuum and Aesthetic Code-Switching in West Indian Literature", in *Shape of That Hurt*, 38.
13. Walcott, "Garden Path", 122.
14. Walcott, *Another Life*, CP, 158.
15. Ibid., 165.
16. Ibid., 183.
17. Naipaul, "Jasmine", 25.
18. Walcott, *Another Life*, CP, 161.
19. Walcott, *Omeros*, 283.
20. Ibid., 14.
21. Walcott, "Garden Path", 125.
22. Walcott, *Arkansas Testament*, 50.

23. Ibid.
24. Ibid., 51.
25. Ibid., 48.
26. Ibid., 51.
27. Ibid., 50–51.
28. Ibid., 51.
29. Ibid., 48.
30. Prints of Holman's painting *The Light of the World* enjoyed great popularity as domestic religious icons in the British colonies in the early twentieth century. When a life-sized replica of Holman's painting toured the Commonwealth between 1905 and 1907, more than seven million people waited in line to see it. See Jeremy Maas, *Holman Hunt and the Light of the World* (London: Scolar Press, 1984), 184–85.
31. V.S. Naipaul, *The Mimic Men* (New York: Macmillan, 1967), 171–72.
32. Ibid., 172.
33. Jamaica Kincaid's novel *See Now Then* (New York: Farrar, Straus and Giroux, 2013) invokes a strikingly similar catalogue of images of loss when the narrator declares: "Mrs. Sweet, looking out at the mountains named Green and Anthony, and the river Paran – its manmade lake interrupting its smooth flow – in the valley, all that remained of a great geologic upheaval, a Then that she was seeing Now and her present will be buried deep in it, so deep that it will never, would never be recognized by anyone who resembled her in any shape or form: not race, not gender, not animal, not vegetable nor any of the other kingdoms, for nothing yet known can or will benefit from her suffering, and all of her existence was suffering: love, love, and love in all its forms and configurations, hatred being one of them" (10). Like all three writers I consider here, Kincaid is extraordinarily invested in the representation and significance of landscape, both its surface features and its genealogical prehistory, and the act of writing functions as both explicit theme and subtext in all her work. In the passage quoted here, her insistent rhetorical negations push back against the claim that Mrs Sweet's words and presence will never come to define the Vermont landscape. Naipaul, though he may harbour similar ambition with respect to Trinidad and Wiltshire, turns away in exhaustion from any such assertion, leaving his readers to decide the fate of his literary legacy.
34. Walcott, "Garden Path", 123.
35. Naipaul, *Overcrowded Barracoon*, 16–17.
36. Naipaul's authorized biographer quotes from a letter Naipaul wrote to his fiancée, Pat, in 1953 after he left Oxford, in which he describes "the everyday racial humiliations he faced in London and his epic uncertainty over his future, displaying raw

wounds to her that he would afterwards try to keep hidden from the world for the rest of his life"; French, *World Is What It Is*, 136. Naipaul fulminates: "Go out & get a clerical job, you write, adding, there are heaps of those. I hate to spring a surprise on you . . . but the people in authority feel my qualifications fit me only for jobs as porters in kitchens, and with the road gangs. My physique decrees otherwise. . . . It is my own fault. Why don't I go back where I came from, and not be a nuisance to anyone? Niggers ought to know their place" (ibid.). Naipaul's need to distinguish himself physically and professionally from less educated immigrants, at a time when his economic prospects were little different from theirs, differentiates his response to racism from that of Walcott, who seems more concerned about his vulnerability, despite his professional privileges, to physical attack in America at the hands of both blacks and whites.

37. Walcott's mixed racial heritage and light skin would not automatically identify him as "black" by Caribbean standards. Bruce King reports that during a phone conversation with Ralph Lennox, who reviewed Walcott's first major poetry reading in the United States in 1964, Walcott had described an exchange with Ralph Ellison in which "Ellison told him that he was not a negro and Walcott said that that was right, he does not feel like one, but did not want to be quoted"; Bruce King, *Derek Walcott: A Caribbean Life* (Oxford: Oxford University Press, 2000), 204.
38. Walcott, *Arkansas Testament*, 102, 109.
39. Walcott, "The Spoiler's Return", *CP*, 432.
40. Walcott, *Arkansas Testament*, 79.
41. Ibid., 88.
42. Naipaul, *Enigma of Arrival*, 5.
43. Ibid., 15.
44. Ibid., 102–3.
45. Bruce King's biography devotes several chapters to this period in Walcott's life. See especially chapters 23 to 25 (405–73). Although King reads the 1980s retrospectively as a period of personal and professional consolidation – Walcott had started working on *Omeros*, the 1986 *Collected Poems* had been a big hit, and Walcott was beginning to reconnect to St Lucia and to establish a relationship with Sigrid Nama – he also describes the writer as lonely in his personal life (468–69), using interviews to make up for the absence of community (471) and still fighting with old and new collaborators about plans for staging plays and creating film scripts in America (417, 459). Walcott was also running into new problems with American students who interpreted his often aggressively direct personal style as sexual harassment (414–16).
46. Walcott, *Omeros*, 187–88.

47. Ibid., 187.
48. Giorgio de Chirico (1888–1978) was a Greek-born Italian artist whose work was first championed, then excoriated, by the surrealist movement. After 1919 he became interested in traditional painting techniques, frequently revisiting the metaphysical themes of his earlier work. The painting *The Enigma of Arrival* was completed in 1912, near the end of his experimental period, and reflects the allegorical style of much surrealist painting of that era. Walcott's review of *Enigma* includes a short diatribe against surrealism, even though he concedes that Naipaul's reliance on a surrealist image does not fall into the clichés often associated with this school. See Walcott, "Garden Path", 124.
49. Naipaul, *Enigma of Arrival*, 98.
50. Ibid., 99.
51. Ibid., 238.
52. Ibid., 239.
53. Ibid., 238–39.
54. Ibid., 239.
55. Walcott, *Omeros*, 54.
56. Ibid., 55.
57. Naipaul, *Enigma of Arrival*, 53.
58. Walcott, *Omeros*, 61.
59. Naipaul, *Enigma of Arrival*, 53.
60. Ibid.
61. Walcott, *Omeros*, 307.
62. Ibid., 308.
63. Walcott, "Season of Phantasmal Peace", *CP*, 464–65.
64. Walcott, *Omeros*, 309.
65. Naipaul, *Enigma of Arrival*, 354.
66. Walcott, *Another Life*, *CP*, 158.
67. Walcott, "North and South", *CP*, 407.
68. Naipaul, *Enigma of Arrival*, 34–35.
69. Walcott, "Garden Path", 125.
70. Ibid., 128.
71. Walcott, *Omeros*, 268.
72. Ibid., 269.
73. Ibid.
74. Ibid., 269–70.
75. Ibid., 270.
76. Walcott, "Garden Path", 123.
77. Walcott, *Arkansas Testament*, 44.

78. Walcott, *Omeros*, 56.
79. Ibid., 57.
80. Ibid., 309.
81. Ibid., 183; Walcott, "Garden Path", 125.
82. Walcott, "Garden Path", 123.
83. From my reading of the manuscript drafts of *Omeros*, Walcott seems to have deliberately excised a number of such scenes, including at least one that draws more explicitly on the breakdown of his marriage to Norline Metevier, and another that would have made Helen a light-skinned mulatto who had more interactions with the narrator.
84. Walcott, "Garden Path", 125.
85. Walcott, *Omeros*, 173.
86. Ibid., 174.
87. Ibid., 208.
88. Ibid., 211.
89. Ibid., 212.
90. In this regard, though it borrows from both Greek and Roman models for its classical allusions, Walcott's *Omeros* most explicitly rewrites Homer's *Odyssey*, placing all its imaginative resources at the service of an achieved final homecoming. As Caryl Phillips points out, even in the early 1980s, when he was most anxious about the consequences of exile, Walcott resisted the idea that exile had to mean a final rupture with home. Phillips quotes the closing lines of the *Midsummer* collection, addressed to Joseph Brodsky, in which Walcott insists that "though no man ever dies in his own country, / the grateful grass will grow thick from his heart" (*CP*, 510). By contrast, Virgil's chronicle in *The Aeneid* of the inaugurating losses and cruel compromises that accompany the search for a new homeland align more closely with Naipaul's *Enigma*. For more on Walcott's classical debt, see Gregson Davis, "'Homecomings without Home': Representations of (Post)colonial *nostos* (Homecoming) in the Lyric of Aimé Césaire and Derek Walcott", in *Homer in the Twentieth Century: Between World Literature and the Western Canon*, ed. Barbara Graziosi and Emily Greenwood (Oxford: Oxford University Press, 2007), 191–209.
91. Walcott, "Garden Path", 122.
92. The episode with the dairyman's son in *Enigma* supplies a mocking riposte to Wordsworth's poem "We Are Seven". It resists that poem's cloying reification of simple English folk, fondly imagined as infinitely open to ethical co-optation by their betters. The list of Caribbean authors whose education steeped them in the poetry and prose of the Romantics and whose writing resists and appropriates a pastoral sublime includes Jamaica Kincaid in *Lucy* (1990; repr., New York:

Farrar, Straus and Giroux, 2002), Merle Collins in *Angel* (Seattle: Seal Press, 1988) and Lamming in *In the Castle of My Skin*.
93. Naipaul, *Enigma of Arrival*, 53.
94. Walcott, *Omeros*, 28, 269.
95. Ibid., 61.
96. In his review of *Omeros*, Brad Leithauser catalogues the seemingly endless varieties of rhyme the work employs, including such arcane forms as triple rhymes, visual rhymes, pararhymes or rim rhymes, anagrammatic rhymes, apocopated rhymes, macaronic rhymes and *rime riche*; Brad Leithauser, "Ancestral Rhyme", *New Yorker*, 11 February 1991, 93. One could assemble a similar catalogue of types of metaphor in the poem, especially its varieties of metonymy. For more on this, see Nicole Matos, " 'Join, Interchangeable Phantoms': From Metaphor to Metonymy in Walcott's *Omeros*", *Small Axe* 10, no. 2 (2006): 40–60.
97. Walcott, "Garden Path", 127–28.
98. Walcott, *Arkansas Testament*, 50.
99. The *double entendre* is Walcott's. In his review he glosses Naipaul's well-known line from *Enigma*, "the island had given me the world as a writer", as "[the island] had given the world me as a writer"; Walcott, "Garden Path", 127.
100. Walcott, *Omeros*, 320–21.
101. Ibid., 320.
102. Ibid., 321.
103. Ibid., 296.

Chapter 9

1. Walcott, *Omeros*, 233.
2. The terms are Brathwaite's, introduced in one of his early critiques of Walcott. See Edward Brathwaite, "West Indian Poetry: A Search for Voices" (lecture in the seminar series "The State of the Arts in Jamaica", University of the West Indies, 14 March 1965). Mervyn Morris cites it and then defends Walcott from its attacks; see "Walcott and the Audience for Poetry", in Hamner, *Critical Perspectives*, 177. Patricia Ismond lays out the perceived differences between the two authors most definitively, in "Walcott versus Brathwaite", 220–36. Meanwhile, Rohlehr addresses the controversy indirectly in "Withering into Truth: A Review of Derek Walcott's *The Gulf and Other Poems*", in Hamner, *Critical Perspectives*, 212–19.
3. Patricia Ismond locates another series of appropriations, this time from Brathwaite's *Mother Poem*, in Walcott's long poem about Michael Manley's Jamaica, *Star Apple Kingdom* (New York: Farrar, Straus and Giroux, 1979); Patricia

Ismond, *Abandoning Dead Metaphors: The Caribbean Phase of Derek Walcott's Poetry* (Kingston: University of the West Indies Press, 2001), 271–73. In one of *Omeros*'s more memorable images, Walcott also repurposes Brathwaite's coral metaphor. The relevant passage in *Arrivants* (232) reads:

> A yellow mote of sand dreams in the polyp's eye;
> the coral needs this pain.
> Look closely:
> the pearl has limestone ridges, hills,
> out of it grows the sun
> and the fat valleys of Haiti,
> . . .
> The coral killers crust my wall of bone

In *Omeros* (296), a similar image acquires new associations:

> strong as self-healing coral, a quiet culture
> is branching from the white ribs of each ancestor,
>
> deeper than it seems on the surface; slowly but sure,
> it will change us with the fluent sculpture of Time

4. Walcott, *Another Life*, CP, 264–65.
5. King offers an extended version of this story. See King, *Derek Walcott*, 455–56.
6. Derek Walcott, "What the Twilight Says", in *What the Twilight Says*, 26.
7. Derek Walcott, "The Caribbean: Culture or Mimicry?", in Hamner, *Critical Perspectives*, 57.
8. Derek Walcott, "Tribal Flutes", in Hamner, *Critical Perspectives*, 44.
9. Walcott, "What the Twilight Says", 35.
10. Derek Walcott, *Dream on Monkey Mountain and Other Plays* (New York: Farrar, Straus and Giroux, 1970), 155; Edward Hirsch, "The Art of Poetry", in Hamner, *Critical Perspectives*, 73.
11. For a discussion of Walcott's early relationships, see Ismond, *Abandoning Dead Metaphors*, 158–59. For Walcott's comments on these early friendships, see Hirsch, "Art of Poetry", 80–82. For his assessment of Lowell's poetry, see "On Robert Lowell", in *What the Twilight Says*, 88–106.
12. Walcott, "The Schooner *Flight*", CP, 355.
13. Walcott, *Omeros*, 15–16.
14. Walcott, *Another Life*, CP, 158–59.
15. Walcott, *Omeros*, 17.
16. Ibid., 18.

17. Walcott, "Tales of the Islands", *CP*, 24–25.
18. Ibid., 25. Critics have discussed the sonnets exhaustively on account of their use of language. Mervyn Morris offers an analysis of their evolution from the time of their first appearance in *Bim* magazine to their publication, five years later, in *In a Green Night* (London: Cape, 1962), which anticipates several of my arguments later in this chapter about the significance of Walcott's revisions to the opening sequence in *Omeros*; Morris, "Walcott and the Audience", 184–86.
19. Anthony Milne, "Derek Walcott", in Hamner, *Critical Perspectives*, 63.
20. Ibid.
21. Ibid.
22. Brathwaite, *Arrivants*, 65.
23. Ibid., 62.
24. Derek Walcott, "A Letter to Chamoiseau", in *What the Twilight Says*, 219.
25. Brathwaite, *Arrivants*, 66.
26. Ibid., 62, 63.
27. Ibid., 67.
28. Ibid., 68–69.
29. Ibid., 44.
30. Ibid., 44–45.
31. Ibid., 42.
32. Ibid., 42, 43.
33. Walcott, "Tribal Flutes", 44.
34. Ibid., 41.
35. Ibid.
36. Ibid., 43.
37. Derek Walcott, "'Rights of Passage': Drama in Itself", *Trinidad Guardian*, 25 April 1973, 5.
38. Ibid.
39. Derek Walcott, "Necessity of Negritude", in Hamner, *Critical Perspectives*, 22.
40. Derek Walcott, "Meanings", in Hamner, *Critical Perspectives*, 48.
41. Walcott, "Tribal Flutes", 44.
42. Walcott, "Drama in Itself", 5.
43. Morris, "Walcott and the Audience", 184.
44. Dennis Scott, "Walcott on Walcott", *Caribbean Quarterly* 14, nos. 1–2 (March–June 1968): 78.
45. Derek Walcott, *Another Life: Fully Annotated*, ed. Edward Baugh and Colbert Nepaulsingh (Boulder: Lynne Rienner, 2004), 163.
46. Walcott, *Arkansas Testament*, 21.
47. Ibid., 10.

48. Walcott, "Muse of History", 49.
49. Ibid.
50. Walcott, *Omeros*, 11.
51. Walcott, "Sainte Lucie", *CP*, 314.
52. Ibid., 317.
53. Ibid., 314.
54. Ibid., 315.
55. Ibid., 316, 318.
56. Walcott, "Tribal Flutes", 42.
57. Walcott, "Sainte Lucie", *CP*, 310.
58. Ibid., 311.
59. Ibid., 309.
60. Ibid., 314.
61. Ibid., 323.
62. Ibid., 307.
63. Ibid.
64. Walcott, "Muse of History", 59.
65. Ibid.
66. Ibid., 54.
67. Ibid., 55, 59.
68. Walcott, "New World", *CP*, 300–301.
69. Ibid., 300.
70. Walcott, "Muse of History", 59.
71. Walcott, "What the Twilight Says", 8.
72. In personal correspondence with me, Paul Breslin notes that Walcott told him he initially thought of writing all of *Omeros* in St Lucian Creole. However, Breslin's studies of early drafts of "Tales of the Islands" and "The Schooner *Flight*" reveal that in actual practice Walcott usually revises "downwards" from Standard to Creole. Both his observations corroborate my argument here about the unique difficulties Walcott faces in moving between Standard English, English Creole and French Creole.
73. Derek Walcott, "Omeros", MS 0564:3:1, Box 20B, Derek Walcott Collection, University of the West Indies Library, St Augustine, Trinidad, n.d.
74. Derek Walcott, "Omeros", MS 0564:4:1, Box 20B, Derek Walcott Collection, University of the West Indies Library, St Augustine, Trinidad, n.d.
75. Walcott, "Sea Grapes", *CP*, 297.
76. Derek Walcott, "Omeros", MS 0564:2:1, Box 20B, Derek Walcott Collection, University of the West Indies Library, St Augustine, Trinidad, n.d.
77. Derek Walcott, "Omeros", MS 0565:5:1, Box 20B, Derek Walcott Collection,

University of the West Indies Library, St Augustine, Trinidad, n.d.
78. Walcott, "Muse of History", 55.
79. Walcott, *Omeros*, 3.
80. Ibid., 6–7.
81. Ibid., 15.
82. Walcott, *Arkansas Testament*, 10; Walcott, *Omeros*, 6.
83. Walcott, *Omeros*, 17.
84. Ibid., 3.
85. Walcott, "Letter to Chamoiseau", 219.
86. Walcott, "Tribal Flutes", 41.
87. Ibid., 42.
88. Ibid., 44.
89. Walcott, "Letter to Chamoiseau", 215.
90. Ibid., 214.
91. Ibid., 223.
92. Ibid., 225.
93. Walcott, "Tribal Flutes", 41.
94. Scott, "Walcott on Walcott", 78.
95. Walcott, *Omeros*, 233.
96. Ibid.
97. Hirsch, "Art of Poetry", 73.
98. Walcott, *Omeros*, 17.
99. Ibid., 233.

Chapter 10

1. Walcott, Poem 14, *Bounty*, 39.
2. Walcott, "Love after Love", *CP*, 328.
3. To be scrupulously even-handed in terms of gender, I should note that *Esquire* magazine has also published the poem. In that version it is superimposed on a full-colour photograph of a fashionably clad Walcott sitting somewhat magisterially – as if for a Kehinde Wiley portrait – and accompanied by this caption: "Derek Walcott has a theory about which he is at least half serious, that the best poets come from islands. Witness Yeats. Witness Philip Larkin. Or Walcott himself. Born in St. Lucia, brought up in Trinidad [sic], educated in Jamaica, Walcott has been publishing poems for nearly forty years; most were recently gathered in a single volume: *Collected Poems 1948–1984* (Farrar, Straus & Giroux). He wears a llama wrap overcoat ($1,038) and reverse-pleated wool trousers ($160). By

Salvatore Ferragamo. Cotton-blend shirt ($32). By Sero. Wool doubleknit pullover sweater ($245). By Jeff Sayre." Derek Walcott, "Love After Love", *Esquire*, August 1986, 99.

4. Walcott, Poem 14, *Bounty*, 39.
5. Ibid.
6. Walcott, "Love after Love", *CP*, 328.
7. Part 4 of King's *Derek Walcott* offers an exhaustive account of this period in Walcott's life. See especially 333–42 for a discussion of the context in which the poems in *Sea Grapes* were produced. King adds to the list of Walcott's woes in the early 1970s a drinking problem (257, 261), anxieties about his family's vulnerability during the 1970 Black Power uprisings in Trinidad (255, 263) and fear of government censorship in its aftermath (275).
8. Anonymous response, 6 July 2009, to 3 June 2009 comment on anonymous post (n.d.), "Love After Love Analysis", http://www.eliteskills.com/analysis_poetry/Love_After_Love_by_Derek_Walcott_analysis.php.
9. "20th Century EuroLite 'Love After Love' ", YouTube video, 6:20, posted by "momomeshmonster", 21 March 2012, https://www.youtube.com/watch?v=acl_maEgOCc.
10. "Love after Love: Derek Walcott", YouTube video, 2:48, posted by "RogerRogerRocket", 12 October 2009, https://www.youtube.com/watch?v=PlljQKq25zs.
11. Anonymous comment, 30 October 2009, on anonymous post (n.d.), "Love after Love Analysis".
12. Walcott, "Love after Love", *CP*, 328.
13. Ibid.
14. T.S. Eliot, *On Poetry and Poets* (1943; New York: Farrar, Straus and Giroux, 2009), 96.
15. W.R. Johnson, *The Idea of Lyric: Lyric Modes in Ancient and Modern Poetry* (Berkeley: University of California Press, 1982), 1. Johnson tracks this meditative form's encroachment through the French and English Romantics (especially Wordsworth's increasingly obscurantist revisions of *The Prelude*) and the Imagist poets to such writers as Sylvia Plath and Delmore Schwartz in the late twentieth century. He shows how at each stage the lyric address contracts, eliminating first *you*, then *I*, until finally we are left with only disconnected images and fractured subjectivities. But eventually he argues for the renaissance of a "singing You" in the work of such poets as Allen Ginsberg and Adrienne Rich, who were part of a New World postwar generation that included both Walcott and Brathwaite. Johnson's argument is less schematic than I have presented it here, as his qualifications clarify: "[I]t is not, of course, merely the restoration of the pronominal form that effects this liberation of the lyric spirit. Much bad poetry, now and

always, has employed the pronominal frame. What there must be in good lyric is 'the sublime,' a 'heartfelt, soulswept elevation.' ... Once that sublimity and elevation have been felt, found, recaptured, what is needed to make them visible and audible is something ... that our ancestors called rhetoric, that is, the vitality of language gathered into and strengthened by the patterned variations of disciplined speech"; ibid., 22–23. His quarrel with the likes of Plath and Schwartz is not on account of their poetic preoccupations with a disintegrating self, which he considers an eloquent representation of their times, but with the way the modernists elevate it from a symptom of the zeitgeist to a repudiation of the possibility of subjectivity.

16. Naipaul, *Mimic Men*, 171.
17. See, for example, Walcott's interview with Edward Hirsch, also cited later in this discussion. Hirsch, "Art of Poetry", 65–83.
18. I am indebted to Adlai Murdoch for alerting me to a similar deployment of the second-person *tu* in francophone Caribbean literature. Murdoch writes: "The two [autobiographical] texts that make use of this discursive strategy are *Ravines du devant-jour* by Raphael Confiant of Martinique ... and *Tu, c'est l'enfance*, by Daniel Maximin of Guadeloupe. ... My reading of their (somewhat different) uses of this pronoun arises out of what I call the key moment of departmentalization, which resulted in a more or less ambivalent identification with both the Caribbean and the French metropole. Resultantly, these authors use this troubled sociopolitical terrain to contest a series of cultural and political conundrums. Beyond issues of alienation and temporal and subjective splitting, their hesitation to use or say 'I' reflects an ongoing attempt to interpellate the larger community through the attainment of a (sometimes unspoken) 'nous'. For Confiant, all this is also informed by his status as a 'Chabin', or mixed race subject, 'un être à part', as he puts it. ... For Maximin, the use of 'tu' is more clearly linked to an older narrator ('je') who addresses his youthful counterpart ('tu'), but key passages [on pages 34, beginning '*Tes ancêtres . . .*' and 46–47, '*Tu connaissais l'épopée de Delgrès . . .*'] bear witness to the family's dedication to local histories of slave resistance and the local revolt against Napoleon's attempt to reimpose slavery in 1802 (facts not taught in school) point to the importance of this [use of *tu* as an] implicit, communal 'nous'." Adlai Murdoch, email message to author, 9 April 2013.
19. Walcott, "Islands", *CP*, 52.
20. Walcott, "Early Pompeian", *CP*, 448.
21. Ibid., 451.
22. Ibid., 449–50.
23. Walcott, "Exile", *CP*, 101–2.
24. See King, *Derek Walcott*, 202–3.

25. Walcott, "Exile", *CP*, 100.
26. At several points in his 1954 novel *The Emigrants* (1954; repr., Ann Arbor: University of Michigan Press, 1994), Lamming describes the view from the deck of the ship on which his characters travel to England. Descriptions of the migrants clearing customs and immigration in England include features similar to those that Brathwaite's poem elaborates: "Some of the passengers had made a queue that moved forward on the upper deck where the passports and other papers were being examined. They had to declare what were their resources, and some of the officials seemed amazed at what they heard. Some of the men had just enough to pay the fare from Plymouth to Paddington. The officials asked what would happen after they reached Paddington, but no one answered with conviction. It seemed a tragic farce. England of all places, they seemed to say. They were bewildered by this exhibition of adventure, or ignorance, or plain suicide" (107–8).
27. Brathwaite, *Arrivants*, 51.
28. Ibid.
29. Ibid.
30. Ibid., 52.
31. Ibid., 53.
32. Ibid., 56.
33. Walcott, "Exile", *CP*, 100.
34. Walcott, *Omeros*, 270.
35. Walcott, "Exile", *CP*, 101.
36. King, *Derek Walcott*, 124; and Bruce King, *Derek Walcott and West Indian Drama* (Oxford: Clarendon, 1995), 17.
37. See Derek Walcott, "The Antilles: Fragments of Epic Memory" (Nobel lecture, 7 December 1992), in *What the Twilight Says*, 65–84. In another of those tantalizing cases of words and ideas refracted between these two writers, Naipaul described his own early memories of watching the Ramlila festival in a 1999 essay in the *New York Review of Books*, subsequently published as "Reading and Writing: A Personal Account", in V.S. Naipaul, *Literary Occasions: Essays*, ed. Pankaj Mishra (New York: Knopf, 2003), 3–31. Naipaul's childhood exposure to the pageant obviously predates Walcott's adult encounter with it. However, the way in which Naipaul re-presents his memory of the pageant, as fragmented but deeply intuited, echoes Walcott's account in the Nobel lecture six years earlier. The timing of this public reminiscence suggests that either Walcott's lecture jogged Naipaul's memory or Walcott's widely circulated claims for what the Ramlila pageant preserved cleared a space for Naipaul to characterize this memory for the first time as a formative experience. At the very least, Naipaul

38. Walcott's review of *Biswas*, titled "A Great New Novel of the West Indies: The Man Who Was Born Unlucky", appeared in the *Sunday Guardian*, 5 November 1961, 17; it is reprinted in Collier, *Derek Walcott*, 1:301–4. King notes that the two men interacted socially when Naipaul visited his family in Trinidad during this period. For a description of Walcott's early reviews of Naipaul, see King, *Derek Walcott*, 196–98.
39. Walcott, "Exile", *CP*, 101, 102.
40. Ibid., 100, 101.
41. Ibid., 102.
42. Walcott, "Oddjob, a Bull Terrier", *CP*, 334.
43. Ibid.
44. Ibid., 335.
45. Mutlu Konuk Blasing, *Lyric Poetry: The Pain and the Pleasure of Words* (Princeton, NJ: Princeton University Press, 2007), 5.
46. Ibid., 2.
47. Ibid., 11.
48. Ibid.
49. Ibid., 45.
50. Ibid., 11.
51. Walcott, *Arkansas Testament*, 10.
52. Blasing, *Lyric Poetry*, 2.
53. Walcott, *Omeros*, 28.
54. Ibid., 291.
55. In *The Idea of Lyric*, Johnson associates Whitman's *Song of Myself* with the resurgence in modern poetry of the choral lyric of antiquity, as opposed to the solo lyric or lyric monologue. He argues that the focus on an alienated, fragmented ethical subject expressed through this solo lyric corresponds with the rise over the past two hundred years of "the name and the idea of selfhood [that] have increasingly come to define only the private individual". He contends that solo and choral lyric modes were originally interdependent: "Human beings have, after all, not only private emotions and selves but also public emotions and selves. For solo lyric and the private emotions that it shapes, the lyric situation is *Ich und Welt* . . . for choral poetry . . . that situation is *Wir und Welt* . . . and, unlike that of solo lyric, this situation does not define opposition or otherness. Its function is not to clarify the limits and the nature of the private self; rather in *Wir und Welt* the choral poet imagines those emotions which lead us to want to understand both the possibility of our communion with each other and the

possibility of our communion with the world." His argument here maps closely onto my distinction between the lyric *I* and the rhetorical *you* with respect to Walcott's poetry. See Johnson, *Idea of Lyric*, 176–77.
56. Walcott, *Omeros*, 223.
57. Few smells have been sanctified enough in lyric poetry to convey specific emotions or values, but Susan Stewart asserts that when they do occur, smells in lyric poems tend to "continually play on the absent situation of writing and the conceit of the speaker's presence in a scene to which the reader has no access". She points out that such poems "make a special use of lyric's triangulation of speaker, addressee, and reader; in this case, the inherent voyeurism of the reader's position is all the more emphasized by the focus on these nonvisual senses so embedded in proximity". They tend to be "erotic – even when they express what might be called an erotic sense of repulsion" and they "often display the irreverent attitude sixteenth-century and later poets came to hold toward Petrarchan conventions". The first part of Stewart's claim makes sense when thinking about *Omeros*, as the poet expresses his passionate love of the St Lucian community by invoking a degree of physical intimacy with his subject that is very private and unmistakably erotic. The absence of satire or irreverence in the tone of Walcott's passage, however, is in keeping with the poem's overall refusal of a notion of the sublime that excludes the possibility of degradation, irascibility or human frailty. See Susan Stewart, *Poetry and the Fate of the Senses* (Chicago: University of Chicago Press, 2002), 27.
58. Walcott, *Omeros*, 75.
59. Walcott, "Love after Love", *CP*, 328.
60. Walcott, *Omeros*, 75.
61. Ibid., 76.
62. Ibid., 75.
63. For a rich discussion of Walcott's use of rhetorical forms, see the chapter "Caribbean Formalism: 'The Grace of Effort'" in Nicole Catherine Matos, "The Grace of Effort: Studies in Contemporary Anglophone Caribbean Form" (PhD diss., University of Massachusetts, 2008).
64. Walcott, *Omeros*, 75.
65. Every time I have taught *Omeros* I have watched this transubstantiation take place. A soldier student who slept through many of my 8:30 a.m. classes took his copy of *Omeros* with him to Iraq, where the rhymes in the battle scenes comforted him at night. A postcolonially angry student, determined to fault Walcott's sympathetic treatment of Plunkett, nonetheless found himself deeply moved by the rhythm of the language when Plunkett's ancestral son dies. An anxious young woman, who despaired of keeping track of the poem's endless

classical allusions, chanted *The Odyssey*'s opening lines with Omeros and the poem's phantom narrator like a child who garbles the Lord's Prayer in church but experienced nevertheless the strange fluttering uplift the shared cadences produced in her heart.

66. Walcott, *Omeros*, 14.
67. Blasing, *Lyric Poetry*, 11.
68. Ibid.
69. Walcott shares this strategy with some rap artists and the Trinidadian Carnival folk figure Pierrot Grenade, whose distinctive form of wordplay involves "spelling" complex multi-syllabic words by treating their component phonemes as separate words. The separate words then tell a story in Creole that reverses or enhances the meaning of the original word. For a discussion of the form, see Al Creighton, "Commoner and King: Contrasting Linguistic Performances in the Dialogue of the Dispossessed", in *West Indian Literature and Its Social Context: Proceedings of the Fourth Annual Conference on West Indian Literature*, ed. M. McWatt (Cave Hill, Barbados: University of the West Indies, 1985).
70. Walcott, *Omeros*, 12–13.
71. Ibid., 280.
72. Walcott comments directly on the apocalyptic overtones of the phrase "and then I saw" when he opens Poem 26 of *The Bounty* with this observation: "The sublime always begins with the chord 'And then I saw,' / following which apocalyptic cumuli curl and divide". The poem defends his work from an over-reliance on a celebratory natural sublime that glosses over the destructive aspects of the Caribbean landscape. Its description – in incorrigibly sublime cadences – of the awe-inspiring force of a Caribbean hurricane ends, tongue in cheek, "Let it be written: The dark days also I have praised". Walcott, Poem 26, *Bounty*, 59.
73. Walcott, *Omeros*, 280.
74. Ibid., 281.
75. Ibid., 283.
76. Ibid.
77. Ibid.
78. Ibid., 284.
79. Ibid.
80. Ibid.
81. Ibid., 286.
82. Ibid.
83. Walcott, "Islands", *CP*, 52.
84. Hirsch, "Art of Poetry", 75.
85. Walcott, "Love after Love", *CP*, 328.

86. Alejo Carpentier, *The Lost Steps*, quoted in Derek Walcott, "Homage to Gregorias", *CP*, 189.
87. Walcott, "Love after Love", *CP*, 328.
88. Walcott, Poem 24, *Bounty*, 57.
89. In his review, William Logan dismisses *The Bounty* as "a retrospective volume, full of elegy and apologia", which, "in its airless and sublime self-indulgence, its dissolution into mere writing, resembles the tedious run-on grandiloquence of *Midsummer* (1984), another book of days"; William Logan, "The Fatal Lure of Home", *New York Times*, 29 June 1977. The comparison to *Midsummer* and the review's added strictures about *Omeros* being an attempt "to shrink the *Iliad* and the *Odyssey* into the tiny sins and squabbles of some Caribbean fishermen and bewildered colonials" dramatizes the distance between some of Walcott's metropolitan readers and his Caribbean readers, for whom the intensely local politics of *Midsummer* and the "tiny sins and squabbles" in *Omeros* are precisely what makes the writing memorable. My point here is that Walcott does not want to be known simply as a gifted lyricist. He aims to write an entire community into aesthetic existence, because he wants those local details to become the stuff of great art.
90. *Derek Walcott: Poetry of Place*, dir. Tony Knox (New York: Films Media Group, 1989), videocassette, 21:34–23:22.
91. André Malraux, *The Psychology of Art*, quoted in Walcott, "The Divided Child", *CP*, 143
92. Bligh's crew on the original expedition mutinied. When he finally got his cuttings to the Caribbean, the slaves refused to eat breadfruit. See William Bligh, *A Voyage to the South Sea* (1792; New York: New American Library, 1962). Several of the essays in Kincaid's *My Garden (Book)* (New York: Farrar, Straus and Giroux, 1999) speak to the paradox that today's Caribbean vegetation, like the people who inhabit the islands, originated mostly in other parts of the world. See especially "To Name Is to Possess", 114–23 (where she discusses Bligh's famous journey); "What Joseph Banks Wrought", 132–41; and "In History", 153–67.
93. Walcott, "The Bounty", *Bounty*, 7.
94. Walcott, *Another Life*, *CP*, 151.
95. Walcott, Poem 28, *Bounty*, 61.
96. Walcott, "Italian Eclogues", *Bounty*, 64.
97. Ibid., 67.
98. Margaret Walcott, personal communication, 25 July 2004. In her remarks, she described visiting the new owners of the property with her grandmother, and being intrigued by her glimpses of the many shy Capildeo grandchildren peeping out at them from inside the house. One wonders if Vidia was among them.

99. Naipaul, *Way in the World*, 375.
100. Walcott, "A Santa Cruz Quartet", *Bounty*, 71.
101. Walcott, "In a Green Night", *CP*, 50.
102. Walcott, "Santa Cruz Quartet", *Bounty*, 72.
103. Ibid.; Derek Walcott, *The Joker of Seville and O Babylon!: Two Plays* (New York: Farrar, Straus and Giroux, 1977), 121.
104. Tracing its origins to the early eighteenth century in southern Spain, the feast of La Divina Pastora, or the Divine Shepherdess, has undergone a cultural evolution since its introduction to Siparia in south Trinidad by Catholic Capuchin missionaries in the mid-eighteenth century. Part of that cultural evolution involves the homage paid to La Divina Pastora, a copper-skinned statue of the Virgin Mary, by both Catholics and Hindus (the latter refer to the statue as Soparee Ke Mai). Believers from both faiths engage in annual and sometimes simultaneous pilgrimages to the shrine, located inside La Divina Pastora Roman Catholic Church in Siparia. Over the years they have been joined by members of the Chinese community, who celebrate the feast by playing the gambling games mah-jong and San Chee, as well as members of the Yoruba-derived Spiritual Baptist sect and Pentecostals. The religious syncretism associated with the shrine fits well into Walcott's culturally eclectic aesthetic project. For a detailed description of the forms of veneration associated today with the shrine, see Richardson Dhalai, "Paying Homage to La Divina Pastora", *Newsday*, 3 March 2013.
105. Walcott, *Joker of Seville*, 121.
106. Walcott, "Santa Cruz Quartet", *Bounty*, 73.
107. Ibid., 77.
108. Walcott, "Parang", *Bounty*, 26.
109. Ibid.
110. Walcott, Poem 14, *Bounty*, 39.
111. Ibid.
112. Walcott, *Joker of Seville*, 145.
113. Walcott, *Omeros*, 281.
114. Walcott, Poem 14, *Bounty*, 39.
115. Ibid.
116. Ibid.
117. Walcott, *Omeros*, 281.
118. Walcott, Poem 14, *Bounty*, 39.
119. Ibid.
120. Blasing, *Lyric Poetry*, 45.
121. Walcott, *Omeros*, 284.
122. Ibid., 75.

Accidents: An Afterword

1. Abraham Cowley, "The Motto", in *The Poems of Abraham Cowley*, ed. A.R. Waller (Cambridge: Cambridge University Press, 1905), 15. Quoted in Richard Helgerson, *Self-Crowned Laureates: Spenser, Jonson, Milton and the Literary System* (Berkeley: University of California Press, 1983), 219. Helgerson cites Cowley in the course of his broader discussion of the ways in which great poets construct personae that ensure they command poetic authority in their own time, as well as posthumously. Helgerson focuses on the self-presentation of Spenser, Ben Jonson and Milton, a triumvirate whose energy, ambition, innovation and sheer chutzpah anticipate that of the three Caribbean writers I discuss. He also demonstrates, as I have attempted to do, how frequently these writers' stylistic achievements draw on tropes central to the literary traditions and cultural expectations from which they endeavour to distinguish themselves.
2. Brathwaite, *Barabajan Poems*, 84.
3. Ibid., 190.
4. Walcott, *Omeros*, 296.

SELECTED BIBLIOGRAPHY

Achebe, Chinua. "Viewpoint". *Times Literary Supplement*, 1 February 1980, 113.
Antoni, Robert. *Divina Trace*. New York: Overlook Press, 1992.
Bakhtin, M.M. *The Dialogic Imagination: Four Essays*. Edited by Michael Holquist. Translated by Caryl Emerson and Michael Holquist. 1981. Reprint, Austin, TX: University of Texas Press, Slavic Series, 2004.
———. *Problems of Dostoevsky's Poetics*. 1984. Reprint, Minneapolis: University of Minnesota Press, 2003.
Bauer, Hermann, and Andreas Prater. *Baroque*. Edited by Ingo F. Walther. London: Taschen Books, 2006.
Baugh, Edward. "Cuckoo and Culture: *In the Castle of My Skin*". *Ariel* 8, no. 3 (July 1977): 23–33.
———. *Derek Walcott, Memory as Vision: Another Life*. London: Longman, 1978.
———. *Frank Collymore: A Biography*. Kingston: Ian Randle, 2009.
Beckles, Hilary. *Black Rebellion in Barbados: The Struggle against Slavery, 1627–1838*. Bridgetown, Barbados: Antilles, 1984.
Bhabha, Homi. "Of Mimicry and Man: The Ambivalence of Colonial Discourse". 1984. In *The Location of Culture*, 121–31. New York: Routledge Classics, 2004.
———. "Signs Taken for Wonders: Questions of Ambivalence and Authority under a Tree Outside Delhi, May 1817". 1985. In *The Location of Culture*, 145–74. New York: Routledge Classics, 2004.
Blasing, Mutlu Konuk. *Lyric Poetry: The Pain and the Pleasure of Words*. Princeton, NJ: Princeton University Press, 2007.
Bligh, William. *A Voyage to the South Sea: For the Purpose of Conveying the Bread-Fruit Tree to the West Indies, Including an Account of the Mutiny on Board the Ship*. 1792. Reprint, New York: New American Library, 1962.
Brathwaite, Doris Monica. *A Descriptive and Chronological Bibliography (1950–1982) of the Work of Edward Kamau Brathwaite*. London: New Beacon, 1988.

Brathwaite, Edward Kamau. *Ancestors*. New York: New Directions, 2001.
———. *The Arrivants: A New World Trilogy*. London: Oxford University Press, 1973.
———. *Barabajan Poems*. New York: Savacou North, 1994.
———. *Contradictory Omens: Cultural Diversity and Integration in the Caribbean*. Kingston: Savacou Mona, 1974.
———. "The Contribution of M.J. Herskovits to Afro-American Studies". *ASAWI Bulletin* 5 (December 1972): 85–94.
———. *The Development of Creole Society in Jamaica, 1770–1820*. Oxford: Clarendon, 1971.
———. *DreamStories*. Introduction by Gordon Rohlehr. Harlow, UK: Longman Caribbean, 1994.
———. *Mother Poem*. New York: Oxford University Press, 1977.
———. "The New West Indian Novelists: Part 2", *Bim* 8, no. 32 (January–June 1961): 271–80.
———. *Other Exiles*. New York: Oxford University Press, 1975.
———. *Roots*. Ann Arbor: University of Michigan Press, 1993.
———. *Shar: Hurricane Poem*. Kingston: Savacou, 1990.
———. *Sun Poem*. New York: Oxford University Press, 1982.
———. *Trench Town Rock*. Providence, RI: Lost Roads, 1994.
———. *X/self*. New York: Oxford University Press, 1987.
———. *The Zea Mexican Diary*. Madison: University of Wisconsin Press, 1993.
Brodber, Erna. *Jane and Louisa Will Soon Come Home*. London: New Beacon, 1980.
Brown, Beverly. "Mansong and Matrix: A Radical Experiment". In *A Double Decolonization: Colonial and Postcolonial Women's Writing*, edited by Kirsten Peterson and Anna Rutherford, 68–79. Coventry, UK: Dangaroo Press, 1986.
Brown, Wayne. "Caribbean Booktalk: Derek Walcott – His Poetry and His People". *Caribbean Affairs* 1, no. 3 (1988): 174–93.
Buhle, Paul, ed. *C.L.R. James: His Life and Work*. London: Allison and Busby, 1986.
Calder-Marshall, Arthur. *Glory Dead*. London: Michael Joseph, 1939.
Caravaggio, Michelangelo. *The Entombment of Christ*. 1602–3. Oil on canvas. Pinacoteca, Vatican.
Césaire, Aimé. *The Original 1939 Notebook of a Return to the Native Land*. Reprint of *Cahier d'un retour au pays natal*, 1939. Translated and edited by A. James Arnold and Clayton Eshleman. Middletown, CT: Wesleyan University Press, 2013.
Chamoiseau, Patrick. *Texaco*. Translated by Rose-Myriam Réjouis and Val Vinokur. New York: Pantheon, 1997.
Cobham-Sander, Rhonda. "'Any Enemy So Was a Compliment': Walcott, Brathwaite and the Formal Possibilities of Creole". In *Interlocking Basins of a Globe: Essays*

on Derek Walcott, edited by Jean Antoine-Dunne, 100–122. Leeds, UK: Peepal Tree, 2013.

———. "The *Caribbean Voices* Programme and the Development of West Indian Short Fiction: 1945–1958". In *The Story Must Be Told: Short Narrative Prose in the New English Literatures*, edited by Peter O. Stummer, 146–58. Würzburg: Königshausen und Neumann, 1985.

———. "Colin Ferguson, Me and I: Anatomy of a Creole Psychosis". *Transition* 67 (Fall 1995): 16–21.

———. "Consuming the Self: V.S. Naipaul, C.L.R. James, and *A Way in the World*". *Anthurium* 5, no. 2 (Fall 2007), art. 5.

———. "K/Ka/Kam/Kama/Kamau: Brathwaite's Project of Self-Naming in *Barabajan Poems*". In *For the Geography of a Soul: Emerging Perspectives on Kamau Brathwaite*, edited by Timothy J. Reiss, 297–315. Trenton, NJ: Africa World Press, 2001.

Collier, Gordon, ed. *Derek Walcott, the Journeyman Years: Occasional Prose, 1957–1974*. Vol. 1, *Culture, Society, Literature, and Art*. New York: Editions Rodopi, 2013.

Collins, Merle. *Angel*. Seattle: Seal Press, 1988.

Cowley, Abraham. *The Poems of Abraham Cowley*. Edited by A.R. Waller. Cambridge: Cambridge University Press, 1905.

Creighton, Al. "Commoner and King: Contrasting Linguistic Performances in the Dialogue of the Dispossessed". In *West Indian Literature and Its Social Context: Proceedings of the Fourth Annual Conference on West Indian Literature*, edited by M. McWatt, 55–68. Cave Hill, Barbados: University of the West Indies, 1985.

———. "Return of the Enigma: Naipaul Goes Home for 75th Birthday". *Stabroek News* (Georgetown, Guyana), 29 April 2007. http://www.landofsixpeoples.com/news702/ns0704299.html.

Cudjoe, Selwyn. *V.S. Naipaul: A Materialist Reading*. Amherst: University of Massachusetts Press, 1988.

Davis, Gregson. "'Homecomings without Home': Representations of (Post)colonial *nostos* (Homecoming) in the Lyric of Aimé Césaire and Derek Walcott". In *Homer in the Twentieth Century: Between World Literature and the Western Canon*, edited by Barbara Graziosi and Emily Greenwood, 191–209. Oxford: Oxford University Press, 2007.

Derrida, Jacques. "'Eating Well', or the Calculation of the Subject: An Interview with Jacques Derrida". In *Who Comes after the Subject?*, edited by Eduardo Cadava, Peter Connor and Jean-Luc Nancy, 96–119. New York: Routledge, 1991.

Dhalai, Richardson. "Paying Homage to La Divina Pastora". *Newsday*, 3 March 2013. http://newsday.co.tt/features/0,174337.html.

Dhondy, Farrukh. *C.L.R. James: A Life*. New York: Pantheon Books, 2001.
Eliot, T.S. *On Poetry and Poets*. 1943. Reprint, New York: Farrar, Straus and Giroux, 2009.
Epstein, Joseph. "A Cottage for Mr Naipaul". *New Criterion* 6, no. 2 (October 1987): 6–15.
Espinet, Ramabai. "Indian Cuisine". *Massachusetts Review* 35, no. 3–4 (Autumn–Winter 1994): 563–73.
Fanon, Frantz. *Black Skin, White Masks*. New York: Grove Press, 1967.
Farred, Grant. *Rethinking C.L.R. James*. Oxford: Blackwell, 1995.
Films Media Group. *Derek Walcott: Poetry of Place*. Directed by Tony Knox. Digital Classics, 1989. Videocassette.
Fisher, Lawrence E. *Colonial Madness: Mental Health in the Barbadian Social Order*. New Brunswick, NJ: Rutgers University Press, 1985.
Ford-Smith, Honor. *My Mother's Last Dance*. Toronto: Sister Vision, 1997.
Freed, Lewis. *T.S. Eliot: The Critic as Philosopher*. West Lafayette, IN: Purdue University Press, 1979.
French, Patrick. *The World Is What It Is: The Authorized Biography of V.S. Naipaul*. New York: Knopf, 2008.
Fuss, Diana. *Identification Papers: Readings on Psychoanalysis, Sexuality, and Culture*. New York: Routledge, 1995.
Goodheart, Eugene. "V.S. Naipaul's Mandarin Sensibility". *Partisan Review* 50, no. 2 (1983): 224–56.
Grimshaw, Anna. *The C.L.R. James Archive: A Reader's Guide*. New York: C.L.R. James Institute and Smyrna Press, 1991.
———. *Special Delivery: The Letters of C.L.R. James to Constance Webb, 1939–1984*. Oxford: Blackwell, 1996.
Hall, Catherine. *Civilising Subjects: Colony and Metropole in the English Imagination, 1830–1967*. Chicago: University of Chicago Press, 2002.
Hamner, Robert D., ed. *Critical Perspectives on Derek Walcott*. Washington, DC: Three Continents, 1993.
Helgerson, Richard. *Self-Crowned Laureates: Spenser, Jonson, Milton, and the Literary System*. Berkley: University of California Press, 1983.
Herskovits, Melville. *Life in a Haitian Valley*. 1937. Reprint, New York: Doubleday, 1971.
———. *The Myth of the Negro Past*. 1941. Reprint, Boston: Beacon Press, 1990.
Hill, Robert. "In England: 1932–38". In *C.L.R. James: His Life and Work*, edited by Paul Buhle, 79. London: Allison and Busby, 1986.
Hirsch, Edward. "The Art of Poetry". 1986. In *Critical Perspectives on Derek Walcott*, edited by Robert D. Hamner, 65–83. Washington, DC: Three Continents, 1993.

"IHS". *Catholic Encyclopedia*. Vol. 7. New York: Robert Appleton, 1910. http://www.newadvent.org/cathen/07649a.htm.

Ismond, Patricia. *Abandoning Dead Metaphors: The Caribbean Phase of Derek Walcott's Poetry*. Kingston: University of the West Indies Press, 2001.

———. "Walcott versus Brathwaite". In *Critical Perspectives on Derek Walcott*, edited by Robert D. Hamner, 220–36. Washington, DC: Three Continents, 1993.

James, C.L.R. *Beyond a Boundary*. 1963. Reprint, Durham, NC: Duke University Press, 1993.

———. *The Black Jacobins: Toussaint L'Ouverture and the San Domingo Revolution*. 1963. Reprint, New York: Vintage, 1989.

———. *The Case for West-Indian Self Government*. New York: University Place Book Shop, 1967.

———. *Minty Alley*. 1936. Reprint, Jackson: University Press of Mississippi, 1997.

Johnson, W.R. *The Idea of Lyric: Lyric Modes in Ancient and Modern Poetry*. Berkeley: University of California Press, 1982.

Kincaid, Jamaica. *The Autobiography of My Mother*. New York: Farrar, Straus and Giroux, 1996.

———. *Lucy*. 1990. Reprint, New York: Farrar, Straus and Giroux, 2002.

———. *My Garden (Book)*. New York: Farrar, Straus and Giroux, 1999.

———. *See Now Then*. New York: Farrar, Straus and Giroux, 2013.

King, Bruce. *Derek Walcott: A Caribbean Life*. Oxford: Oxford University Press, 2000.

———. *Derek Walcott and West Indian Drama – Not Only a Playwright but a Company: The Trinidad Theatre Workshop, 1959–1993*. Oxford: Clarendon, 1995.

Lamming, George. *Of Age and Innocence*. London: Allison and Busby, 1981.

———. *In the Castle of My Skin*. New York: McGraw-Hill, 1953.

———. *The Emigrants*. 1954. Reprint, Ann Arbor: University of Michigan Press, 1994

———. *The Pleasures of Exile*. 1960. Reprint, New York: Schocken, 1984.

———. *Season of Adventure*. London: Michael Joseph, 1960.

Leithauser, Brad. "Ancestral Rhyme". Review of *Omeros*, by Derek Walcott. *New Yorker*, 11 February 1991, 91–95.

Logan, William. "The Fatal Lure of Home". Review of *The Bounty*, by Derek Walcott. *New York Times*, 29 June 1997. http://www.nytimes.com/books/97/06/29/reviews/970629.29logant.html.

Lorimer, Joyce, ed. *Sir Walter Ralegh's Discoverie of Guiana*. London: Hakluyt Society, 2006.

Lovelace, Earl. *Is Just a Movie*. Chicago: Haymarket Books, 2012.

Maas, Jeremy. *Holman Hunt and the Light of the World*. London: Scolar Press, 1984.

Matos, Nicole Catherine. "The Grace of Effort: Studies in Contemporary Anglophone

Caribbean Form". PhD dissertation, University of Massachusetts, 2008. http://scholarworks.umass.edu/dissertations/AAI3325129/.

———. "'Join, Interchangeable Phantoms': From Metaphor to Metonymy in Walcott's *Omeros*". *Small Axe* 10, no. 2 (2006): 40–60. http://muse.jhu.edu/journals/small_axe/v010/10.2matos.html.

McLemee, Scott, ed. *C.L.R. James on the Negro Question*. Jackson: University Press of Mississippi, 1996.

Mittelholzer, Edgar. *Sylvia*. London: NEL Books, 1968.

Morgan, Mary. "The Silver Feather". In *For the Geography of the Soul: Emerging Perspectives on Kamau Brathwaite*, edited by Timothy J. Reiss, 317–31. Trenton, NJ: Africa World Press, 2001.

Morris, Mervyn. "Walcott and the Audience for Poetry". In *Critical Perspectives on Derek Walcott*, edited by Robert D. Hamner, 174–92. Washington, DC: Three Continents, 1993.

Naipaul, V.S. *The Adventures of Gurudeva*. 1976. Reprint, New Delhi: Buffalo, 2001.

———. *An Area of Darkness*. 1964. Reprint, New York: Vintage, 2002.

———. *A Bend in the River*. New York: Knopf, 1979.

———. *The Enigma of Arrival*. 1987. Reprint, New York: Vintage, 2012.

———. *Finding the Center: Two Narratives*. New York: Knopf, 1984.

———. *Guerrillas*. 1975. Reprint, New York: Vintage, 1980.

———. *A House for Mr Biswas*. 1961. Reprint, New York: Knopf, 1995.

———. *In a Free State: A Novel*. New York: Knopf, 1973.

———. *India: A Million Mutinies Now*. 1990. Reprint, New York: Vintage, 2011.

———. *Literary Occasions: Essays*. Edited by Pankaj Mishra. New York: Knopf, 2003.

———. *The Loss of El Dorado*. 1969. Reprint, New York: Vintage, 2003.

———. *The Middle Passage: Impressions of Five Societies – British, French, and Dutch – in the West Indies and South America*. New York: Vintage, 1981.

———. *Miguel Street*. 1959. Reprint, New York: Vintage, 2002.

———. *The Mimic Men*. New York: Macmillan, 1967.

———. *The Overcrowded Barracoon and Other Articles*. Harmondsworth, UK: Penguin, 1976.

———. Review of *Of Age and Innocence* by George Lamming. *New Statesman* 56 (6 December 1958): 826.

———. *A Way in the World: A Novel*. New York: Vintage, 1995.

Nancy, Jean-Luc. Introduction. In *Who Comes after the Subject?*, edited by Eduardo Cadava, Peter Connor, and Jean-Luc Nancy, 1–8. New York: Routledge, 1991.

Nixon, Rob. "London Calling: V.S. Naipaul and the License of Exile". *South Atlantic Quarterly* 87, no. 1 (Winter 1988): 1–37.

O'Brien, Conor Cruise, Edward Said and John Lukacs. "The Post-Colonial Intellectual: A Discussion with Conor Cruise O'Brien, Edward Said and John Lukacs". *Salmagundi* 70/71 (Spring–Summer 1986): 65–81.

Phillips, Caryl. "No Man Ever Dies in His Own Country". Review of *The Arkansas Testament*, by Derek Walcott. *Los Angeles Times Book Review*, 6 September 1987, 1–9. http://articles.latimes.com/1987-09-06/books/bk-6413_1_walcott-poem-collections.

———. "The Voyage In". Review of *A Way in the World*, by V.S. Naipaul. *New Republic* 210, no. 24 (13 June 1994): 40–45.

Rahim, Jennifer, and Barbara Lalla, eds. *Created in the West Indies: Caribbean Perspectives on V.S. Naipaul*. Kingston: Ian Randle, 2011.

Rhys, Jean. *Wide Sargasso Sea*. New York: Norton, 1982.

Risden, Winnie. Review of *Masks*, by Kamau Brathwaite. *Caribbean Quarterly* 14, no. 1–2 (March–June 1968): 145–47.

Rohlehr, Gordon. *Pathfinder*. Port of Spain: College Press, 1981.

———. *The Shape of That Hurt and Other Essays*. Port of Spain: Longman Trinidad, 1992.

———. "West Indian Poetry: Some Problems of Assessment". 1971. In *My Strangled City and Other Essays*, 107–32. Port of Spain: Longman Trinidad, 1992.

———. "Withering into Truth: A Review of Derek Walcott's *The Gulf and Other Poems*". In *Critical Perspectives on Derek Walcott*, edited by Robert D. Hamner, 212–19. Washington, DC: Three Continents, 1993.

Scott, David. *Refashioning Futures: Criticism after Postcoloniality*. Princeton, NJ: Princeton University Press, 1999.

Scott, Dennis. "Walcott on Walcott". *Caribbean Quarterly* 14, no. 1–2 (March–June 1968): 77–82, 120–26.

Selvon, Samuel. *The Lonely Londoners*. 1956. Reprint, Harlow, UK: Longman, 1987.

Sheppard, Jill. *The "Redlegs" of Barbados: Their Origins and History*. Millwood, NY: KTO Press, 1977.

Stewart, Susan. *Poetry and the Fate of the Senses*. Chicago: University of Chicago Press, 2002.

Tennyson, Alfred. *In Memoriam: Authoritative Text – Criticism*, edited by Erik Irving Graly. New York: W.W. Norton, 2004.

Walcott, Derek. *Another Life: Fully Annotated*. Edited by Edward Baugh and Colbert Nepaulsingh. Boulder: Lynne Rienner, 2004.

———. *The Arkansas Testament*. New York: Farrar, Straus and Giroux, 1987.

———. *The Bounty*. New York: Farrar, Straus and Giroux, 1997.

———. *Collected Poems*. New York: Farrar, Straus and Giroux, 1986.

———. *Dream on Monkey Mountain and Other Plays*. New York: Farrar, Straus and Giroux, 1970.

———. "A Great New Novel of the West Indies: The Man Who Was Born Unlucky". In *Derek Walcott, the Journeyman Years: Occasional Prose, 1957–1974*. Vol. 1, *Culture, Society, Literature, and Art*, edited by Gordon Collier, 301–4. New York: Editions Rodopi, 2013.

———. *The Joker of Seville and O Babylon!: Two Plays*. New York: Farrar, Straus and Giroux, 1977.

———. "Omeros". MSS 0564:1:1–0564:4:1 and 0565:5:1 (n.d.). Box 20B, Derek Walcott Collection. University of the West Indies Library, Trinidad.

———. *Omeros*. 2nd ed. New York: Farrar, Straus and Giroux, 1992.

———. "'Rights of Passage': Drama in Itself". *Trinidad Guardian*, 25 April 1973, 5.

———. "West Indian Poetry: A Search for Voices". Lecture in seminar series "The State of the Arts in Jamaica". University of the West Indies, 14 March 1965.

———. *What the Twilight Says: Essays*. New York: Farrar, Straus and Giroux, 1998.

Whitman, Walt. "Song of Myself". 1855. In *Song of Myself and Other Poems*, edited by Robert Hass, 7–133. Berkeley, CA: Counterpoint Press, 2010.

Williams, Eric. *Capitalism and Slavery*. 1944. Reprint, Chapel Hill: University of North Carolina Press, 1994.

———. *Inward Hunger: The Education of a Prime Minister*. Chicago: University of Chicago Press, 1971.

Worcester, Kent. *C.L.R. James: A Political Biography*. Albany: State University of New York Press, 1995.

Zobel, Joseph. *La rue Cases-Nègres*. 1974. Reprint, Paris: Présence africaine, 1984.

INDEX

Achebe, Chinua, 17, 251n13
Africa. *See under* Brathwaite; Naipaul; Walcott
Allen, Jim. *See* Vere Allen de
Applewhite, Charles, 234–35
Aston, Alisdair, 123
Auden, W.H., 33–34, 138
Awoonor, Kofi, 245n9

Bakhtin, M.M., 92–93
Barbados. *See under* Brathwaite; Naipaul; Walcott
Barbados Advocate, 80
Barrell, John, 126–128
Baugh, Edward, *vii*, 39, 262n31, 263n33
BBC. *See* British Broadcasting Corporation
Beacon, 31, 250n6
Beckles, Hilary, 95, 260n20
Bhabha, Homi, 127
Bim, 10, 80–81, 182, 246n9, 256n7, 273n18
Blackman, Margot, 80
Black Power movement, 38, 168, 189, 276n7
Blake, William, 33–34
Blasing, Mutlu K., 216–18, 222–23, 231, 238

Bligh, William, 231, 282n92
Bonaparte, Napoleon, 277n18
Brathwaite, Beryl Emmeline, 111, 113
Brathwaite, Carlisle, 100
Brathwaite, Doris Monica, 3, 70–71, 76, 247n28, 258n33. *See also under* Brathwaite: relationships: wife; Brathwaite: *Zea Mexican Diary*
Brathwaite, Edward Hilton, 100–101, 104–105, 109, 111, 113, 121, 129, 260n2, 261n25
Brathwaite, Henry Lawson, 100, 260n2
Brathwaite, James Edward, 260n2
Brathwaite, Lawson Edward, 260n2
BRATHWAITE, KAMAU (formerly Edward): Barbados Scholarship, 8; *Bim*, editor for, 81; crises, personal, 69–71, 78, 124–125, 255nn3–4, 256n12; experiments with language, 14, 88, 92–93, 101–102, 122–124, 174–177, 181–182, 190–199; fame, deals with, 15, 129; feminist criticism of, 78–79, 89, 256n16; Harrison College, 8; Harvard University lecture, 69; legacy, literary, 2, 13, 70, 80, 110, 120; Haitian Vodun, 74–75; historian, 70–72, 79–80, 107, 110,

293

BRATHWAITE, KAMAU (*continued*) 116–117, 130, 176, 179, 182, 256n7; International Prize for Literature, 245n9; music, influenced by, 72–73, 89, 112, 177; New York University, 78, 80; Oedipus complex, 107, 121–122; Pembroke, 123; racial inclusivity, 114, 264n40; renamed Kamau, 75, 81–84, 100, 107, 110, 130, 262n25; representation of whiteness, 71, 91, 97, 111–114, 118–120, 122–124, 128; reviews *House for Mr Biswas*, 117, 250n9; reviews *Of Age and Innocence*, 257n20; Sir Winston Scott Memorial Lecture, 72, 84, 256n7; University of Cambridge, 8, 123–126, 128; University of West Indies, 16; video style, 17, 69, 72–73, 78, 97, 103
—relationships (people/places): African culture, 72, 75, 83–84, 95, 117, 118, 128–129, 259n12, 264n40; African heritage/history, 71–72, 110, 188, 263n39; African landscape, 71–72, 187; aunt, 112–113, 119, 128; Barbadian/Barabajan/Bajan landscape, 1, 72, 88, 101, 113, 118, 121, 174–175, 260n5; Barbadian/Barabajan/Bajan society, 72, 80–81, 85–86, 95, 97; Collymore, 100, 111–114, 117, 119–120, 128, 130, 263n33; England, landscape, 123, 125; Europe, 201–211; father and father figures, 13, 71, 99–111, 113–114, 117, 120–121, 127–130, 260n5, 261n25; grandfather, 103, 105, 120–121, 127–130; great-uncle, 103, 105; Jamaican history, 95; Jamaican landscape, 3, 16, 70, 72; Jamaican society, 95–96, 247n29, 258n33; Kenya, 81–82; mother and mother figures, 106–107, 111–113, 201; Naipaul, contrast with, 79, 80, 96–97, 99, 113, 114, 121, 125, 126, 127, 129; Naipaul, praises, 247n29; readers, 15–17, 76, 134; Roach, 265n48; St Vincent, 83; Walcott, contrast with, 94, 96, 99, 108, 111, 113, 114–117, 119, 127, 129–130, 134–135, 167–171, 174, 176–177, 181–201, 204, 206, 209–212, 214, 218, 247n29; Walcott, critiques, 271n2; Walcott, parodied by, 169, 179–180, 188–189, 247n29; wife, 70–71, 76, 111–112, 258n33

—works: "All God's Chillun", 178, 179, 180; *Ancestors*, 103; "Ancestors", 100, 103–104, 105, 120, 121, 129; "Angel/Engine", 73–75, 89, 92, 95; *Arrivants: A New World Trilogy*, 70, 75, 88, 100, 103–104, 120–121, 168, 182, 187, 188, 201, 211, 241, 272n3 (reviews, 182); *Barabajan Poems*, 8, 11, 12, 17, 69–104, 107, 110–114, 120–129, 134, 217, 241–42, 247n29, 256n7, 257n16, 258n1, 260n5, 262n29, 264n40; "Clips", 121; *Contradictory Omens*, 264n40, 264n48; "Crossing", 101, 129; "Day the First Snow Fell", 122–123, 125–126; *Development of Creole Society in Jamaica*, 95; *DreamStories*, 70–71, 246n10, 255n3, 256n12, 259n19; "Dust", 88, 101, 174–176, 178–182, 194, 195, 198 (reviews, 178, 180–181); "Emigrants", 209, 212; "Fleches", 104–110, 112–114, 119, 121–122, 129; "Francina", 179; "Hex", 76–78; *Islands*, 71, 179; "Jazz and the West Indian Novel", 10; "Legba", 83, 88; "Love Axe", 10, 246n9; *Masks*, 168, 179 (reviews, 255n6); *Mother Poem*, 73, 76, 82, 118, 242, 259n19,

271n3; "Nametracks", 82; "Negus", 169, 179, 247n29; "New West Indian Novelists: Part II", 80; "Noom", 101, 118, 128; "Ogun", 100, 103, 104, 105; *Rights of Passage*, 71, 170, 178–179, 180–182, 201 (reviews, 170, 174, 176, 178, 180, 185, 188, 198, 201); *Roots*, 117, 265n48; "Roots", 117; *Shar*, 69, 70, 71, 255nn2–3; *Sun Poem*, 71, 82, 88, 92, 93, 99, 101–104, 118, 120, 121, 262n29; "Stone Sermon", 75; *Trench Town Rock*, 70, 255n4; "Twist", 180; "West Indian Poetry", 271n2; "Wings of a Dove", 176–178, 180, 184 (reviews, 176, 180); *X/Self*, 70, 256n12; *Zea Mexican Diary*, 1–2, 70, 71, 77–78, 246n10, 255n4, 257n20

Brathwaite, Michael Kwesi, 260n2
Breslin, Paul, *vii*, 274n72
British Broadcasting Corporation, 8, 31, 169, 180, 230, 247n29
Brodber, Erna, 78, 243
Brodsky, Joseph, 13, 136, 171, 233–36, 266n7, 270n90
Broodhagen, Karl, 114
Brown, Beverly, 256n16
Brown, Wayne, 136–137, 139, 145
Buhle, Paul, 252n23

Calder-Marshall, Arthur, 30, 31
calypso/calypsonian, 10, 37, 38, 146, 164, 184, 190, 248n29, 251n18, 262n25
Campell, George, 9, 164
Capildeo, Rudranath, 16, 282n98
Captain Bligh. *See* Bligh, William
Caravaggio, Michelangelo Merisi da, 115–116, 264nn44–45
Caribbean Nights programme, 169, 180, 247n29. *See also* British Broadcasting Corporation
Caribbean Voices programme, 8, 9, 10, 31, 246n25. *See also* British Broadcasting Corporation
Carnegie, James, 78
Carnegie, Mary, 78
Césaire, Aimé, 197–198, 200, 270n90; *Cahier d'un retour au pays natal*, 168, 178, 182, 198
Chamoiseau, Patrick, 175, 197–20; *Texaco*, 197–199
Chapman, Matthew J., 72, 120
Chaucer, Geoffrey, 17, 174
Chirico, Giorgio de: *Enigma of Arrival* (painting), 148, 150, 269n48
Christ, Jesus, 108, 115–116, 119, 128, 141, 261n23, 264n44
Cimabue, 231
Cipriani, Arthur A., 250n3
Clare, John, 232
Coetzee, J.M., 17, 245n9
Collier, Gordon, 247n27
Collins, Merle, 271n92
Colly. *See* Collymore, Frank
Collymore, Frank, 80–81, 100, 111–114, 117, 118–120, 128, 130, 251n18, 256n7, 262n31, 263n33. *See also under* Brathwaite: relationships
Columbus, Christopher, 210–211, 217
Condé, Maryse, 78
Confiant, Raphael, 277n18
Constantine, Learie, 250n3
Cowley, Abraham, 240, 284n1
Cox, Brian, 123
Crane, Hart, 178, 200
Creighton, Al, 255n7, 281n69
Creole (language), 5, 168, 173–174, 181, 183, 186, 190, 200, 206–207, 216, 218, 223–24, 281n69; English, 87, 97, 172–173, 176, 183–185, 187,

Creole (language) (*continued*)
194–195, 197, 199, 207, 258n1, 274n72; English, Barbadian, 181, 193; English, Jamaican Patwah, 81, 176–177; English, St Lucian, 14, 191, 197, 274n72; French, 95, 139, 140, 172–173, 183–187, 192–194, 196–197, 207, 223, 274n72; French, St Lucian, 185, 199–200, 274n72. *See also* Brathwaite: experiments with language. *See also* English, Standard. *See also* Walcott: experiments with language

creole (people), 5, 34, 36, 90–91, 95, 217, 252n20; culture, 37–43, 63–64, 117, 251n18

Cudjoe, Selwyn, 251n13

Dante, Alighieri, 174, 181, 192
Davis, Gregson, 270n90
Delacroix, Eugène, 142
Demas, William, 54
Derrida, Jacques, 6–7, 63–64, 83
Dhalai, Richardson, 283n104
Dhondy, Farrukh, 249n3, 250n9
Dickens, Charles, 138, 162
Donne, John, 138
Dyson, Tony, 123

Edward VII (king), 109, 261n25
Edward VIII (king), 109, 111, 261n25
Eliot, T.S., 178, 181, 194, 200, 206
Ellison, Ralph, 268n37
England. *See under* Brathwaite; Naipaul; Walcott
English, Standard, use in Caribbean, 5, 97, 173–174, 176–177, 183–184, 186–188, 191–195, 199, 207, 218, 274n72. *See also* Creole (language)
Epstein, Joseph, 251n13

Espinet, Ramabai, 251n18
Esquire, 275n3

Fanon, Frantz, 4, 13, 34, 96, 130, 246n12; Fanon's paradigm, 4–6, 63, 65, 127
Farah, Nuruddin, 245n9
Fisher, Lawrence, 246n19
Forde, Freddie, 104
Foucault, Michel, 127
French, Patrick, 54, 249n2, 249n3, 254n14, 266n5, 268n36
Fuss, Diana, 4–5, 246n12

Ginsberg, Allen, 276n15
Giroux, Robert, 182
Goodheart, Eugene, 251n13
Gordimer, Nadine, 17
Gottlieb, Bob, 123
Guevara, Che, 115–116, 119
Gunn, Thom, 123

Haley, Alex, 82
Hallam, Arthur, 25
Hall, Catherine, 126–128
Hardwick, Elizabeth, 171
Harris, Wilson, 8, 164
Haward, Patricia, *viii*, 249n2
Hawkins, John, 50–52, 56
Hawthorne, Nathaniel, 138
Heaney, Seamus, 136, 171, 266n7
Hearne, John, 164
Heidegger, Martin, 6
Helgerson, Richard, 284n1
Herbert, Cecil, 164
Herron, Carolivia, 12, 69, 70, 78, 79, 80
Herskovits, Melville, 263n39
Hill, Robert, 252n23
Hirsch, Edward, 170, 229, 272n11
Holman Hunt, William, 141, 267n30

Homer, 13, 93–94, 138, 195, 223, 225–28, 237; *Iliad*, 282n89; *Odyssey*, 139, 270n90, 281n65, 282n89
Homer, Winslow, 158
Hughes, Ted, 123
Hunte, Julian, 264n40

Ismond, Patricia, 247n29, 271nn2–3, 272n11

Jamaica. *See under* Brathwaite; Naipaul; Walcott
James, C.L.R., 12, 15, 30–32, 34, 38, 40, 41, 43, 45–49, 59, 60–61, 62, 63, 134, 164, 249n3, 250n4, 250n9, 251nn13–14, 252n23, 254n14. *See also under* Naipaul: relationships
James, Cynthia, 78
Jeyifo, Biodun, *vii*, 250n3
Johnson, W.R., 206, 276n15, 279n55
Jonson, Ben, 284n1
Joyce, James, 174

Keats, John, 51, 55
Kincaid, Jamaica, 62, 78, 164, 259n16, 267n33, 270n92, 282n92
King, Bruce, 268n37, 268n45, 272n5, 276n7, 279n38
Kingsley, Charles, 138
Kitchener, Herbert. *See* Lord Kitchener

Lacan, Jacques, 205, 220
Lamming, George, 8, 9–10, 38, 39–40, 42, 104, 114, 164, 181, 194, 200, 243, 250n6, 252n20; coo-coo, in work, 39, 262n29 (*see also under* Naipaul); *Emigrants*, 209, 278n26; *In the Castle of My Skin*, 8–9, 38–39, 178, 180, 262n29, 271n92 (reviews, 39); *Of Age and Innocence*, 257n20 (reviews, 9–10, 253n5, 257n20); *Pleasures of Exile*, 212; *Season of Adventure*, 90; *Water with Berries*, 259n19. *See also under* Naipaul: relationships
Larkin, Phillip, 275n3
Leithauser, Brad, 271n96
Lennox, Ralph, 268n37
Logan, William, 282n89
Lord Kitchener, 164
Lovelace, Earl, 190, 254n9
Lowell, Robert, 171, 272n11
Lukacs, John, 251n13

Maas, Jeremy, 267n30
MacDermott, Thomas, 263n31
MacLeish, Archibald, 178, 200
Mais, Roger, 164, 200; *Brother Man*, 178, 180
Malraux, André, 231
Manley, Michael, 271n3
Marley, Bob, 141, 164, 177, 190
Marshall, Harold, 114
Marshall, Paule, 78
Marvell, Andrew, 234–36
Matos, Nicole, 271n96, 280n63
Maximin, Daniel, 277n18
McKay, Claude, 243
Mighty Sparrow, 164, 251n18
Mighty Spoiler, 190
Milne, Anthony, 173
Milosz, Czeslaw, 266n7
Milton, John, 284n1
Mittelholzer, Edgar, 8, 9, 164, 250n6; *Sylvia*, 90–91
Morgan, Mary, 245n9
Morris, Mervyn, 271n2, 273n18
Morrison, Toni, 78
Murdoch, Adlai, 277n18

Naipaul, Patricia, 267n36

Naipaul, Seepersad, 31–32, 113, 245n8, 250n6
Naipaul, Shiva, 3, 164, 245n8
NAIPAUL, V.S.: *Carribean Voices*, editor for, 9, 10, 246n25; coo-coo, in work, 34–39, 41, 44, 45, 63, 64, 65, 129, 240–41, 244, 251n18, 262n29 (*see also under* Lamming); fame, deals with, 12, 15, 31, 47, 62; exile, 135, 138, 142–144, 147, 150, 162, 213; legacy, literary, 2, 27–28, 58–59, 62, 66, 134, 165–166, 267n33; Makerere University, 30, 249n2; New York University, 3; Oxford University, 3, 8, 34, 113, 245n8, 249n2, 267n36; Queens Royal College, 8, 31, 54, 61, 255n7; race, attitudes towards, 34, 36–38, 48–49, 53–55, 58, 63, 155, 251n13, 268n36; Ramlila pageant, 278n37; representation of Trinidad/Trinidadians, 10, 12, 14, 22, 23, 26–27, 29, 30–31, 33–38, 41, 42, 51–58, 142; reviews *Beyond a Boundary*, 32; reviews *Of Age and Innocence*, 9–10, 253n5; Trinidad Island Scholarship, 8; University of West Indies, 249n3
—relationships (people/places): African culture/politics, 36, 40, 42, 52–53, 64, 252n20; African heritage/history, 39, 65, 249n7; African landscape, 23, 26, 30, 46, 53, 56, 58, 61, 147; Barbadian history, 36; Barbadian landscape, 17, 39; Brathwaite, contrast with, 79, 80, 96–97, 99, 113, 114, 121, 125, 126, 127, 129; Brathwaite, critiques, 247n29; England landscape, 25, 27, 32, 135, 137–138, 142–145, 149–151, 162, 213, 254n3; father, 3, 99, 245n8; Jamaican culture, 38; Jamaican landscape, 17; James, influenced by, 31–32, 134, 250n4; Lamming, influenced by, 8–10, 38, 252n20, 262n29; readers, 12, 15–17, 28–29, 33–34, 47–49, 54–55, 58–59, 60–63, 65–66, 134, 143–144, 147, 164; siblings, 3, 245n8; St Vincent history, 36; Trinidadian culture/politics, 26, 30, 36–38, 40–42, 51, 56, 64, 65, 95, 117, 250n3, 251n18, 252n20, 252n23; Trinidadian history, 22, 26, 31, 33, 35–36, 65, 95, 135, 252n23; Trinidadian landscape, 12, 17, 21, 22, 28, 29, 39, 55, 60–61, 64, 135–136, 137, 143–144, 147, 149–151, 153, 157, 254n3, 266n5, 267n33; Trinidadian society, 56, 58, 60, 63, 253n5, 255n7, 279n38; Walcott, contrast with, 96, 134–140, 142–166, 206–207, 214, 218, 234; wife, 267n36; Wiltshire landscape, 143, 149, 150–154, 162, 267n33
—works: *Area of Darkness*, 58; *Bend in the River*, 22 (reviews, 251n13); "Crocodiles of Yamoussoukro", 22, 52; *Enigma of Arrival*, 1, 13, 56, 62, 64, 135, 137, 143–159, 163–164, 217, 245n8, 265n5, 270n90, 270n92 (reviews, 27, 62, 135–136, 139–140, 142, 147, 149–150, 157–159, 162–165, 247n29, 269n48, 271n99); *Finding the Center*, 253n5; *Guerrillas*, 23, 56; *House for Mr Biswas*, 9, 234, 245n8 (reviews, 117, 214, 250n9, 279n38); *In a Free State*, 22; *India: A Million Mutinies Now*, 58; "Jasmine", 2, 31–32, 143; *Loss of El Dorado*, 22, 135, 266n5; *Middle Passage*, 33, 36, 61, 254n3; *Miguel Street*, 23, 55, 262n25; *Mimic Men*, 10, 56, 57, 142–143, 150,

160, 207; *Mystic Maseur*, 250n9; "Prologue to an Autobiography", 23, 245n8, 253n5; "Reading and Writing", 278n37; *Way in the World*, 8, 17, 21–48, 50–59, 60–65, 80, 121, 134, 234, 240, 250n4, 251n13 (reviews, 48, 240)
Nama, Sigrid, 268n45
Nancy, Jean-Luc, 3
New Republic, 135, 164, 248n29
Newsday, 283n104
New Statesman, 9, 249n2, 250n9
New York Review of Books, 278n37
New York Times, 229, 282n89
Ngũgĩ wa Thiong'o, 82, 245n9
Nietzche, Friedrich, 216
Nixon, Rob, 251n13

O (magazine), 202
O'Brien, Conor Cruise, 251n13
O'Neale, Bobby, 100
Ovid, 233, 236

Padmore, George, 34
Perse, St John, 197–198, 200
Petrarch, 207, 227, 280n57
Phillips, Amaryllis Rebecca, 262n31
Phillips, Caryl, 48, 266n7, 270n90
Plath, Sylvia, 276n15
Poe, Edgar Allan, 57
Pound, Ezra, 178
Prince, Mary, 78

Quincy, Thomas de, 126–128

Raleigh, Walter, 11–12, 21–28, 30–31, 33, 46, 50–52, 56, 57, 63, 134, 234, 248n7
Ramchand, Kenneth, 15, 248n33, 253n28

Raphael, Frederick, 123
Rastafarian, 5–6, 95, 177–178, 207, 242
Ravenscroft, Arthur, 123
Redcam, Tom. *See* MacDermott
Redgrove, Peter, 123
Reed, Alistair, 123
Rhys, Jean, 90, 164; *Wide Sargasso Sea*, 90
Rich, Adrienne, 276n15
Risden, Winnie, 255n6
Roach, Eric, 164, 265n48
Rodney, Walter, 254n14
Rohlehr, Gordon, *vii*, 10, 70, 137, 255n3, 256n7, 256n12, 256n16, 257n33, 259n19, 260n5, 265n48, 271n2
Ruskin, John, 33–34

Saadawi, Nawal El, 245n9
Said, Edward, 251n13, 253n28
Savacou Publications, 69, 77, 246n9
Schwartz, Delmore, 276n15
Scott, David, 264n39
Scott, Dennis, 182
Seacole, Mary, 78
Selvon, Samuel, 8, 114, 164; *Lonely Londoners*, 212
Shakespeare, William, 17, 82, 138, 230, 234; *Tempest*, 76
Shelley, Percy Bysshe, 173, 176
Sheppard, Jill, 259n20
Simmons, Harold, 2, 14–15, 168, 171, 181, 245n6, 263n33
Skeete, Monica, 114
Spenser, Edmund, 284n1
Soyinka, Wole, 17
Stewart, Susan, 280n57
St Lucia. *See under* Creole (language); Walcott
St Omer, Dunstan, 187, 263n33. *See also under* Walcott: relationships

Sunday Guardian, 279n38
Swanzy, Henry, 8, 9, 31
Synge, John Millington, 174

Tennyson, Alfred Lord, 24–25, 27, 51, 125
Thomas, Edward, 163
Thoreau, Henry David, 160
Trinidad/Trinidadian. *See under* Brathwaite; Naipaul; Walcott. See also *creole* (people)
Trinidad and Tobago Guardian. *See under* Walcott
Trinidad Theatre Workshop, 16, 170, 180, 204, 234, 236. *See also* Walcott: relationships: theatre

Vere Allen de, James, 30, 249n2
Virgil, 130, 233, 236; *Aeneid*, 270n90

Walcott, Alix, 133–134, 232
WALCOTT, DEREK: art, influenced by, 9, 138, 139, 141–142, 160, 181, 220–22, 227, 230–31; British Colonial Development and Welfare Organization scholarship, 8; Commonwealth Literature Conference, 188; crises, personal, 203–204, 276n7; exile/expatriate, 135, 138–139, 141, 144, 145, 147, 151–154, 156, 162–163, 170, 209, 212, 214–15, 233, 239, 270n90; experiments with language, 136–137, 140, 159–162–164, 168, 172, 173–174, 181–182, 184–200, 205–207, 218–26, 271n96 (*see also* Creole [language]); fame, deals with, 15; ghosts, in work, 133–134, 139, 140, 146, 147–148, 152, 158, 161, 166, 220, 222–27, 234; legacy, literary, 2, 134, 165–166, 201, 208, 218, 220–21, 226–27, 229, 233, 236, 239; MacArthur Foundation "genius grant", 136, 167; Nobel Prize, 2, 167, 229, 232; Nobel Prize lecture, 214, 222, 278n37; racial identity, struggle with, 145–146, 268n37; Ramlila pageant, 214, 278n37; representation of whiteness, 114–116, 119, 129; reviews "Dust", 178, 180–181; reviews *Enigma of Arrival*, 27, 62, 135–136, 139–140, 142, 147, 149–150, 157–159, 162–165, 247n29, 269n48, 271n99; reviews *House for Mr Biswas*, 214, 250n9, 279n38; reviews *Rights of Passage*, 170, 174, 176, 178, 185, 188, 198, 201; reviews "Wings of a Dove", 176, 180; rhetorical "you", use of, 14, 203–215, 217–23, 226, 229, 233–34, 236, 280n55; St Lucian Artists' Guild, 171; St Mary's College, 8; theatre, involvement with, 16, 139, 170, 180–181, 184, 195, 213, 218, 222, 268n45; *Trinidad and Tobago Guardian*, critic for, 10, 170; University of West Indies, 8, 191

—relationships (people/places): African culture/politics, 158, 168; African history, 134, 188, 231; African landscape, 13, 154, 167–168, 187; America, 135–136, 138, 140, 145, 159–160, 203, 229, 268n36, 268n45; Barbadian landscape, 17; Berlin, 209; Boston, 134, 136, 145, 154, 159–160, 162; Brathwaite, contrast with, 94, 96, 99, 108, 111, 113, 114–117, 119, 127, 129–130, 134–135, 167–171, 174, 176–177, 181–201, 204, 206, 209–212, 214, 218, 247n29; Brathwaite, parody of, 169, 179–180,

188–189, 247n29; Brathwaite, poem dedicated to, 187; Brathwaite, praises, 174, 178, 198; Collymore, 114; England landscape, 143, 151, 209, 212; Europe, 138, 154; father and father figures, 2, 147–148, 156, 220–21; friendships, early, 272n11; Jamaican culture/politics, 177, 271n3; Jamaican landscape, 17, 275n3; mother and mother figures, 2, 133–134, 232; Naipaul, contrast with, 96, 134–140, 142–166, 206–207, 214, 218, 234; Naipaul, critiques, 170, 181, 198; Naipaul, poem about, 209, 212–13, 215; Nama, 268n45; readers, 14, 15–17, 133–134, 141, 147, 164, 204, 238, 282n89; Simmons, 168, 171, 263n33; St Lucian culture, 171, 138, 184 (see also Creole [language]); St Lucian history, 135, 157, 161, 200; St Lucian landscape, 8, 13, 17, 108, 134, 138–140, 145, 148, 151, 159–160, 162, 183, 187, 224, 227, 233, 268n45, 275n3, 280n57; St Omer, 187, 263n33; Trinidadian culture, 184, 213–14, 281n69, 283n104; Trinidadian history, 276n7; Trinidadian landscape, 136, 139, 145, 234–36, 275n3; wife, *vii*, 207, 234, 282n98
—works: *Another Life*, 9, 14, 111, 135, 138, 139, 154, 168, 170–172, 181–182, 207, 231–32, 245n6, 263n33, 266n5; "Antilles: Fragments of Epic Memory", 278n37; *Arkansas Testament*, 137–141, 145–147, 228 (reviews, 136–137, 266n7); *Bounty*, 8, 13, 14, 203, 229–38, 281n72 (reviews, 229, 282n89); "Caribbean: Culture or Mimicry", 170, 181; *Castaway and Other Poems*, 145, 248n29; "Che", 115–116, 119; *Collected Poems*, 268n45, 275n3; "Cul de Sac Valley", 183, 217; "Divided Child", 231; "Early Pompeian, 208, 215; "Exile", 208–209, 211–15, 217, 237; "For Adrian", 146; *Fortunate Traveller*, 153, 248n29; "Great New Novel of the West Indies", 279n38; *Gulf*, 145 (reviews, 271n2); *In a Green Night*, 235, 273n18; "Islands", 207, 215, 228; "Italian Eclogues", 233; *Joker of Seville*, 235–37; "Laventille", 219, 248n29; "Light of the World", 140–141, 143–144, 146, 158, 161, 164, 218; "Love after Love", 202–206, 220, 221, 222, 229, 233, 239, 275n3; "Meanings", 181; *Midsummer*, 136, 270n90, 282n89; "Muse of History", 116, 188; "Names", 187–188, 247n29; "New World", 189–190; "North and South", 154; "Oddjob, a Bull Terrier", 215; *Omeros*, 1, 8, 94, 133–136, 139, 140, 145, 147–148, 151–156, 158–168, 171–173, 183–184, 190–196, 198–200, 205, 212, 218–30, 233, 237, 243, 268n45, 270n90, 272n3, 273n18, 274n72, 280n57, 280n65, 282n89 (reviews, 271n96); "Poem 14", 203, 237–238; "Poem 26", 281n72; "Sainte Lucie", 184–187, 192, 193, 196, 228; "Santa Cruz Quartet", 234–235; "Schooner *Flight*", 10, 171, 184, 190, 274n72; *Sea Grapes*, 184, 187, 188–189, 192–193, 201, 203, 228–29, 247n29, 276n7; "Season of Phantasmal Peace", 153; "Spoiler's Return", 146, 184, 190, 248n29; *Star Apple Kingdom*, 10, 271n3; "Sunday in the Old Republic", 137; "Tales of the Islands", 173, 176, 182, 193,

WALCOTT, DEREK (*continued*) 274n72; "Three Musicians", 228; *Ti-Jean and His Brothers*, 16, 170, 213, 232; "Tomorrow, Tomorrow", 146; *Twenty-Five Poems*, 15; "What the Twilight Says", 169, 170
Walcott, Margaret, *vii*, 207, 234, 282n98
Walcott, Pamela, 171
Walcott, Roderick, 2, 171
Walcott, Warwick, 113, 220
Walker, Alice, 78
Warner, Maureen, 78

Weldon, Catherine, 160, 162
Wheatley, Phyllis, 240
Whitman, Walt, 219, 228, 279n55
Williams, Eric, 40, 252n23
Winfrey, Oprah, 202
Wooding, Selby, 54, 254n14
Worcester, Kent, 47–48, 251n14, 252n23
Wordsworth, William, 163, 231, 270n92, 276n15

Yeats, William B., 232–33, 275n3

www.ingramcontent.com/pod-product-compliance
Lightning Source LLC
Chambersburg PA
CBHW032332230426
43664CB00039B/105